Parasha
and
Other Poems

Ivan Turgenev

Translated by Michael Pursglove

ALMA CLASSICS

ALMA CLASSICS
an imprint of

ALMA BOOKS LTD
Thornton House
Thornton Road
Wimbledon Village
London SW19 4NG
United Kingdom
www.almaclassics.com

For the publication date of the individual poems, see the Introduction
This translation first published by Alma Classics in 2022
Translation and Notes © Michael Pursglove, 2022

Extra Material © Alma Books Ltd

Printed in Great Britain by CPI Group (UK) Ltd, Croydon CR0 4YY

MIX
Paper | Supporting
responsible forestry
FSC
www.fsc.org   FSC® C171272

ISBN: 978-1-84749-891-5

Contents

Introduction   5

Parasha and Other Poems   1

  PARASHA   3

  ANDREI   53

    PART ONE   55

    PART TWO   91

  A CONVERSATION   127

  THE LANDOWNER   169

  THE VILLAGE PRIEST   205

  Note on the Text   229

  Notes   229

Extra Material   233

  Ivan Turgenev's Life   235

  Ivan Turgenev's Works   245

  Select Bibliography   257

Other books by IVAN TURGENEV
published by Alma Classics
(translated by Michael Pursglove)

A Nest of the Gentry

The Diary of a Superfluous Man

Fathers and Children

Faust

Memoirs of a Hunter

On the Eve

Rudin

Smoke

Virgin Soil

Ivan Turgenev (1818–83)

Pauline Viardot

Louis Viardot

"Paulinette",
Turgenev's daughter

Marya Savina as Verochka in
A Month in the Country

Bougival, France, where Turgenev spent the end of his life

Turgenev's funeral procession in Petersburg in 1883

Drawing of Ivan Turgenev
by Adolph Menzel

Introduction

Ivan Turgenev, one of the major Russian prose writers of the nineteenth century, began his career as a poet. Turgenev's first literary venture, *Steno*, was written between September 1834, when he was fifteen, and December 1834, when he was just past his sixteenth birthday. It was heavily based on Byron's *Manfred* (1816–17), and, like it, was described as "A Dramatic Poem" (*Dramaticheskaya poema*). It was not published in Turgenev's lifetime, but its two elements – drama and verse – were the mainstay of his literary output for the next thirteen years. In that time he wrote short lyrics, of which over fifty have survived, and published the first two of the ten plays he was to write in his moderately successful career as a playwright. However, it was the four narrative poems he published in this period which brought him to the notice of the public.

Although Turgenev turned his back on his own poetry in 1847 and, in a letter of 1875, disowned it altogether, he did not in fact lose interest in the subject. For instance, quotations from the classic Russian authors, notably Pushkin and Lermontov, are scattered liberally throughout his novels. He was instrumental in producing the first book of Tyutchev's poetry in 1850, although his insistence on "correcting" what he regarded as metrical lapses caused considerable difficulties for subsequent editors. For a time, in the 1850s, Turgenev was close to the major poet of the time, Nikolai Nekrasov, the editor of the *Contemporary* journal, although the two later fell out and Turgenev famously, and rather unfairly, commented in 1868 that "poetry never spent a night in his verse".

The five poems in this collection are arranged in order of publication.

Parasha. Written at the beginning of 1843. Published 1843.
Andrei. Written in the first half of 1845. Published in *Notes of the Fatherland*, 1845.
A Conversation (*Razgovor*). Completed August 1844. Published 1845.
The Landowner (*Pomeshchik*), Written March 1845. Published in Nekrasov's *Petersburg Collection*, 1846.
The Village Priest (*Pop*). Completed June 1844. Published 1917.

These are all narrative poems, although Turgenev chose to call *Parasha* "A Story in Verse" (*Rasskaz v stikhakh*), no doubt responding to the fact that Pushkin called his *Eugene Onegin*, which greatly influenced Turgenev's poem, "A Novel in Verse" (*Roman v stikhakh*). The word *poema* in Russian is a somewhat elusive term, but, whatever else it means, it implies two things: length and a story of life, contemporary or historical. The word is often translated as "narrative poem". How long a work has to be to qualify as a narrative poem is uncertain, and there is, of course, no maximum length. All five poems in this collection would qualify easily, although only two were actually designated as *poemy* by Turgenev himself: the shortest, *A Village Priest*, with 360 lines, and the longest, *Andrei*, with 1262 lines. Belinsky preferred to call *The Landowner* a "physiological sketch" rather than a narrative poem.

These translations are mimetic – that is to say, they mimic, as far as possible, the metre, rhyme and stanzaic format of the original. Turgenev uses iambic metre in all five poems. Line lengths vary from hexameter (the first sixteen lines of *A Conversation*), to pentameter (*Parasha*, *Andrei* and *The Village Priest*) and tetrameter (*The Landowner*, *A Conversation*, Dunyasha's song and both the letter scene in *Andrei* and the Satan scene in *Parasha*). Stanza lengths are different in the four *poemy* published in Turgenev's lifetime. A thirteen-line stanza, apparently Turgenev's own invention, in *Parasha*, an eight-line stanza ("*ottava rima*") in *Andrei*, a sixteen-line stanza in *The Landowner* and a variable stanza length in *A Conversation*. Turgenev again used the *ottava rima*, borrowed from Byron's *Beppo*, in *A Village Priest*. The *ottava rima* involves two triple rhymes, while the first five lines of the *Parasha* stanza contain a single set of triple rhymes. Not only does this provide a considerable headache for the translator into English, it also caused Turgenev problems: in the last stanza of *The Landowner* he speaks, with evident relief, of the "the end of this uneasy quest for rhymes". Although rhymes are easier in an inflected language like Russian – some would claim too easy – the first few stanzas of *Parasha* alone provide several examples of very perfunctory rhymes. For example he rhymes *nei* with *ei*, two different cases of the same pronoun (stanza 11), and *nei* with the virtually meaningless interpolation *ei-ei* (stanza 4). A good many rhymes in the subsequent poems are similarly sketchy.

It was Vissarion Belinsky's pioneering review of *Parasha* which made Turgenev famous and launched him on his long literary career. Belinsky's review occupied eleven pages of the May 1843 issue of *Notes of the Fatherland*, much of it taken up with twenty quotations from the work, some of them lengthy. He summarizes its plot in a single line ("A provincial landowner marries his neighbour, a young lady – that's all there is"), and claims to have read the poem several times. His main contention is that Turgenev's arrival on the poetic scene demonstrates that Russian poetry had not died with the death of Lermontov in 1841, but merely slept. He concedes that Turgenev owes much to both Pushkin and Lermontov, but refutes any suggestion of servile plagiarism on his part, pointing out what he regards as the original features of *Parasha*. These include the sheer ordinariness of Viktor, whose first words to Parasha are to ask her the time, and whom he describes as a "horribly prosaic" figure. Indeed, he describes Turgenev himself as "prosaic", which he sees as a virtue. Belinsky's eulogy concludes:

> The poem is permeated with such a strict unity of thought, tone and colouring, and is so well balanced that it reveals an author who has not only a creative talent, but a mature and powerful talent capable of mastering its subject. In general, it must be noted, a propos of this poem, what great progress our society and our poetry have made recently.

The anonymous critics of two other journals (possibly Nikolai Nekrasov in both cases) followed Belinsky's lead in according the poem lavish praise. Turgenev also received praise for the work from a rather more unlikely source – his own mother, who, in general, disapproved strongly of his literary aspirations. In a letter she said of the work that it "smells of wild strawberries" – meaning, presumably, that in her view, it captured the essence of the Russian countryside.

Belinsky's comments on Turgenev's next three narrative poems, while obviously enthusiastic, are rather more muted and qualified than his comments on *Parasha*. *Andrei*, for instance, he described in 1846 as one of the outstanding works published in that year, but a year later he thought it less successful than Turgenev's other work, although he did concede that there was "much that is good in it, because there are many authentic sketches of ordinary Russian life". Of *Conversation*, which may have been originally dedicated to him, he wrote:

> Strong, energetic and simple lines fashioned à la Lermontov, which are at the same time sumptuous and poetical, constitute by no means the only virtue of Mr Turgenev's work: it always contains ideas which bear the stamp of reality and modernity – and, as the ideas of a gifted individual, they are always original.

He was clearly more enthused by *The Landowner*, describing it as a "light, lively, brilliant improvisation, full of intelligence, irony, wit and grace [...] – a *jeu d'esprit*, if you will, but one which succeeds far better than the author's other poems. Bold, epigrammatic verse, cheerful irony, authentic pictures combined with overall restraint – everything demonstrates that Mr Turgenev has found a true outlet for his talent, has found his voice, and that there is no need for him to abandon verse." The chief theorist of the Slavophiles, Konstantin Aksakov, was a good deal less enthusiastic, however, taking strong exception to the picture in stanza 28 of the "very clever Muscovite" with the "hat much liked by Slavophiles", and assuming, rightly, that it was directed at him.

There were, of course, other reviews of Turgenev's narrative poems. Their tone is fairly predictable. Those written by critics of a more liberal bent – Apollon Grigoryev and Pyotr Pletnyov, for instance – were positive. Those on the right – notably Faddei Bulgarin, the *bête noire* of liberals – were virulently hostile, claiming for instance that *The Landowner* was an unsuccessful imitation of Pushkin, or even a parody of Pushkin.

Village priests and their wives were often the butt of bawdy folk poetry; Turgenev's *The Village Priest* is in the same vein, though much more elegantly phrased than its folk counterparts. Belinsky was no doubt aware of the existence of this mildly erotic narrative poem, which was circulated among the author's friends, of whom he was one. However, its eroticism was not sufficiently mild to pass the censorship of tsarist Russia, which also objected to any disparaging references to village priests. As a result, the work was not published in Turgenev's lifetime. Fragments were published in Russia in 1884 and 1885, and a full version appeared in Geneva in 1887, followed by another in Berlin in 1910. So un-Turgenevan did one commentator feel the work to be that he ascribed it to M.A. Longinov (1823–75), an erstwhile friend of Turgenev, whose literary output included both erotica and pornographic poems. Those familiar with Turgenev's prose, which struck Victorian readers, and probably strikes modern readers, as the epitome of restraint and good taste, will no doubt be surprised to find the occasional "unprintable" word in the poem. Early editors went to some lengths to rewrite the offending passages. Not until 1917 was the work published in full in Russia, thanks mainly to the efforts of the literary historian Mikhail Gershenzon (1869–1925). To Gershenzon, too, belongs the only substantial article in Russian on Turgenev's narrative poems, which appeared as a chapter of the book *Images of the Past* (*Obrazy proshlogo*). His view of Turgenev's *poemy* is generally favourable, although he does make an exception of *The Conversation*, his section on this beginning with the words: "If *Parasha* is a corner of a blossoming and fragrant steppe, then *The Conversation* is a desolate and tedious wasteland." He goes on to call the poem a "tasteless and tedious diatribe". Of English-language commentators on Turgenev, only F.F. Seeley has devoted any space to the narrative poems.

In its day *The Conversation* also provoked much criticism. Here Turgenev does what he was to do many times in his subsequent career – divide humanity into two contrasting types. In the future it was to be Khor and Kalinych, Hamlet and Don Quixote, Fathers and Children – and even, in *Rudin*, "bob-tailed and long-tailed". In *Conversation* the old man represents the generation of those who fought Napoleon and went on to nurture the Decembrists, while the younger man represents what Turgenev himself later called the "superfluous man". Which type does Turgenev favour? This was the question posed by critics, who came up with opposing answers depending on their own philosophical or political bent. The answer, as always in Turgenev, is: "neither". Indeed, although most critics of the time looked backwards from these narrative poems to the age of Pushkin and Lermontov, there is much in them which looks forward, to the great prose writer that Turgenev was to become.

None of the five works in this collection appear to have been translated hitherto into any language – certainly not into English. The translator is grateful to Alma Books, specifically to Will Dady and Christian Müller, for turning somewhat untidy electronic files into a polished finished product, and to Alessandro Gallenzi, publisher, novelist, Russianist and Turgenev enthusiast, for taking on this project.

– Michael Pursglove, 2022

Parasha
and
Other Poems

PARASHA

A STORY IN VERSE

1

Читатель, бью смиренно вам челом.
Смотрите: перед вами луг просторный,
За лугом речка, а за речкой дом,
Старинный дом, нахмуренный и черный,
Раскрашенный приходским маляром...
Широкий, низкий, с крышей безобразной,
Подпертой рядом жиденьких колонн...
Свидетель буйной жизни, лени праздной
Двух или трех помещичьих племен.
За домом сад: в саду стоят рядами
Всё яблони, покрытые плодами...
Известно: наши добрые отцы
Любили яблоки — да огурцы.

2

Не разберешь — где сад, где огород?
В саду ж был грот (невинная затея!)
И с каждым утром в этот темный грот
(Я приступаю к делу, не робея)
Она — предмет и вздохов и забот,
Предмет стихов моих довольно смелых,
Она являлась — в платьице простом,
И с книжкою в немножко загорелых,
Но милых ручках... На скамью потом
Она садилась... помните Татьяну?
Но с ней ее я сравнивать не стану;
Боюсь — рукой читатели махнут
И этой сказки вовсе не прочтут.

1

I humbly bow my head before you, reader.
Before you lies a big wide meadow. Look!
A house, a river, both beyond the meadow.
The house is venerable, both grim and black,
And painted by a local decorator,
Both low and broad, and with a hideous roof
Propped up by columns, most of them askew.
It saw the idleness and life uncouth
Of owners one, or maybe two, or three.
Beyond the house, an orchard where there stood
Long lines of apple trees bedecked with fruit.
Our ancestors give many good examples
Of how they loved both cucumbers and apples.

2

A kitchen garden? Orchard? Who could tell?
A grotto stood there, innocent construction!
And every morning came to this dark dell
(I broach the subject quite without compunction)
My verses' theme, a well-known local belle,
A girl who wore a plain and simple dress,
Whose hands, though by the sun made slightly brown,
Were very good to look at nonetheless,
Who on a bench to read a book sat down –
Does this Tatyana* call at all to mind?
I similarities with her can't find,
And fear that readers will not pay due heed
And to the end my story will not read.

5

3

Но кто она? и кто ее отец?
Ее отец — помещик беззаботный
Сперва служил, и долго; наконец,
В отставку вышел и супругой плотной
Обзавелся; теперь большой делец!
Живет в ладу с своими мужичками...
Он очень добр и очень плутоват,
Торгуется и пьет чаек с купцами.
Как водится, его супруга — клад;
О! сущий клад! и умница такая!
А женщина она была простая,
С лицом, весьма похожим на пирог;
Ее супруг любил как только мог.

4

У них одна лишь дочь была... Мы с ней
Уж познакомились. Никто красоткой
Ее б не назвал, правда; но, ей-ей
(Ее два брата умерли чахоткой), —
Я девушки не видывал стройней.
Она была легка — ходила плавно;
Ее нога, прекрасная нога,
Всегда была обута так исправно;
Немножко велика была рука;
Но пальцы были тонки и прозрачны...
И даже я, чудак довольно мрачный,
На эту руку глядя, иногда
Хотел... Я заболтался, господа.

5

Ее лицо мне нравилось... оно
Задумчивою грустию дышало;
Всегда казалось мне: ей суждено
Страданий в жизни испытать немало...
И что ж? мне было больно и смешно;
Ведь в наши дни спасительно страданье...
Она была так детски весела,
Хотя и знала, что на испытанье
Она идет, — но шла, спокойно шла...
Однажды я, с невольною печалью,
Ее сравнил и с бархатом и с сталью...
Но кто в ее глаза взглянул хоть раз —
Тот не забыл ее волшебных глаз.

3

But who is she? Who can her father be?
A landlord with a comfortable life,
He served the government for long, then he
Retired and found himself a well-off wife.
Now of big business he's a devotee!
He lives in harmony with all his peasants...
He's very kind, but sly beyond all measure.
He does some trading and drinks tea with merchants.
As often is the case, he'd wed a treasure –
A treasure, and considerable brain!
And yet his wife was homely, simple, plain.
Her face was reminiscent of a pie.
Her spouse loved her as much as he could try.

4

They had a single daughter, whom we've met,
But as for her, I cannot but admit
To call her beautiful would bend the truth.
(TB dispatched two brothers in their youth.)
But on such grace my eyes I've never set.
Her gait was easy, and she seemed to cruise
On pretty feet, and set a fine example
By wearing the most elegant of shoes.
It may be thought her hands were rather ample –
Her fingers, though, were delicate and slim.
And even I, eccentric, somewhat grim,
On seeing this, would sometimes have a yen...
But I have talked too freely, gentlemen.

5

Her face attracted me, being with a sort
Of pensive melancholia suffused;
It always seemed to me it was her lot
To suffer in this life and be ill-used.
All this both pained me and amused. So what?
Such suffering is salutary today.
Her joy so childish was, so innocent,
Although she knew that trials lay in her way,
She on and on without complaining went.
Whoever met but one sole time her gaze
Did not forget the magic of her eyes.

6

Взгляд этих глаз был мягок и могуч,
Но не блестел он блеском торопливым;
То был он ясен, как весенний луч,
То холодом проникнут горделивым,
То чуть мерцал, как месяц из-за туч.
Но взгляд ее задумчиво-спокойный
Я больше всех любил: я видел в нем
Возможность страсти горестной и знойной,
Залог души, любимой божеством.
Но, признаюсь, я говорил довольно
Об этом взгляде: мне подумать больно,
Что — может быть — читающий народ
Всё это неестественным найдет.

7

Она в деревне выросла... а вы,
Читатель мой, — слыхали вы, наверно,
Что барышни уездные (увы!).
Бывают иногда смешны безмерно.
Несправедливость ветреной молвы
Известна мне; но сознаюсь с смиреньем,
что над моей степнячкой иногда
Вы б посмеялись: над ее волненьем
В воскресный день — за завтраком, когда
Съезжались гости, — над ее молчаньем,
И вздохами, и робким трепетаньем...
Но и она подчас бывала зла
И жалиться умела, как пчела.

8

Я не люблю восторженных девиц...
По деревням встречаешь их нередко;
Я не люблю их толстых, бледных лиц,
Иная же — помилуй Бог — поэтка.
Всем восхищаются: и пеньем птиц,
Восходом солнца, небом и луною...
Охотницы до сладеньких стишков,
И любят петь и плакать... а весною
Украдкой ходят слушать соловьев.
Отчаянно все влюблены в природу...
Но барышня моя другого роду;
Она была насмешлива, горда,
А гордость — добродетель, господа.

6

Her look was one of gentleness and might,
But with no transient sparkle did it glow:
One moment it was clear as spring sunlight,
The next, with haughtiness shot through and through,
Then glimmered like the clouded moon at night.
Of all her looks, her look of calm and thought
I loved the most of all. In it I'd see
The hint of passions searing, burning hot,
A pledge of soul loved by the deity.
But I admit I've had enough to tell
About these looks. It makes me feel unwell
That you may possibly, my gentle reader,
All I have said unnatural consider.

7

She grew up in the countryside. And you,
My gentle reader, doubtless will have heard
Provincial girls – I fear it's all too true –
Are sometimes quite excessively absurd.
That rumour is unjust I always knew –
With due humility I have to own
That my steppe girl you'd with derision treat
On Sundays, for the agitation shown
When guests would come to have a bite to eat.
You'd mock her for her taciturnity,
Her sighs and tremulous timidity…
But when aggrieved, or angry, sometimes she
Knew how to sting as well as any bee.

8

I do not like emotional young maids…
To meet such in the country is not rare;
I do not like their faces, plump and fading;
Some may be poetesses, God us spare!
They take delight in all: the song of birds,
The rising of the sun, the moon, the sky…
Enthusiasts for sentimental poets,
They love to sing and weep, and on the sly,
To listen to the nightingales' sweet notes.
They are in love with all by Nature wrought…
But my young lady was a different sort:
Yes, she was full of pride, contemptuous,
But, gentlemen, such pride is virtuous.

9

Она читала жадно... и равно
Марлинского и Пушкина любила
(Я сознаюсь в ее проступках)... но
Не восклицала: «Ах, как это мило!»
А любовалась молча. Вам смешно?
Не верите вы в русскую словесность —
И я не верю тоже, хоть у нас
Весьма легко приобрести известность...
Российские стихи, российский квас
Одну и ту же участь разделяют:
В порядочных домах их не читают
А квас не пьют... но благодарен я
Таким чтецам, как барышня моя.

IO

Для них пишу... но полно. Каждый день —
Я вам сказал — она в саду скиталась.
Она любила гордый шум и тень
Старинных лип — и тихо погружалась
В отрадную, забывчивую лень.
Так весело качалися березы,
Облитые сверкающим лучом...
И по щекам ее катились слезы
Так медленно — Бог ведает о чем.
То, подойдя к убогому забору,
Она стояла по часам... и взору
Тогда давала волю... но глядит,
Бывало, всё на бледный ряд ракит.

II

Там, — через ровный луг — от их села
Верстах в пяти, — дорога шла большая;
И, как змея, свивалась и ползла
И, дальний лес украдкой обгибая,
Ее всю душу за собой влекла.
Озарена каким-то блеском дивным,
Земля чужая вдруг являлась ей...
И кто-то милый голосом призывным
Так чудно пел и говорил о ней.
Таинственной исполненные муки,
Над ней, звеня, носились эти звуки...
И вот — искал ее молящий взор
Других небес, высоких, пышных гор...

9

She read as much as possible, and put
Marlinsky's works* and Pushkin's on a par
(I readily admit her lapses)... but
She did not cry "How nice these authors are!",
But silently admired. Is that so odd?
In Russian literature you don't believe,
And nor do I, although I find with us
Celebrity is easy to achieve.
Both Russian poetry and Russian kvass
Have run into a serious reverse.
In decent circles they don't favour verse
And don't drink kvass, but first I must begin
By thanking readers like my heroine.

10

I write for them. Enough. For days and days,
I've told you – in the garden she would roam.
She loved the shade and sound of ancient trees;
Among the limes oblivion would come;
Beneath them she would sink in leisured ease.
The swaying of the birches brought much cheer,
Irradiated with a glowing ray,
And down her cheeks would roll tear after tear
So slowly... no one knew the reason why.
One moment she approached a broken fence
And stood for hours, giving every chance
To eyes that wished to see – but all she saw
Was nothing but pale willows in a row.

11

Across a meadow, from her village distant
About three miles, there ran the great high road,
Which twisted round, contorted like a serpent,
And clipped the edges of a distant wood,
And to it made her inner soul subservient.
With wondrous beams of light illuminated,
A world unknown now started to appear,
A voice which called, with kindness permeated,
So wonderfully sang and spoke to her.
And, overfilled with some mysterious pain,
There rang above her head the same refrain...
She sought to find with her beseeching eyes
The peaks of lush green hills, and other skies...

12

И тополей и трепетных олив...
Искал земли пленительной и дальной;
Вдруг русской песни грустный перелив
Напомнит ей о родине печальной;
Она стоит, головку наклонив,
И над собой дивится, и с улыбкой
Себя бранит; и медленно домой
Пойдет, вздохнув... то сломит прутик гибкой,
То бросит вдруг... Рассеянной рукой
Достанет книжку — развернет, закроет;
Любимый шепчет стих... а сердце ноет,
Лицо бледнеет... В этот чудный час
Я, признаюсь, хотел бы встретить вас,

13

О, барышня моя... В тени густой
Широких лип стоите вы безмолвно;
Вздыхаете; над вашей головой
Склонилась ветвь... а ваше сердце полно
Мучительной и грустной тишиной.
На вас гляжу я: прелестью степною
Вы дышите — вы нашей Руси дочь...
Вы хороши, как вечер пред грозою,
Как майская томительная ночь.
Но — может быть — увы! воспоминаньем
Вновь увлечен, подробным описаньем
Я надоел — и потому готов
Рассказ мой продолжать без лишних слов.

14

Моей красотке было двадцать лет.
(Иной мне скажет: устрицам в апреле,
Девицам лет в пятнадцать — самый цвет...
Но я не спорю с ним об этом деле,
О разных вкусах спорить — толку нет.)
Ее Прасковьей звали; имя это
Не хорошо... но я — я назову
Ее Парашей... Осень, зиму, лето
Они в деревне жили — и в Москву
Не ездили, затем что плохи годы,
Что с каждым годом падают доходы.
Да сверх того Параша — грех какой! —
Изволила смеяться над Москвой.

12

And poplar trees and olives' trembling crowns…
She wanted an enchanted land to find –
Then suddenly a Russian song's sad sound
Would her of Russia's mournful land remind.
She used to stand there with her head cast down
And wonder at herself, and harsh words speak
Against herself, and smile, then slowly wend
Her way back home, and then a thin branch break
And cast aside with a distracted hand.
She tried to read, but did not even start.
No whispered verses helped, for she was sick at heart.
Her face turned pale, and in that wondrous second,
I own the thought of meeting with you beckoned.

13

My fair young lady, in the heavy shade
Of spreading limes you stand, and stay tight-lipped;
You heave a sigh, and then above your head
A branch droops downwards and your heart is gripped
By total silence, agonizing, sad.
I look at you and feel the steppe-land charm
Which you exude… you are a child of ours…
You're like the evening before a storm,
Like enervating summer night-time hours.
But maybe I've let memory distract:
Again a recitation of mere fact
Has bored you all. And so I am prepared
To carry on without another word.

14

My heroine had twenty summers passed.
(Some say that oysters in the month of April,
Like maidens at fifteen, are at their best…
But over that opinion I'll not quarrel:
It makes no sense to quarrel over taste.)
Her name – Praskovya – simply will not do,
So I to her the name Parasha give.*
Her family spent winters (summers too)
In rural Russia, choosing not to live
In Moscow, after many a bad year
In which their income slumped from low to poor.
And more than that, Parasha – what a crime! –
Was pleased to laugh at Moscow all the time.

15

Москва — Москва — о матушка Москва!
Но я хвалить тебя не смею, право;
Я потерял бывалые права́...
Твои ж сыны превспыльчивого нрава,
И в них мои смиренные слова
Возбудят ревность — даже опасенья.
И потому к Параше молодой,
О матушка, прошу я снисхожденья...
А если, о читатель дорогой,
Навеянный приятностью рассказа,
Отрадный сон закрыл вам оба глаза, —
Проснитесь — и представьте себе день...
Прежаркий день... (Я посажу вас в тень.)

16

Прежаркий день... но вовсе не такой,
Каких видал я на далеком юге...
Томительно-глубокой синевой
Всё небо пышет; как больной в недуге.
Земля горит и сохнет; под скалой
Сверкает море блеском нестерпимым —
И движется, и дышит, и молчит...
И все цвета под тем неумолимым
Могучим солнцем рдеют... дивный вид!
А вот — зарывшись весь в песок блестящий,
Рыбак лежит... и каждый проходящий
Любуется им с завистью — я сам
Им тоже любовался по часам.

17

У нас не то — хоть и у нас не рад
Бываешь жару... точно — жар глубокий...
Гроза вдали сбирается... трещат
Кузнечики неистово в высокой
Сухой траве; в тени снопов лежат
Жнецы; носы разинули вороны;
Грибами пахнет в роще; там и сям
Собаки лают; за водой студеной
Идет мужик с кувшином по кустам.
Тогда люблю ходить я в лес дубовый,
Сидеть в тени спокойной и суровой
Иль иногда под скромным шалашом
Беседовать с разумным мужичком.

15

Oh, Moscow! Moscow! Moscow! Moscow mine!
Although I do not dare to sing your praise –
The rights which once were mine I have forgone…
Your sons are men of most impulsive ways:
In them my least successful five-foot line
Aroused their jealousy and good cause gave
For fear. And so towards my young Parasha
I, Moscow, your indulgence humbly crave.
And if, my dearest readers throughout Russia,
You by my pleasant story are enthused
And my sweet dreams your two eyes have shut closed,
Awake! See in your mind a day of heat
(And I'll conduct you to a shady seat).

16

A scorching day, although not such as were
Endured by many like me in the south…
The whole sky is a sickening azure there,
And, like a fevered invalid, the earth
Is scorched and parched. Beneath the cliff the glare
Of sun on sea is quite insufferable –
The waters do not speak, but breathe and stir…
And, seared beneath a sun implacable,
All tints are red and bright beyond compare!
Completely buried in the glistening sand,
See, over here there lies a fisherman,
Admired and envied by each passer-by –
I too regarded him admiringly.

17

With us it's not the same, though we dislike,
It's true, the scorching heat, the heat which saps…
A storm is coming. Grasshoppers still make
Their frantic chirring in the tall dry grass.
The sheaves give shade, and there the reapers take
Their rest. Then come a sound of cawing crows,
A smell of mushrooms in the woods. A dog
Occasionally barks. A peasant goes
To fetch some fresh cold water in a jug.
I love to go then to an oaken glade
And sit in peaceful, unrelenting shade,
And sometimes in a modest peasant hut
With the sagacious householder to chat.

18

В такой-то день — Параша в темный грот
(О нем смотрите выше) шаг за шагом
Пришла; пред ней знакомый огород,
Знакомый пруд; а дальше за оврагом
Знакомый лес на холмике... Но вот
Что показалось ей немного странным:
В овраге под кустом сидел один
Охотник; резал хлеб ножом карманным,
Он по всему заметно — господин;
Помещик; он в перчатках — и красиво
Одет... Вот он поел, потом лениво
Собаку кликнул, шапку снял, зевнул,
Раздвинул куст, улегся — и заснул.

19

Заснул... Параша смотрит на него,
И смотрит, признаюсь, с большим вниманьем.
К ним ездили соседи... но его
Лицо ей незнакомо; описаньем
Теперь мы не займемся, оттого
Что уж и так с излишеством речист я...
Он спит, а ветер тихо шевелит
Его густые волосы, и листья
Над ним шушукают; он сладко спит...
Параша смотрит... он недурен, право.
О чем же вдруг так мило, так лукаво
Она смеется? Я б ответил — но
Мне женский смех постигнуть не дано.

20

И час прошел... и предвечерний зной
Внезапно начал стынуть... уж и тени
Длиннее стали... Вот — охотник мой
Проснулся, стал лениво на колени,
Надел небрежно шапку, головой
Тряхнул — хотел подняться... и остался...
Он увидал Парашу — о друзья!
Глядел, глядел — с смущеньем засмеялся,
Вскочил, взглянул поспешно на себя,
Потом через овраг легко и смело
Перебежал... Параша побледнела,
Но до забора он дошел и стал,
И с вежливой улыбкой шапку снял.

18

On such a day Parasha made her way
To the dark grotto (we've described the scene).
In front of her a well-known garden lay,
A pond, and then, beyond, a small ravine,
A forest on a hill – and, strange to say,
She saw a sight she thought was very odd:
Beneath a bush was sitting all alone
A hunter with a penknife, slicing bread.
It was quite clear he was a *gospodin*,
A landowner. He wore clothes à la mode
And gloves, and ate, and indolently called
His gun-dog to him, yawned, his hat then doffed,
Made space, lay down, immediately dropped off.

19

He fell asleep. Parasha, I confess
Regarded him with great attentiveness.
Her neighbours used to call on her, but his
Was not a face she knew. Descriptiveness
We will avoid. I am aware of this –
That I have often overused my voice.
He slept, his hair by gentle breezes swept,
And from the leaves there came a rustling noise
Above his head, as on and on he slept…
Parasha looks – he's not at all bad really,
So why, in such a manner, pleasant, wily,
The sudden laugh? I'd make a quick response,
But female mirth has foxed me more than once.

20

An hour passed, and midday heat began
To yield to coolness. Shadows grew in size.
Just take a look. You'll see my hunting man
Has woken up and rises to his knees,
In careless fashion dons his hat and then
Attempts to stand, and gives his head a shake.
He sees Parasha, and – hear this, my friends –
He looks and looks, and gives himself a look,
Then up he jumps. Now finally he stands.
Through the ravine, with step both light and bold,
He ran, at which Parasha's features paled –
But when he reached the fence, he paused awhile,
And then removed his hat with courteous smile.

21

Она стояла, вспыхнув вся... и глаз
Не подымая... Сильно и неровно
В ней билось сердце. «Умоляю вас, —
Так начал он, и очень хладнокровно, —
Скажите мне, теперь который час?»
Сперва она немножко помолчала
И отвечала: «Пятый» — а потом
Взглянула на него; но он, нимало
Не изменясь, спросил: «Чей это дом?»
Потом весьма любезно извинился
Бог знает в чем и снова поклонился,
Но не ушел... сказал, что он сосед
И что с ее отцом покойный дед

22

Его был очень дружен... что он рад
Такой нежданной встрече; понемногу
И двадцать раз сказавши «виноват!»
(У нас заборы плохи, слава Богу),
Через забор он перебрался в сад.
Его лицо так мило улыбалось
И карий глаз так ласково сиял,
Что ей смешным и странным показалось
Дичиться... Он ей что-то рассказал,
Над чем она сперва довольно звонко,
Потом потише засмеялась... с тонкой
Усмешкой посмотрел он ей в глаза —
Потом ушел, пробормотав: «Comm'ça!»

23

И вслед она ему смотрела... Он
Через плечо внезапно оглянулся,
Пожал плечьми — и, словно приучен
К победам, равнодушно улыбнулся.
И ей досадно стало... Громкий звон
Раздался в доме... Чай готов... Небрежно
Она, вернувшись, рассказала всё
Отцу... Он засмеялся безмятежно,
Заговорил про старое житье,
Про деда... Но уездный заседатель.
Вдовец, Парашин древний обожатель,
Разгневался и покраснел, как рак,
И объявил, что их сосед — чудак.

21

She stood and blushed, and raised her eyes no more –
Her heart was palpitatingly unruly
Within her soul. He said: "I you implore,"
Addressing thus Parasha very coolly.
"Please tell me, if you will, what is the hour?"
At first Parasha into silence sank,
Then answered she: "It's five o'clock", whereat
She cast her eyes on him, but drew a blank.
He nothing did, but asked: "Whose house is that?"
Apologetic was in the extreme
(God knows for what), then bowed a second time,
But did not leave, explained he was a neighbour,
And that his late grandfather knew her father –

22

And knew him well... that he was very glad
Of this chance meeting. In his own good time
He "sorry" twenty times at least then said.
The garden fence he now began to climb
(Thank Heavens fences here are very bad).
Across his features spread a smile which beamed,
And there was kindness in each hazel eye,
So much that oddly comical it seemed
To make such show of being very shy.
He something said that made Parasha laugh
Out loud. He answered with no more than half
A smile, and added in an undertone
"*Comm'ça*"* – and in a moment he was gone.

23

She watched him as he went. A glance he threw
Across his shoulder at her all at once,
Then shrugged, as if such victories weren't new,
And smiled with absolute indifference.
She grew annoyed. The bell for tea rang through
The house. Returning there, she casually
Reported to her father in detail.
He merely laughed at all this placidly
And of the olden days began the tale,
About her grandsire... But an office bearer,
A widower, Parasha's old admirer,
Got really angry and, red as any beetroot,
Said that their neighbour was a total idiot.

24

А я б его не назвал чудаком...
Но мы об нем поговорить успеем;
Параша села молча под окном
И, подпершись рукой — мы лгать не смеем,
Всё думала да думала о нем.
Алеет небо... над травой усталой
Поднялся пар... недвижны стали вдруг
Верхушки лип; свежеет воздух вялый,
Темнеет лес, и оживает луг.
Вечерний ветер веет так прохладно,
И ласточки летают так отрадно...
На церкви крест зарделся, а река
Так пышно отражает облака...

25

Люблю сидеть я под окном моим
(А в комнате шумят, смеются дети),
Когда над лесом темно-голубым
Так ярко пышет небосклон... о, в эти
Часы я тих и добр — люблю, любим...
Но кто поймет, кто скажет, чем так чудно
Томилось сердце барышни моей...
Состарившись — и тяжело и трудно
Припоминать блаженство прежних дней —
Тех дней, когда без всякого усилья
Любовь, как птица, расширяет крылья...
И на душе так страстно, так светло...
Но это всё прошло, давно прошло.

26

Да, вы прошли и не вернетесь вновь,
Часы молитв таинственных и страстных,
Беспечная, свободная любовь,
Порывы дум, младенчески прекрасных...
Всё, всё прошло... горит упорно кровь
Глухим огнем... а, помнится, бывало,
Верхом я еду вечером; гляжу
На облака, а ветер, как опахало,
В лицо мне тихо веет — я дышу
Так медленно — и, благодати полный,
Я еду, еду, бледный и безмолвный...
Но, впрочем, кто ребенком не бывал
И не забыл всего, что обожал?

24

But as for me, I would not call him that,
And he will be our subject by and by.
Parasha silent by the window sat,
And, head in hands – we cannot tell a lie –
Was thinking of him with her every thought.
The sky turned red. Above the tired grass
A vapour rose. Unmoving stood the limes –
The fetid atmosphere again felt fresh.
The wood grows dark, the lea its life reclaims,
The evening breeze a breath of coolness brings,
And swallows fly aloft on joyful wings.
Atop the church, a crimson crucifix –
A river which the clouds above reflects.

25

While children play below, I sit and see
Above the dark-blue forest there is light
On the horizon. Only then for me
Will there be pleasure in love's benefit,
And I'll be calm and kindly once again.
But who will understand what made the heart
Miraculously shrink within my miss?
As years advance, it's painful and it's hard
To resurrect of former days the bliss,
Those days when love, completely undeterred
On outstretched wings soared higher than a bird,
And in my soul the light of passion shone –
But all that's gone, irrevocably gone.

26

Yes, all that's gone, and never to return,
The hours of passionate and secret prayer
And love unfettered, free from all concern,
And sudden meditations, young and fair,
All gone, quite gone, but stubborn blood will burn
With a dull flame... and then I call to mind
An evening ride when I my gaze bestow
Upon the clouds, but, like a fan, the wind
Caresses me with gentleness. So slow
My breaths become, and, with a sense of grace
I ride, deprived of speech and pale of face...
But who, however, has not been a child,
And quite forgotten all they once extolled.

27

Он обещал прийти — твердит она...
И хочет и не может оторваться;
Но неужель Параша влюблена?
Не думаю — но не могу ручаться...
А вот и ночь: и вкралась тишина,
Как поцелуй томительно протяжный,
Во всё земное... «Спать пора, сосед!»
Сказал отец, а мать с улыбкой важной
Его зовет на завтрашний обед.
Параша в сад таинственный и темный
Пошла — и понемногу грусти томной
Вся предалась... Но он-то, что же он?
Я вам скажу — он вовсе не влюблен.

28

Хотите ль знать, что он за человек?
Извольте: он богат, служил в военной;
Чужим умом питался весь свой век,
Но ловок был и вкрадчив. Изнуренный,
Скучающий, направил он свой бег
В чужие страны; с грустною улыбкой
Везде бродил, надменный и немой;
Но ум его насмешливый и гибкой
Из-за границы вынес целый рой
Бесплодных слов и множество сомнений,
Плоды лукавых, робких наблюдений...
Он надо всем смеялся; но устал —
И над собой смеяться перестал.

29

Мы за границу ездим, о друзья!
Как казаки в поход... Нам всё не в диво;
Спешим, чужих презрительно браня,
Их сведений набраться торопливо...
И вот твердим, без страсти, без огня,
Что и до нас дошло, но что, быть может,
Среди борений грозных рождено,
Что там людей мучительно встревожит,
Что там погубит сердце не одно...
Не перейдя через огонь страданья,
Мы не узнаем радостей познанья —
И, наконец, с бессмысленной тоской
Пойдем и мы дорогой столбовой.

27

"He promised that he'd come," she keeps on saying…
He tries, but can't his bid for freedom make.
But can Parasha really be love's plaything?
I do not know, but would not risk a stake.
It's night, and silence earth has permeated
As if it were a kiss, protracted, painful.
"And so, my neighbour, time to say goodnight,"
Said Father, while Mama, with smile disdainful
To come to lunch is quick him to invite.
Parasha's in the garden's secret gloom,
And slowly yields to sadness wearisome.
Now tell me what his feelings for her were:
He did not feel a single thing for her.

28

You seek to know what sort of life he led?
Well, he was rich, served in the military,
And all his life on others' wisdom fed.
But he was crafty, suave, and, being weary,
With nothing else to do, abroad he fled.
He wandered everywhere; his smile was mournful,
But he himself was arrogant and mute;
His intellect, both flexible and scornful
From foreign parts a massive number brought
Of useless words and multifarious doubts,
Of crafty, timid scrutiny the fruits.
He laughed at everything, but then he tired:
No more was mockery of self required.

29

Dear friends! We now are travelling abroad,
Like Cossacks on campaign, by nothing fazed;
We with contempt all foreigners upbraid,
Then from their words we benefit in haste…
So we repeat the things which we have heard
With no enthusiasm, but which are
The fruits of fearsome struggles undergone
Which grievously alarm the people there,
And will destroy the heart of more than one.
If no ordeal by fire we undergo,
The joys of knowledge we will never know –
And, bearing languor's idiotic load,
We too will set off down that well-marked road.

30

Но к делу. Он, как я вам доложил,
В отставке был. Пока он был на службе,
Он выезжал, гулял, плясал, шалил,
Приятелей обыгрывал — по дружбе —
И был, как говорится, очень мил.
Он был любезен, влюбчив, но спокоен
И горделив... а потому любим;
И многих женщин был он недостоин,
Обманутых и позабытых им.
Он весел был, но весел безотрадно;
Над чудаком смеялся беспощадно,
Но в обществе не славился умом
И не был «замечательным лицом».

31

А между тем его любили... Он
Пленял людей беспечностью свободной
И был хорош собой — и одарен
Душой самолюбивой и холодной.
Он, я сказал, не очень был умен,
Но всем ему дарованным от Бога
Владел вполне... и презирал людей
А потому имел довольно много
«Испытанных и преданных» друзей.
Он с ними вместе над толпой смеялся
И от толпы с презреньем отчуждался).
И думали все эти господа,
Что, кроме их, всё вздор и суета.

32

Он всё бранил от скуки — так!..
Не предаваясь злобе слишком детской,
Скажу вам, в бесы метил мой остряк;
Но русский бес не то, что чёрт немецкий.
Немецкий чёрт, задумчивый чудак,
Смешон и страшен; наш же бес, природный,
Российский бес и толст и простоват,
Наружности отменно благородной
И уж куда какой аристократ!
Не удивляйтесь: мой приятель тоже
Был очень дружен не с одним вельможей
И падал в прах с смеющимся лицом
Пред золотым тельцом — или быком.

30

But back to business. He, as I have said,
Was in retirement. While not yet retired,
A life of visits, merriment he led;
His friends he fleeced, as friendship's bonds required,
And was well liked, as everyone agreed,
And amorous, and thought adorable,
And haughty, and so generally loved.
His way with women was deplorable,
And many were forgotten or deceived.
He humour had, but humour lacking cheer,
And laughed quite ruthlessly at all things weird.
For wit in the beau monde he was not famous –
In fact was something of an ignoramus.

31

But people loved him all the same. He lifted
Their spirits with his boundless lack of care;
He was a handsome fellow, and was gifted
With a self-confident and chilly air.
He was not very bright, I have insisted,
But everything that's granted man from God
He had in spades… and people he disdained,
And therefore he possessed a goodly lot
Of people who were held to be his friend.
Together they would of the crowd make fun,
Then that same crowd contemptuously shun.
And all these worthy gentlemen would think
That everything, apart from them, was junk.

32

He cursed the world and all he found in it…
I do not wish too childishly to cavil;
I tell you, quite a devil was this wit.
The Russian devil is no German devil:
Your German devil is a thoughtful sprite –
He's funny, scary too, while sprites home-grown,
Our Russian sprites are simpletons, and fat,
Of aspect very noble and high-flown,
And every inch the real aristocrat!
My friend, do not be too surprised to see,
Was in cahoots with more than one grandee,
And, laughing heartily, in stitches fell
Before the golden calf – or golden bull.

33

Вам гадко... но, читатель добрый мой,—
Увы! и я люблю большого света
Спокойный блеск и с радостью смешной
Любуюсь гордым холодом привета —
Всей этой жизнью звонкой и пустой.
На этот мир гляжу я без желанья,
Но первый сам я хохотать готов
Над жаром ложного негодованья
Непризнанных, бесхвостых «львиц и львов»!
Да сверх того вся пишущая братья
На «свет и роскошь» сыпала проклятья...
А потому см<отри> творенья их;
А я сегодня — что-то очень тих.

34

Люблю я пышных комнат стройный ряд,
И блеск и прихоть роскоши старинной...
А женщины... люблю я этот взгляд
Рассеянный, насмешливый и длинный;
Люблю простой, обдуманный наряд...
Я этих губ люблю надменный очерк,
Задумчиво приподнятую бровь;
Душистые записки, быстрый почерк,
Душистую и быструю любовь.
Люблю я эту поступь, эти плечи,
Небрежные, заманчивые речи...
Узнали ль вы, друзья, скажите мне,
С кого портрет писал я в тишине?

35

«Но,— скажут мне,— вне света никогда
Вы не встречали женщины прекрасной?»
Таких особ встречал я иногда —
И даже в двух влюбился очень страстно;
Как полевой цветок, они всегда
Так милы, но, как он, свой легкий запах
Они теряют вдруг... и, Боже мой,
Как не завянуть им в неловких лапах
Чиновника, довольного собой?
Но сознаюсь, и сознаюсь с смущеньем,
Я заболтался вновь и с наслажденьем
К моей Параше я спешу — спешу
И вот ее в гостиной нахожу.

33

You find it loathsome, but, my reader good,
Alas! I too adore the beau monde's glitter,
And with a comic gladness I salute
The arrogance and chill of greetings bitter,
This life of noisy, empty platitude.
This world I contemplate with no desire.
But I am quite prepared to let be mocked
Disapprobation's counterfeited fire
From social lions with their tails half-docked.
What's more, the writing confraternity
Would curse excesses of society.
So therefore take a look at what they write –
But I today will stay completely mute.

34

I love a lavish room and stylish suite,
And luxury capricious and old-fashioned…
And women – I so love their glance to meet:
Distracted, mocking, lengthy and impassioned.
I love attire that's plain, considered, neat…
I love the outline of a haughty moue,
The eyebrow which they questioningly lift,
The hasty scribble of sweet billets-doux,
And love which is both sweet-scented and swift.
I love a graceful movement; I love arms,
Those casual and captivating charms…
So tell me, do you recognize, dear friend,
From whom it is this portrait I have penned?

35

Outside society, it will be said,
No woman you have met appeals to you.
Such women I have on occasion met –
I even fell in love with one or two.
As fair as flowers in spring are they, and yet
Their fragrance they will very quickly lose.
They can but fade away, good Heavens above,
When they are clutched in the ungainly paws
Of some official brimming with self-love.
But I confess, confess ashamedly,
I've let my tongue run right away with me.
To my Parasha now my steps I bend,
And in the living room it's her I'll find.

36

Она сидит близ матери... на ней
Простое платье; но мы замечаем
За поясом цветок. Она бледней
Вчерашнего, взволнована. За чаем
Хлопочет няня; батюшка моей
Параши новый фрак надел; к окошку
Подходит часто: нет, не едет гость!
А обещал... И что же? понемножку
Ее берет девическая злость...
Ее прическа так мила, перчатки
Так свежи — видно, все мои догадки
Не ложны... «Что, мой друг, ты так грустна?»
Спросила мать — и вздрогнула она

37

И слабо улыбнулась... и идет
К окну; садится медленно за пяльцы;
И, головы не подымая, шьет,
Но что-то часто колет себе пальцы.
И думает: «Ну что ж? он не придет...»
От тонкой шеи, слабо наклоненной,
Так гордо отделялася коса...
Ее глаза — читатель мой почтенный,
Я не могу вам описать глаза
Моей слегка взволнованной девицы —
Их закрывали длинные ресницы...
Я на нее глядел бы целый век;
А он не едет — глупый человек!

38

Но вдруг раздался топот у крыльца —
И всходит «он». «Насилу! как мы ради!»
Он трижды щеки пухлые отца
Облобызал... потом приличья ради
К хозяйке к ручке подошел... с чепца
До башмаков ее окинул взглядом
И быстро усмехнулся, а потом
Параше низко поклонился — рядом
С ней сел — и начал речь о том о сем...
Внимательно старинные рассказы
Хозяев слушал... три, четыре фразы
С приветливой улыбкой отпустил —
И стариков «пленил и восхитил».

36

Beside her mother sitting, she had on
A very simple dress, but at her waistline she
Had placed a flower. She appeared more wan
And worried than the day before. Then tea
Was served. Parasha's father chose to don
A new frock coat. He frequently approached
The window, but of guest could see no sign.
He'd promised. Now the bitterest reproach
Begin to occupy Parasha's mind.
Her coiffure was so nice, her gloves so fresh,
And everything, it's clear, bore out my guess.
"My darling, why are you so sad?" asked Mother,
And in reply Parasha gave a shudder,

37

Then faintly smiled, and to the window went,
Then sat down slowly and began to sew,
And over her embroidery stayed bent,
And pricked her fingers frequently somehow,
And thought: "How so? What can him now prevent?"
Down from her slender neck, submissively inclined,
Her plaited hair had proudly come away.
Her eyes' description, reader, you will find
I'm utterly unable to convey,
Because the eyes of this most anxious maiden
Were by a pair of long eyelashes hidden.
My gaze forever could upon her fall –
And still he did not come, the stupid fool!

38

Then in the hall the sound of steps rang out,
And *he* appeared: "At last! We are so pleased!"
Three times he kissed her father in salute,
And then the hand of his hostess he squeezed
And pressed it to his lips – to be polite.
He gazed at her, from mob cap to her feet.
His smile was brief, sarcastic – whereupon
He bowed low to Parasha, took a seat
Beside her and of this and that began
To talk. He listened with attention to his host,
And phrases, three or four of them at most,
With an ingratiating smile let fall,
And managed both her parents to enthral.

39

С Парашей он ни слова... на нее
Не смотрит он, но все его движенья,
Звук голоса, улыбка — дышит всё
Сознанием внезапного сближенья...
Как нежен он! Как он щадит ее!
Как он томится тайным ожиданьем!..
Ей стало легче — молча на него
Она глядит с задумчивым вниманьем,
Не понимая сердца своего...
И этот взгляд, и женский и ребячий,
Почувствовал он на щеке горячей —
И, предаваясь дивной тишине,
Он наслаждался страстно и вполне.

40

Не нравится он вам, читатель мой...
Но в этот миг он был любим недаром;
Он был проникнут мирной простотой,
Он весь пылал святым и чистым жаром,
Он покорялся весь душе другой.
Он был любим — как скоро! Но, быть может,
Я на свою Парашу клевещу...
Скажите — ваша память мне поможет,—
Как мне назвать ту страстную тоску,
Ту грустную, невольную тревогу,
Которая берет вас понемногу...
К чему нам лицемерить — о друзья! —
Ее любовью называю я.

41

Но эта искра часто гаснет... да;
И, вспыхнувши, горит довольно странно
И смертных восхищает — не всегда.
Я выражаюсь несколько туманно...
Но весело, должно быть, господа,
Разгар любви следить в душе прекрасной,
Подслушать вздох, задумчивую речь,
Подметить взгляд доверчивый и ясный,
Былое сбросить всё, как ношу с плеч...
Случайности предаться без возврата
И чувствовать, что жизнь полна, богата
И что способность праздного ума
Смеяться надо всем — смешна сама.

39

But no word to Parasha. He avoids
Her glances, but his each and every movement,
His voice, his smile, his everything exudes
A consciousness of sudden close involvement.
How tenderly from blame he her excludes,
Yet secret expectations cause him tension!...
Her load was lightened, and without a word
She fixed her eyes on him with rapt attention.
The promptings of her heart were vague and blurred...
The look she cast, so womanly and meek,
He was aware of on his burning cheek –
And, yielding to a silence unalloyed,
He to the full all passion's bliss enjoyed.

40

But you, dear reader, he may not attract,
But he was loved– no wonder – at that moment,
And for simplicity he nothing lacked,
And was consumed by chaste and sacred ferment
In making with another such contact.
How quickly he was loved, but it may be
I am not being fair to my Parasha.
So tell me – here I need your memory –
What should I call that anguish and that passion
Which takes possession of us by degrees...
That melancholy feeling of unease?
Why should I play the hypocrite, my friend?
I gave that feeling love's name in the end.

41

This spark will often fade to nothing... yes,
Then flare again, then smoulder rather oddly,
And mortals try to please – with scant success.
I have expressed myself a trifle badly,
But, gentlemen, you must find happiness
In following the kindling of love's fire,
In eavesdropping on sighs, on words well said,
In intercepting glances, trusting, clear,
In casting off the past, a burden shed,
In leaving all to chance and not resiling,
In finding life fulfilling and beguiling,
In thinking those who seek all things to mock
Themselves become a general laughing stock.

42

И так они сидели рядом... С ней
Заговорил он... Странен, но понятен
Параше смысл уклончивых речей...
Она его боится, но приятен
Ей этот страх — и робости своей
Она едва ль не радуется тайно.
Шутя, скользит небрежный разговор;
И вдруг глаза их встретились случайно —
Она не тотчас опустила взор...
И встала, без причины приласкалась
К отцу... ласкаясь, тихо улыбалась,
И, говоря о нем, сказала: «он».—
Читатель, я — признайтесь — я смешон.

43

А между тем ночь наступает... в ряд
Вдали ложатся тучи... ровной мглою
Наполнен воздух... липы чуть шумят;
И яблони над темною травою,
Раскинув ветки, высятся и спят —
Лишь изредка промчится легкий трепет
В березах; там за речкой соловей
Поет себе, и слышен долгий лепет,
Немолчный шёпот дремлющих степей.
И в комнату, как вздох земли бессонной,
Влетает робко ветер благовонный
И манит в сад, и в поле, и в леса,
Под вечные, святые небеса...

44

Я помню сам старинный, грустный сад,
Спокойный пруд, широкий, молчаливый...
Я помню: волны мелкие дрожат
У берега в тени плакучей ивы;
Я помню — много лет тому назад —
Я в том саду хожу в траве высокой
(Дорожки все травою поросли),
Заря так дивно рдеет... блеск глубокий
Раскинулся от неба до земли...
Хожу, брожу, задумчивый, усталый,
О женщине мечтаю небывалой...
И о прогулке поздней и немой —
И это всё сбылось, о Боже мой!

42

And so they sat together. Soon he struck
Up conversation with her. Strange but clear
To her his words, although somewhat oblique.
She was afraid of him, but liked her fear,
And found she could her shyness also like,
Experiencing no clandestine regret.
A jesting conversation they kept up,
And suddenly by chance their glances met,
But she was slow to let her glances drop...
She gave her father an uncalled-for hug,
And, as she did so, gave a smiling shrug.
In mentioning her suitor, called him *he* –
I own, dear reader, this is comedy.

43

Meanwhile the night comes on, and distant rows
Of clouds are forming. Through the air is spread
A mist. The limes make scarcely any noise,
And apple trees above the darkening sward
Their branches stretch, then rise, then doze.
Through birches runs a sudden and brief tremor;
Beyond the stream a nightingale is heard;
Together with this unremitting clamour
Come whispers when the sleeping steppe is stirred.
Sweet-smelling breezes through the window fly,
As if the earth has breathed a timid sigh
And tempted one to garden and green place
Beneath the heaven's endless sacred space.

44

I call to mind a garden, dismal, old,
A tranquil stretch of water, silent, broad...
Remember how the little ripples rolled
Against the shore, beneath the willow's shade –
Remember how, in years gone by untold,
In that same garden I would wander round
Through grasses tall (the paths were overgrown)...
A wondrous dawn glowed red, and from the ground
To highest heaven its crimson hues were thrown...
Reflective, weary, I would walk and roam,
And of a woman like no other dream,
Of evening walks when neither spoke a word –
Good grief! All this has actually occurred!

45

«А не хотите ль в сад? — сказал старик,—
А? Виктор Алексеич! вместе с нами?
Сад у меня простенек, но велик;
Дорожки есть — и клумбочки с цветами».
Они пошли... вечерний, громкий крик
Коростелей их встретил; луг огромный
Белел вдали... недвижных туч гряда
Раскинулась над ним; сквозь полог темный
Широких лип украдкою звезда
Блеснет и скроется — и по аллее
Идут они: одна чета скорее,
Другая тише, тише всё... и вдруг
С супругой добродетельный супруг

46

Отстал... О хитрость сельская! Меж тем
Параша с ним идет не слишком скоро...
Ее душа спокойна — не совсем:
А он не начинает разговора
И рядом с ней идет, смущен и нем.
Боится он внезапных объяснений,
Чувствительных порывов... Иногда
Он допускал возможность исключений,
Но в пошлость верил твердо и всегда.
И, признаюсь, он ошибался редко
И обо всем судил довольно метко...
Но мир *другой* ему был незнаком.
И он — злодей! — не сожалел о нем.

47

«Помилуйте, давно ль ваш Виктор был
И тронут и встревожен и так дале?»
Приятель мой — я вам сказать забыл —
Клялся в любви единственно на бале —
И только тем, которых не любил.
Когда же сам любовной лихорадки
Начальный жар в себе он признавал,
Его терзали, мучили догадки —
Свою любовь, как клад, он зарывал,
И с чувствами своими, как художник,
Любил один возиться мой безбожник...
И вдруг — с уездной барышней — в саду...
Едва ль ему отрадней, чем в аду.

45

"The garden then?" It is the old man speaking.
"Please, Viktor Alexeich, be our guest.
My garden is quite large, though simple-looking –
It has both paths and flowers at their best."
So off they went. Crepuscular loud croaking
Of corncrakes greeted them, while banks of cloud,
Above a meadow gleaming white afar,
Were overcast, and, through a gloomy shroud
Of spreading lime trees, furtively a star
Would shine and disappear – and so they go
Along the avenue: one couple slow,
The other rather quicker. In an instant
The virtuous spouse, together with her husband,

46

Hung back. Oh, rural wiliness! Meanwhile,
Parasha joined *him* in a dawdling walk…
Her soul was tranquil – not completely tranquil,
But he did not initiate their talk,
And, walking at her side, was mute and ill
At ease, of sudden sentiment afraid,
And suchlike bursts of feeling. Now and then
He granted that exceptions could be made;
His firm belief in *poshlost** was not vain.
And, I admit, mistakes with him were rare,
And when he made a judgement, he took care.
But he declined another world to visit,
And he – the villain – did not even miss it.

47

"Pray tell me, had your Viktor long been what
Is known as 'touched', 'disturbed', 'in someone's thrall'?"
My friend – to tell you this I quite forgot –
Would only swear to love when at a ball,
And only to whomever he was not
In love. When he within himself the fire
Of love's first stirrings to himself confessed,
Conjecture, supposition at him tore,
And love was buried like a treasure chest.
My godless friend was like an artist prone
To toying with emotions when alone,
And with this most provincial of young ladies
He would have been more comfortable in Hades.

35

48

Но постепенно тает он... Хотя
Почтенные родители некстати
Отстали, но она — она дитя;
На этом тихом personичике печати
Лукавства нет; и вот — как бы шутя
Ее он руку взял... и понемногу
Предался вновь приятной тишине...
И думает с отрадой: «Слава Богу,
До осени в деревне будет мне
Не скучно жить — а там... но я взволнован.
Я, кажется, влюблен и очарован!»
Опять влюблен? Но почему ж? — Сейчас,
Друзья мои, я успокою вас.

49

Во-первых: ночь прекрасная была,
Ночь летняя, спокойная, немая;
Не свети́ла луна, хоть и взошла;
Река, во тьме таинственно сверкая,
Текла вдали... Дорожка к ней вела;
А листья в вышине толпой незримой
Лепечут; вот — они сошли в овраг,
И, словно их движением гонимый,
Пред ними расступался мягкий мрак...
Противиться не мог он обаянью —
Он волю дал беспечному мечтанью
И улыбался мирно и вздыхал...
А свежий ветер в глаза их лобызал.

50

А во-вторых: Параша не молчит
И не вздыхает с приторной ужимкой;
Но говорит, и просто говорит.
Она так мило движется — как дымкой,
Прозрачной тенью трепетно облит
Ее высокий стан... он отдыхает;
Уж он и рад, что с ней они вдвоем.
Заговорил... а сердце в ней пылает
Неведомым, томительным огнем.
Их запахом встречает куст незримый,
И, словно тоже страстию томимый,
Вдали, вдали — на рубеже степей
Гремит, поет и плачет соловей.

48

He melted, though discomfited that both
Her worthy parents chose to lag behind,
But she was very young – a child, in truth:
No cunning was there in her face or mind.
To take her hand he seemed a trifle loath,
But take her hand he did, and gradually
He gave himself to silence once again,
And thought with mounting pleasure: "Glory be,
Till autumn country living will be fun,
But there... but I'm upset and agitated.
I seem to be in love, exhilarated!"
In love again? But why? I ask. And lest
You fret, my friends, I'll set your mind at rest.

49

In the first place, it was a lovely night –
A tranquil, soundless night, a night of summer;
Although the moon was up, it gave no light;
A distant stream, with enigmatic glimmer,
Flowed ever on. A path led to its side;
The leaves addressed their whispers to the heavens,
Then to the depths of a ravine they fluttered;
As if they were by that dispersal driven,
The tender shades of night before them scattered.
Their charm he set his face against in vain,
And, carefree, dreaming, sought not to remain.
He smiled a smile serene, and heaved long sighs,
And cooling breezes kissed them on the eyes.

50

And secondly Parasha does not baulk
At talking, nor heaves sighs with sweet grimace,
But talks – how plain and simple is her talk!
She moves so well, like a translucent haze.
A trembling shadow makes for her a cloak...
And now he is a man completely calm,
And glad he finds himself alone with her.
He spoke, and in her heart rose up a flame,
And unfamiliar, agonizing fire.
And unseen flowers bathed them with their scent,
As if with passion likewise they were spent;
A nightingale upon the steppe's far bourn
Sang plaintively and wistfully in turn.

51

И, может быть, он начал понимать
Всю прелесть первых трепетных движений
Ее души... и стал в нем утихать
Крикливый рой смешных предубеждений.
Но ей одной доступна благодать
Любви простой, и детской и стыдливой...
Нет! о любви не думает она —
Но, как листок блестящий и счастливый,
Ее несет широкая волна...
Всё — в этот миг — кругом ей улыбалось,
Над ней одной всё небо наклонялось.
И, колыхаясь медленно, трава
Ей вслед шептала милые слова...

52

Они всё шли да шли... Приятель мой
Парашей любовался молчаливо;
Она вся расцветала, как весной
Земля цветет и страстно и лениво
Под теплою, обильною росой.
Облитое холодной, влажной мглою,
Ее лицо горит... и понял он,
Что будет он владеть ее душою,
Что он любим, что сам он увлечен.
Она молчит — подобное молчанье
Имеет всем известное названье...
И он склонился — и ее рука
Под поцелуем вспыхнула слегка.

53

Читайте дальше, дальше, господа!
Не бойтесь: я писатель благонравный.
Шалил мой друг в бывалые года,
Но был всегда он малый «честный, славный»
И не вкушал незрелого плода.
Притом он сам был тронут: да признаться,
Он постарел — устал; не в первый раз
Себе давал он слово не влюбляться
Без цели... иногда в свободный час
Мечтал он о законном, мирном браке...
Но между тем он чувствует: во мраке
Параша вся дрожит... и мой герой
Сказал ей: «Не вернуться ль нам домой?»

51

Perhaps he had begun to understand
The stirrings of her soul in all their charm.
Within his inner soul a comic band
Of blatant misconceptions grew less warm.
But she alone the blessing had attained
Of artless feeling, childlike, diffident…
No! Love was never present in her thought.
She, like a favoured leaf, and radiant,
Was borne away upon a billow broad…
The world at large was smiling on her now,
To her alone the heavens seemed to bow,
And, swaying in slow motion, all the grass
To her in whispers spoke of happiness.

52

Thus they continued on. A paean of praise
My friend upon Parasha mutely heaped.
She blossomed, as the earth does on spring days
When, in abundant, warming dewdrops steeped,
It passionately, idly, comes ablaze.
Surrounded by a clammy, chilly mist,
Her face was burning. He knew well enough
That she would soon be by himself possessed,
That he was loved, and was in love himself.
When silences like she adopted fall,
They bear a name familiar to all.
He bent his head – beneath his kiss her hand
Grew warmer than a gently burning brand.

53

Please read on, gentlemen, read more;
Don't worry – I will always morals hallow.
My friend was dissolute in days of yore,
But always was a decent sort of fellow,
And unripe fruits he always would ignore.
Yet he himself was touched, it must be granted.
He'd aged, was tired, nor was it the first time
He'd promised that his love would not be flaunted
Without good reason. Sometimes he would dream
About a marriage as ordained by law,
But in the mean time in the dark he saw
Parasha tremble: this made him suggest
To go back home for them would be the best.

54

Они пошли домой; но — признаюсь —
Они пошли дорогой самой длинной...
И говорили много: я стыжусь
Пересказать их разговор невинный
И вовсе не чувствительный — клянусь.
Она болтала с ним, как с старым другом,
Но голос бедной девушки слегка
Звенел едва исчезнувшим испугом,
Слегка дрожала жаркая рука...
Всё кончено: она ему вверялась,
Сближению стыдливо предавалась...
Так в речку ножку робкую дитя
Заносит, сук надежный ухватя.

55

И, наконец, они пришли домой.
За ужином весьма красноречиво
И с чувством говорил приятель мой.
Старик глядит на гостя, как на диво;
Параша тихо подперлась рукой
И слушает. Но полночь бьет; готова
Его коляска; он встает; отец
Его целует нежно, как родного;
Хозяйка чуть не плачет... наконец
Уехал он; но в самый миг прощанья
Он ей шепнул с улыбкой: «До свиданья»,
И, уходя совсем, из-за дверей
Он долгим взглядом поменялся с ней.

56

Он едет; тихо всё... глухая ночь;
Перед коляской скачет провожатый.
И шепчет он: «Я рад соседям... дочь
У них одна; он человек богатый...
Притом она мила...» Он гонит прочь
Другие, неуместные мечтанья,
Отзвучия давно минувших дней...
Не чувствуя ни страха, ни желанья,
Она ходила в комнатке своей;
Ее душа немела; ей казалось,
Что в этот миг как будто изменялось
Всё прежнее, вся жизнь ее, — и сон
Ее застиг; во сне явился — он.

54

They set off homeward, but I have to say
It was the longest route by which they went.
I cannot easily to you convey
Their conversation, young and innocent,
Devoid of sentiment in any way.
She chatted to him, as with old friends she might.
The poor girl's voice, however, had the sound
Of one somewhat affected by a fright;
A gentle tremor ran through her warm hand...
The deed is done: in him she put her trust,
Consenting to becoming his at last.
Just so a child its foot will slowly ease
To test the water – then a stout branch seize.

55

Back home returned the couple in the end.
His talk was very eloquent and warm,
And feeling marked these speeches of my friend,
Seen by her father as, in human form,
A demigod. Parasha gently leant
Upon her arm; it's midnight; his calèche awaits;
He rises, and her father tenderly
Bestows on him a family embrace.
His wife is close to tears, and finally
He left, but at the moment of farewell
He whispered *au revoir* and gave a smile,
And, as he left her, from behind the door,
A long exchange of glances had with her.

56

He travelled on – all quiet at dead of night;
A horseman the calèche precedes at speed.
Then Viktor says, "My plans my neighbours suit,
With just one daughter; he is rich indeed,
And she's so nice." He quickly puts aside
All other inappropriate ideas
And every echo of the days of yore.
In her is no desire, no hidden fears,
And in her little room she paced the floor;
Her soul was muted. To her it now appeared
That all her past a new form had acquired,
As had her life. She now lived in a dream,
And in that dream she saw quite clearly – *him*.

57

Он... грустно мне; туманятся слезой
Мои глаза... гляжу я: у окошка
Она сидит на креслах; головой
Склонилась на подушку; с плеч немножко
Спустилася косынка... золотой
И легкий локон вьется боязливо
По бледному лицу... а на губах
Улыбка расцветает молчаливо.
Луна глядит в окно... невольный страх
Меня томит; мне слышится: над спящей,
Как колокольчик звонкий и дрожащий,
Раздался смех... и кто-то говорит...
И голосок насмешливо звенит:

«В теплый вечер и ульях чистых
Зреют светлые со́ты;
В теплый вечер лип душистых
Раскрываются цветы;
И когда по ним слезами
Потечет прозрачный мед —
Вьется жадно над цветами
Пчел ликующий народ...
Наклоняя сладострастно
Свой усталый стебелек,
Гостя милого напрасно
Ни один не ждет цветок.
Так и ты цвела стыдливо,
И в тебе, дитя мое,
Созревало прихотливо
Сердце страстное твое...
И теперь в красе расцвета,
Обаяния полна,
Ты стоишь под солнцем лета
Одинока и пышна.
Так склонись же, стебель стройный,
Так раскройся ж, мой цветок;
Прилетел жених... достойный —
В твой забытый уголок!»

57

I grieve to say that he… my eyes are misted
By tears. I looked: she by the window sat,
Upon a pillow she her forehead rested.
Below her shoulders hung a braided plait.
Across her pallid lineaments lay twisted
A timid lock of soft and golden hair…
With eyes and lips she hesitantly smiled,
A smile which silently burst into flower.
The moon shone through the window. Fears assailed
Me, and I heard the ring of bell-like laughter,
Which echoed round about the sleeping daughter.
And then there came the voice of someone speaking,
A voice enunciating words of mocking:

"Warmth of evening in the hives
Ripens the bright honeycombs;
Warmth of evening fragrance breathes
Into blossoms on the limes;
When the liquid honey flows
From inside them like sweet tears,
And rejoicing swarms of bees
Greedily ransack the flowers…
Every blossom will incline
Sensuously its weary stem;
Such a guest comes not in vain,
And is no surprise to them.
Thus in blossom, yet demure,
Passion in your heart had you,
O my child, a heart mature,
Which capriciousness outgrew;
Now that you are in your prime,
Full of charm and fascination,
In your splendid isolation,
Here you stand in summer time.
So then, bow, you flower of beauty,
And your gorgeous flower head open.
He has come, your worthy suitor,
To your corner, long forgotten."

58

Но, впрочем, это кончиться ничем
Могло... он мог уехать — и соседку,
Прогулку и любовь забыть совсем,
Как забываешь брошенную ветку.
Да и она, едва ль... но между тем
Как по́ саду они вдвоем скитались —
Что́, если б он, кого все знаем мы,
Кого мы в детстве, помнится, боялись,
Пока у нас не развились умы, —
Что́, если б бес печальный и могучий
Над садом тем, на лоне мрачной тучи
Пронесся и над любящей четой
Поник бы вдруг угрюмой головой, —

59

Что б он сказал? Он видывал не раз,
Как Дон Жуан какой-нибудь лукаво
Невинный женский ум, в удобный час,
Опутывал и увлекал... и, право,
Не тешился он зрелищем проказ,
Известных со времен столпотворенья...
Лишь иногда с досадой знатока
Он осуждал его распоряженья,
Давал советы изредка, слегка;
Но всё ж над ней одной он мог смеяться.
А в этот раз он стал бы забавляться
Вполне и над обоими. Друзья,
Вы, кажется, не поняли меня?

60

Мой Виктор не был Дон Жуаном... ей
Не предстояли грозные волненья.
«Тем лучше, — скажут мне,— разгар страстей
Опасен»... точно; лучше, без сомненья,
Спокойно жить и приживать детей —
И не давать, особенно вначале,
Щекам пылать... склоняться голове...
А сердцу забываться — и так дале.
Не правда ль? Общепринятой молве
Я покоряюсь молча... Поздравляю
Парашу и судьбе ее вручаю —
Подобной жизнью будет жить она;
А кажется, хохочет сатана.

58

But nothing might have come of this, however –
He might have left, forgetting promenade
And neighbour, now potentially his lover,
As you forget a twig which you discard.
And as for her, she scarcely… but together
They through the parkland briskly bowled along –
But what if he, a being we all know,
Of whom we were afraid when we were young,
Before our intellect had time to grow…
What if this demon, sorrowful and proud,
Above the parkland on a lowering cloud
Passed by, then made towards the couple,
A tilting of his head portending trouble.

59

What would his words have been, being not unused
To seeing some Don Juan on the sly
Make sure a female mind was quite confused,
Distracted? And, as no one could deny,
Of liking tricks he could not be accused,
Which had been practised since the world's foundation.
Occasionally he used piqued expertise
To criticize our Viktor's stipulations.
He sometimes gave *him* bits of mild advice;
At *her* expense alone could he make fun,
And he by now would no doubt have begun
To laugh at length at both of them. My friends,
It seems no one amongst you understands.

60

My Viktor was not a Don Juan and strife
Was not a thought which now before her lay.
"So much the better," will be said, "for passions rife
Are dangerous." It's better, they will say
To bring up children, lead a quiet life,
And not allow, especially at the start,
Your cheeks to redden or your head to drop,
Nor yet oblivion to grip your heart,
Et cetera. I yield to general vox pop
Without a word, and I congratulate
Parasha, whom I now leave to her fate.
A life like this is destined to be hers,
But Satan laughs his head off, it appears.

61

Мой Виктор перестал любить давно...
В нем сызмала горели страсти скупо;
Но, впрочем, тем же светом решено,
Что по любви жениться — даже глупо.
И вот в кого ей было суждено
Влюбиться... Что ж? он человек прекрасный
И, как умеет, сам влюблен в нее;
Ее души задумчивой и страстной
Сбылись надежды все... сбылося всё,
Чему она дать имя не умела,
О чем молиться смела и не смела...
Сбылося всё... и оба влюблены...
Но всё ж мне слышен хохот сатаны.

62

Друзья! я вижу беса... на забор
Он оперся — и смотрит; за четою
Насмешливо следит угрюмый взор.
И слышно: вдалеке, лихой грозою
Растерзанный, печально воет бор...
Моя душа трепещет поневоле;
Мне кажется, он смотрит не на них —
Россия вся раскинулась, как поле,
Перед его глазами в этот миг...
И как блестят над тучами зарницы,
Сверкают злобно яркие зеницы;
И страшная улыбка проползла
Медлительно вдоль губ владыки зла.

63

Я долго был в отсутствии; и вот
Лет через пять я встретил их, о други!
Он был женат на ней — четвертый год
И как-то странно потолстел. Супруги
Мне были ради оба. Мой приход
Напомнил ей о прежнем — и сначала
Ее встревожил несколько... она
Поплакала; ей даже грустно стало,
Но грусть замужней женщины смешна.
Как ручеек извилистый, но плавный,
Катилась жизнь Прасковьи Николавны;
И даже муж — я вам не всё сказал —
Ее весьма любил и уважал.

61

My Viktor had for long from love abstained;
From childhood passions burned in him, but dully;
Society, moreover, now maintained
That marrying for love was downright silly.
And this the man with whom it was ordained
She fall in love. Why not? A catch first-rate,
As best he could, he was by her distracted;
Her soul was contemplative, passionate,
And all its hopes were soon to be enacted,
Plus everything which had no nomenclature,
About which she to pray would never venture;
And so the two became a loving pair –
However, that is Satan's laugh I hear.

62

I see the demon, friends, against the fence.
He's leaning, watching, eyes fixed on the pair –
Derisive, saturnine his sombre glance.
Just listen to the forest howl afar:
Torn limb from limb, it utters mournful plaints.
My soul to tremors cannot help but yield;
It seems it isn't them whom he surveys –
The whole of Russia stretches like a field
In next to no time, there before his gaze.
As summer lightning bolts the storm clouds touch,
Malevolently his bright pupils flash.
A terrifying smile now slowly slips
Across the Prince of Darkness's cruel lips.

63

Some five long years went by before we met
Again. My friends, just think of that.
It was four years since he his bride had wed,
In which time he had grown extremely fat.
Our meeting pleased them. My arrival led
To memories of the past, and worries too,
At least at first, and so she sought relief
In bitter tears, and quite despondent grew.
But there was something comic in her grief.
"A stream which flows meandering but smooth"
Describes Parasha's life sunk in its groove –
Her husband even, I can now reveal,
Respected her, and loved her a great deal.

64

Сперва он тешился над ней; потом
Привык к ним ездить; наконец — женился;
Увидев дочь под свадебным венцом,
Старик отец умильно прослезился —
И молодым построил славный дом,
Обширный — по-старинному удобно
Расположенный... О друзья мои,
Поверьте: в жизни всё правдоподобно...
Вы, может быть, мне скажете: любви,
Ее любви не стоил он... Кто знает?
Друзья, пускай другой вам отвечает;
Пора мне кончить; много я болтал;
И вам я надоел, и сам устал.

65

Но — Боже! то ли думал я, когда,
Исполненный немого обожанья,
Ее душе я предрекал года
Святого, благодатного страданья?
С надеждами расставшись навсегда,
Свыкался я с суровым отчужденьем,
Но в ней ласкал последнюю мечту
И на нее с таинственным волненьем
Глядел, как на любимую звезду...
И что ж? я был обманут так невинно,
Так просто, так естественно, так чинно,
Что в истине своих желаний я
Стал сомневаться, милые друзья.

66

И вот что ей сулили ночи той,
Той летней ночи страстные мгновенья,
Когда с такой тревожной быстротой
В ее душе сменялись вдохновенья...
Прощай, Параша!.. Время на покой;
Перо к концу спешит нетерпеливо...
Что ж мне сказать о ней? Признаться вам,
Ее никто не назовет счастливой
Вполне... она вздыхает по часам
И в памяти хранит как совершенство
Невинности нелепое блаженство!
Я скоро с ней расстался... и едва ль
Ее увижу вновь... ее мне жаль.

64

At first at her expense he would amuse
Himself, but finally to wed resolved.
On seeing his daughter take her marriage vows,
Her aged father into tears dissolved,
And built the two young people a fine house,
Old-fashioned, spacious and quite comfortable.
O friends, you really do have to believe
That anything in life is plausible.
Perhaps he was not worthy of her love,
You'll say to me, but who can know or tell?
My friends, let someone else take up the tale,
It's time for me to end: too long I've chattered
And bored you all to death – I too am shattered.

65

Did I think *that* when I was in a lather,
Unspoken admiration proffering,
When I was forecasting a plethora
Of sanctified and blissful suffering?
Abandoning my every hope for ever,
I grew accustomed to grim alienation,
But I clung fast to my last dream in her,
And gazed at her with secret admiration,
As I would contemplate a favourite star –
And yet I was so innocently gulled,
So simply, comprehensively was fooled,
That truthfulness and dearest wishes I
Came to regard with some dubiety.

66

They promised her a night like that, no less,
A summer night, and moments of emotion,
A time when, with alarming rapidness,
When inspiration follows inspiration.
Farewell, Parasha! Now it's time to rest,
My pen to finish grows importunate.
What should I say of her? I must concede
The world would not have thought her fortunate
At all. For hours and hours on end she sighed,
And in her memory has kept long since
The awkward blessedness of innocence.
We went our separate ways, and it is pretty
Unlikely we shall meet – the more's the pity.

67

Мне жаль ее... быть может, если б рок
Ее повел другой — другой дорогой...
Но рок, так всеми принято, жесток;
А потому и поступает строго.
Припомнив взгляд любимый, я бы мог,
Я бы хотел сказать, чем, расставаясь
С Парашей, вся душа томится... но —
На серебристом снеге разгораясь,
Блестят лучи; скрипит мороз; давно
Пора на свежий воздух, на свободу...
И потому я кланяюсь народу
Читателей — снимаю свой колпак
Почтительно и выражаюсь так:

68

Читатель мой, прощайте! Мой рассказ
Вас усыпил иль рассмешил — не знаю;
Но я, хоть вижусь с вами в первый раз,
Дальнейшего знакомства не желаю...
Всё оттого, что уважаю вас,
Свои ошибки вижу я: их много;
Но вы добры, я слышал, и меня
По глупости простите ради Бога!
А вы, мои любезные друзья,
Не удивляйтесь: страстию несчастной
С ребячьих лет страдал ваш друг прекрасный.
Писал стихи... мне стыдно; так и быть!
Прошу вас эти бредни позабыть!

69

А если кто рассказ небрежный мой
Прочтет — и вдруг, задумавшись невольно,
На миг один поникнет головой
И скажет мне спасибо: мне довольно...
Тому давно — стоял я над кормой,
И плыли мы вдоль города чужого;
Я был один на палубе... волна
Вздымала нас и опускала снова...
И вдруг мне кто-то машет из окна.
Кто он, когда и где мы с ним видались,
Не мог я вспомнить... быстро мы промчались —
Ему в ответ и я махнул рукой —
И город тихо скрылся за горой.

67

I pity her. Perhaps if destiny
Had led her down another, different path...
But destiny is cruel, we all agree,
And therefore sometimes acts with undue wrath.
Remembering her glance it might well be
I would have said how loath I was to go
From my Parasha, how much it hurt, and yet –
The moonlight shone upon the silvery snow,
The hoar frost crackled – high time to forget
What now is past, to breathe fresh air and freedom.
I therefore pay respect to all my readers.
My nightcap now respectfully I doff,
And with these last reflections I sign off:

68

Farewell to you. The tale which I relate
Has bored you rigid, or amused, who knows?
Although this is the first time that we've met,
This is as far as our acquaintance goes.
This is because you with respect I treat,
And author am of many a mistake –
But I have heard that you are very kind:
Forgive my foolishness, for Heaven's sake!
And as for you, my most affectionate friends,
Be not surprised that passion unrequited
From childhood my entire existence blighted.
I blush to say I turned to verse. So what?
I ask you to forget about the lot.

69

Should anyone my narrative have read,
And suddenly, struck by a passing thought,
For just a little while has bowed his head
And thanked me – that is all I ever sought.
Our ship was sailing past some unknown town;
I took my station in the helmsman's stead;
I stood alone on deck. The waves combined
To raise us up and then to set us down,
When from a window someone waved and signed.
Who was this person, when did we meet last,
I could not think, and soon we had sailed past.
I waved my hand in answer to them too –
The town behind the hill sank out of view.

ANDREI

A POEM IN TWO PARTS

Часть первая

«Дела давно минувших дней».

1

«Начало трудно», — слышал я не раз.
Да, для того, кто любит объясненья.
Я не таков, и прямо свой рассказ
Я начинаю — без приготовленья...
Рысцой поплелся смирный мой Пегас;
Друзья, пою простые приключенья...
Они происходили вдалеке,
В уездном, одиноком городке.

2

Подобно всем уездным городам,
Он правильно расположен; недавно
Построен; на горе соборный храм
Стоит, неконченный; домá забавно
Свихнулись набок; нет конца садам
Фруктовым, огородам; страх исправно
Содержатся казенные места,
И площадь главная всегда пуста.

3

В уютном, чистом домике, в одной
Из улиц, называемой «Зеленой»,
Жил человек довольно молодой,
В отставке, холостяк, притом ученый.
Как водится, разумной головой
Он слыл лишь потому, что вид «мудреный»
Имел да трубки не курил, молчал,
Не выходил и в карты не играл.

Part One

"The deeds of days which are long past."*

1

It's hard to start, they've told me more than once –
Not least for those who favour explanations.
I'm not one such, and will my tale commence
With no preliminary preparations...
My Pegasus has set off briskly hence.
Adventures are the theme of my narration...
A cut-off township saw them come about –
A little place, provincial and remote.

2

Provincial towns like this were one and all
Correctly laid out by a local builder.
Atop the hill there stands the cathedral,
Unfinished – and the houses out of kilter
Look odd. Fruit orchards in an endless sprawl,
So many they the onlooker bewilder.
The public offices are all still there,
But there is no one in the central square.

3

A cosy cottage, comfortable and clean,
Which on a street called "Green Lane" is located,
Was where a young retired man was seen.
A bachelor he was, and educated,
As is the way, he was adjudged a "brain"
Because he seemed to be "sophisticated",
Did not go out and was the silent type,
Did not play cards, nor did he smoke a pipe.

4

Но не было таинственности в нем.
Все знали его чин, его фамилью.
Он года три в Москве служил; потом
Наскучив должностной... и прочей гилью,
Вернулся в отчий запустелый дом.
Все комнаты наполненные пылью
Нашел (его домашние давно
Все померли), да старое вино

5

В подвале, да запачканный портрет,
Да в кладовой два бабушкиных платья.
На воле рос он с самых ранних лет;
Пока служил он — связи да занятья
И вспомнить ему не́ дали, что нет
Родной груди, которую в объятья
Принять бы мог он... нет ее нигде...
Но здесь, в родимом и пустом гнезде,

6

Ему сначала было тяжело...
Потом он полюбил уединенье
И думал сам, что счастлив... но назло
Рассудку — часто грустное томленье
Овладевало им. Его влекло
Куда-то вдаль — пока воображенье
Усталое не сложит пестрых крыл, —
И долго после, молчалив, уныл,

7

Сидел он под окошком. Впрочем, он,
Как человек без разочарованья,
Не слишком был в отчаянье влюблен
И не лелеял своего страданья.
Начнет, бывало, думать... что ж? не стон,
Зевота выразит его мечтанья;
Скучал он не как байронов Корсар,
А как потомок выходцев-татар.

8

Скучал он — да; быть может, оттого,
Что жить в деревне скучно; что в столицах
Без денег жить нельзя; что ничего
Он целый день не делал; что в девицах

4

But he was not a mystery man in fact:
His surname was well known, as was his rank.
Three years he worked in Moscow, but he lacked
All interest in work and suchlike junk,
And to his empty manor house went back.
He found the rooms were full of dust, and dank;
His servants all had long since passed away;
His cellar only held some old Tokay,

5

A portrait hidden under layers of grime,
And in a cupboard two of grandma's dresses.
He'd grown up unconstrained from childhood time.
In Moscow both his contacts and his interests
No real opportunity gave him
To think about a mother's fond caresses.
Such nowhere were for him made manifest
But in the empty patriarchal nest.

6

At first he did not think that things were right,
But then he came to like his solitude,
Considered himself happy, but in spite
Of what his reason told him, lassitude
Took hold of him and focused his delight
Elsewhere, until he felt the pinions fold
Of vivid, colourful imagination,
And afterwards felt only desolation.

7

He by the window sat, but being a man
Who did not feel to disillusion drawn,
And on despair had never been too keen,
And did not think himself to suffering born,
He now to ponder weighty things began
Which did not make him groan, but rather yawn.
Un-Corsair-like* the fashion, he grew bored,
More like that of descendants of the Horde.

8

Yes, he was bored. Perhaps this was because
The rustic life is dull and lack of pay
Makes life in Petersburg a total loss,
Perhaps because he nothing did all day,

Не находил он толку... но всего
Не выскажешь никак — пока в границах
Законности, порядка, тишины
Держаться сочинители должны.

9

Так, он скучал; но молод был душой,
Неопытен, задумчив, как писатель,
Застенчив и чувствителен — большой
Чудак-дикарь и несколько мечтатель.
Он занимался нехотя собой
(Чему вы подивитесь, о читатель!),
Не важничал и не бранил людей
И ничего не презирал, ей-ей.

10

Хотел любви, не зная сам зачем;
В нем силы разгорались молодые...
Кипела кровь... он от любви совсем
Себе не ждал *спасенья*, как иные
Девицы да студенты. Между тем
Мгновенья проходили золотые —
И минуло два года — две весны...
(Весной все люди чаще влюблены.)

11

И вот опять настала та пора,
Когда, на солнце весело сверкая,
Капели падают... когда с утра
По лужам дети бегают, играя...
Когда коров гоняют со двора,
И травка зеленеет молодая,
И важный грач гуляет по лугам,
И подступает речка к берегам.

12

Прекрасен русский теплый майский день...
Всё к жизни возвращается тревожно;
Еще жидка трепещущая тень
Берез кудрявых; ветер осторожно
Колышет их верхушки; думать — лень,
А с губ согнать улыбку невозможно...
И свежий, белый ландыш под кустом
Стыдливо заслоняется листом.

Or maybe it could be the reason was
He had no time for girls – I just can't say,
Not least because, like any decent author,
I keep within the rules of law and order.

9

So he was bored, and yet was young in heart,
And thoughtful, like a writer, and unworldly,
Both sensitive and timid, and in part
A man who dreamt his dreams a touch absurdly.
He did not bother much with his own thought –
Should this my readers strike so very oddly?
Nor did he put on airs, or folk berate –
Held nothing in contempt, I'm pleased to state.

10

He wanted love, did not himself know why,
Within him youthful passion flowed in torrents;
His blood was seething, but from love's power he
Did not expect salvation, as do students.
Meanwhile he felt his life was going by,
A life which promised precious golden moments,
And two years passed, one spring and then another,
And springtime is the time for any lover.

11

And now that time of year came round again
When cheerfully, in a sun-drenched display,
There falls a shower of shining drops of rain,
And through the puddles children run and play,
When cattle from the cattle yard are ta'en,
And shoots of grass in green the fields array,
And self-important rooks strut o'er the meads,
And swollen rivers overflow their sides.

12

Such days in May the Russian scene enhance,
And into every vein the new life drips.
The trembling birch-tree shade is not yet dense;
A gentle, cautious breeze the tree crowns clips.
To spend this time in thinking makes no sense,
And yet the smile remains upon one's lips.
The lilies of the valley, fresh and white,
Beneath the bushes bashful faces hide.

13

Поедешь зеленями на коне...
Вздыхает конь и тихо машет гривой —
И как листок, отдавшийся волне,
То медленной, то вдруг нетерпеливой,
Несутся мысли... В ясной вышине
Проходят тучки чередой ленивой...
С деревни воробьев крикливый рой
Промчится... Заяц жмется под межой,

14

И колокольня длинная в кустах
Белеется... Приятель наш природу
Весьма любил и в четырех стенах
Не мог остаться в ясную погоду...
Надел картуз — и с палкою в руках
Пешком пустился через грязь и воду...
Была в числе всех улиц лишь одна
«Дворянская» когда-то мощена.

15

Он шел задумчиво, повеся нос.
По лужицам ступая деликатно,
Бежал за ним его легавый пес.
Мечтатель шел; томительно-приятно
В нем сердце билось — и себе вопрос
Он задавал: зачем так непонятно,
Так грустно-весел он, как вдруг один
Знакомец, не служащий дворянин,

16

Нагнал его: «Андрей Ильич! Куда-с?»
«Гуляю, так; а вы?» — «Гуляю тоже.
Вообразите — не узнал я вас!
Гляжу, гляжу... да кто ж это, мой Боже!
Уж по собаке догадался, да-с!
А слышали вы — городничий?» — «Что же
С ним сделалось?» — «Да с ним-то ничего.
Жену свою прибил он за того

17

Гусарчика —вы знаете...» — «Я? Нет!»
«Не знаете? Ну как же вам не стыдно?
Такой приятный в обществе, брюнет.
Вот он понравился — другим завидно,

13

Across a sea of greenery you ride.
Your steed will quietly toss its head and mane.
And, like the leaves which on the wave tops float,
Now slowly, now impatiently again,
Your thoughts are borne, while in the clear blue height
The clouds process in slow and lazy line,
And flocks of sparrows from the village flit,
And hares beneath the fences huddled sit,

14

And in the trees a bell tower, white and tall.
Of Nature was our friend extremely fond.
He did not like to stay indoors at all,
And never in his own four walls remained.
He set off on his way through mud and squall
With cap on head and stout stick in his hand.
Among the local streets there was just one,
Known as "Dvoryanskaya"* and paved with stone.

15

With eyes downcast his pensive way he wound,
Through puddles stepping in a manner comely.
Behind him ran his shaggy hunting hound.
A dreamer he, within whom wearisomely,
Yet pleasantly, a heart began to pound.
Repeatedly he asked himself how come he
Was happy and yet sad. All of a sudden an
Acquaintance and a fellow nobleman

16

Approached. "Andrei, where are you going to?"
"Just for a stroll. And you?" "Me too. Why not?
I did not realize that it was you.
I looked and looked. Who can it be? My God!
I recognized the dog, and then I knew.
But have you heard about the mayor?" "So what
Has happened?" "He is quite all right,
But that hussar was what caused him to beat

17

His wife. You know about it?" "No."
"You don't? You really ought to be ashamed.
A pleasant fellow, hair of brown. A beau
And popular. And jealousy consumed

Послали письмецо да весь секрет
И разгласили... Кстати, нам обидно
С женой, что не зайдете никогда
Вы к нам; а жили, помнится, всегда

18

Мы с вашим батюшкой в большом ладу».
«А разве есть у вас жена?» — «Прекрасно!
Хорош приятель, признаюсь! Пойду
Всем расскажу...» — «Не гневайтесь напрасно».
(Ну, — думал он, — попался я в беду.)
«Не гневаться? Нет, я сердит ужасно...
И если вы хотите, чтоб я вас
Простил совсем, пойдемте к нам сейчас».

19

«Извольте... но нельзя ж так...» — «Без хлопот!»
Они пошли под ручку мимо праздных
Мещанских баб и девок, у ворот
Усевшихся на лавках, мимо разных
Заборов, кузниц, домиков... и вот
Перед одним из самых безобразных
Домов остановилися... «Здесь я
Живу, — сказал знакомец, — а судья

20

Живет вон там, подальше. Вечерком
Играем мы в картишки: заседатель,
Он, я да Гур Миняич, вчетвером».
Они вошли; и закричал приятель
Андрея: «Эй! жена! смотри, кто в дом
Ко мне зашел — твой новый обожатель
(Не правда, что ли?)... вот, сударь, она,
Авдотья Павловна, моя жена».

21

Ее лицо зарделось ярко вдруг
При виде незнакомого... Стыдливо
Она присела... Радостный супруг
Расшаркался... За стулья боязливо
Она взялась... Ее немой испуг
Смутил Андрея. Сел он молчаливо
И внутренно себя бранил — и, взор
Склонив, упрямо начал разговор.

The town. Soon everyone was in the know.
But, by the way, I'm rather underwhelmed,
You never come to see my wife and me,
Despite the fact, as I remember, we

18

Together with your father got on well."
"So do you really have a wife?" "That's great!
You are my dearest friend. I'll go and tell
The tale to everybody." "Please don't get
Annoyed for nothing." (Well, I'm in a hole,
He thought.) "Annoyed? I'm very much upset,
And if you really want me to forgive
You, come with me to visit us forthwith."

19

"But, by your leave, can I just come?" "That's fine."
So arm in arm the two friends passed a bevy
Of damsels and old women in a line,
Passed several little cottages and smithies,
Passed several picket fences, whereupon
They stopped before the most rebarbative
Of houses. Andrei's new friend lived there.
"The judge lives over there," he said. "It's where

20

We like to occupy the evening hour
By playing cards – me and the president,
The judge and Gur Minyaich, making four."
They entered, and at once his new-found friend
Yelled, "Wife! Just take a look who's come to our
Abode. May I your new admirer here present?
(I think I've got that right. At least, she's caught you –
That is to say, my lovely wife Avdotya.)"*

21

At once a colouring suffused her face
When she the stranger saw. She timorously
Sat down, while her delighted lawful spouse
Bowed low all round. Avdotya nervously
Moved chairs. Her nerves seemed to confuse
Andrei, who merely sat there wordlessly,
And cursed himself, and then his gaze averted,
And awkwardly a conversation started.

22

Но вот, пока зашла меж ними речь
О том, что людям нужно развлеченье
И что здоровье надобно беречь,
Взглянувши на нее, в одно мгновенье
Заметил он блестящих, белых плеч
Роскошный очерк, легкое движенье
Груди, зубов-жемчужин ровный ряд
И кроткий, несколько печальный взгляд.

23

Заметил он еще вдоль алых щек
Две кудри шелковистые да руки
Прекрасные... Звенящий голосок
Ее хранил пленительные звуки —
Младенчества, как говорят, пушок.
А за двадцать ей было... пользу скуки
Кто может отрицать? Она, как лед,
От порчи сберегает наш народ.

24

Пока в невинности души своей
Любуется наш юноша стыдливый
Чужой женой, мы поспешим о ней
Отдать отчет подробный, справедливый
Читателям. (Ее супруг, Фаддей
Сергеич, был рассеянный, ленивый,
Доверчивый, прекрасный человек...
Да кто ж и зол в наш равнодушный век?)

25

Она росла печальной сиротой;
Воспитана была на счет казенный...
Потом попала к тетушке глухой,
Сносила нрав ее неугомонный,
Ходила в летнем платьице зимой —
И разливала чай... Но брак законный
Освободил несчастную: чепец
Она сама надела, наконец.

26

Но барыней не сделалась. Притом
Авдотья Павловна, как институтка,
Гостей дичилась, плакала тайком
Над пошленьким романом; часто шутка

22

And so between them started a debate
About the recreation people need,
About how one should stay in a fit state.
Meanwhile, in gazing at her, he espied
The outline of a pair of shoulders white,
The movement of her bosom as she breathed,
Of teeth, a pearly-white and gleaming set,
A mild look in her eyes, full of regret.

23

He saw the way her cheeks began to mantle,
Two ringlets and a pair of graceful hands...
He heard a voice both immature and brittle,
Which still retained its captivating sounds
And was what people call both young and gentle.
Who can deny that boredom knows no bounds
For someone over twenty. It like ice
Preserves all Russian people from all vice.

24

While in his heart of hearts our bashful youth
Admired a wife in manner innocent,
I am at pains to document the truth
So readers get an accurate account.
Faddei, the husband, was a man of sloth,
A little vague, but counted excellent,
Inclined to be entirely unsuspicious...
Who in this listless age can be dubbed vicious?

25

She grew up as a most unhappy orphan,
And at the state's expense was educated...
But then a deaf old auntie took her over,
Whose restless manner left her quite frustrated.
In winter, summer clothes were all her cover;
She poured out tea, but then was liberated
By lawful wedlock. Now she could don
The cap denoting status newly won.

26

But higher circles could not her accept.
And she, a product of a boarding school,
Fought shy of guests, and on the quiet wept
When reading trashy novels. Often cruel

Ее пугала... Но в порядке дом
Она держала; здравого рассудка
В ней было много; мужа своего
Она любила более всего.

27

Но, как огонь таится под золой,
Под снегом лава, под листочком розы
Колючий шип, под бархатной травой
Лукавый змей и под улыбкой слезы, —
Так, может быть, и в сердце молодой
Жены таились пагубные грезы...
Мы посвящаем этот оборот
Любителям классических острот.

28

Но всё ж она любила мужа; да,
Как любят дети, — кротко, без волнений,
Без ревности, без тайного стыда,
Без тех безумных, горьких сожалений
И помыслов, которым иногда
Предаться совестно, без подозрений, —
Безо всего, чем дерзостную власть
Свою не раз обозначала страсть.

29

Но не была зато знакома ей
Восторгов нескончаемых отрада,
Тоска блаженства... правда; но страстей
Бояться должно: самая награда
Не стоит жертвы, как игра — свечей...
Свирепый, буйный грохот водопада
Нас оглушает... Вообще всегда
Приятнее стоячая вода.

30

И если грусть ей в душу как-нибудь
Закрадывалась — это мы бедою
Не назовем... ведь ей же хуже, будь
Она всегда, всегда своей судьбою
Довольна... Грустно ей, заноет грудь,
И взор заблещет томною слезою —
Она к окошку подойдет, слегка
Вздохнет да поглядит на облака,

Asides would scare her, but she kept
Her house in order. She was no one's fool,
Had lots of common sense, adored her man
As much as any human being can.

27

But just as fire persists beneath the ash,
As snow hides lava, roses spikes,
Just as a downy layer of velvet grass
Conceals the lair of cunning poisonous snakes,
It could be, in the heart of this young lass,
A soul-destroying flight of fancy lurks.
These several similes we dedicate
To those who love our classic authors' wit.

28

She loved her lawful husband all the same,
As children do, without dissimulation,
Without all envy and all secret shame,
Without all bitter, mad recriminations,
Or schemes which sometimes bring upon one blame,
Without suspicions, nor yet hesitations,
Nor anything whereby consuming passion
Has shown its power on more than one occasion.

29

However, she had been quite unaware
Of sensual delights the consolation,
Of bliss the trials. All true, but she a fear
Of passions had. They were no compensation
For sacrifice, and candles are worth more
Than any game. The deafening sensation,
The crashing thunder of the waterfall
Do not match standing water overall.

30

But if her soul acquainted was with grief
At sundry times, disastrous it was not.
Things would have been much bleaker for her if
She always had been happy with her lot.
She's sorrowful; her heart aches, bosom heaves,
The tears that dim her eyes are burning hot;
She to the window goes and gives a sigh,
Then glances upwards at the cloud-filled sky

31

На церковь старую, на низкий дом
Соседа, на высокие заборы —
За фортепьяно сядет... всё кругом
Как будто дремлет... слышны разговоры
Служанок; на стене под потолком
Играет солнце; голубые шторы
Сквозят; надувшись весь ручной
Снегирь свистит — и пахнет резедой

32

Вся комната... Поет она — сперва
Какой-нибудь романс сантиментальный...
Звучат уныло страстные слова;
Потом она сыграет погребальный
Известный марш Бетховена...но два
Часа пробило; ждет патриархальный
Обед ее; супруг, жену любя,
Кричит: «Уха простынет без тебя».

33

Так жизнь ее текла; в чужих домах
Она бывала редко; со слезами
Езжала в гости, чувствовала страх,
Когда с высокопарными речами
Уездный франт в нафабренных усах
К ней подходил бочком, кося глазами...
Свой дом она любила, как сурок
Свою нору — свой «home», свой уголок.

34

Андрей понравился соседям. Он
Сидел у них довольно долго; и споры
Пускался; словом, в духе был умен,
Любезен, весел... и хотя в узоры
Канвы совсем, казалось, погружен
Был ум хозяйки, — медленные взоры
Ее больших и любопытных глаз
На нем остановились — и не раз.

35

Меж тем настала ночь. Пришел Андрей
Ильич домой в большом недоуменье.
Сквозь зубы напевал он: «Соловей
Мой, соловей!» — и целый час в волненье

31

And sees the church, and squat house of her neighbour,
The towering shapes of lofty palisades,
And sits at the pianoforte. Slumber
Envelops all around. The serving maids
Are talking audibly. Across the timber
Of ceiling sunbeams play and penetrate
The sky-blue blinds. There sings a bullfinch tame
And mignonettes disperse their sweet perfume

32

Throughout the room. She then at first began
To sing some kind of sentimental romance,
A mournful song, a passionate refrain.
She next began to play a funeral march,
A well-known piece composed by Beethoven.*
But then, at two o'clock, came time for lunch.
Her husband didn't want his wife to scold,
So simply said: "Your soup is getting cold."

33

And so her life continued on. She shied
Away from visiting, in tears would baulk
At meeting guests. Was always terrified
When listening to the highfalutin talk
Of some provincial fop with whiskers dyed,
Or seeing him give her a sideways look.
As marmots burrows, so she loved her *dom*,
Her little corner of the world, her "home".

34

Andrei was liked by neighbours, and would sit
Some time with them. Prolonged discussions he
Would start. His mood was good, and he was bright,
Although in doing her embroidery
It seemed the lady of the house was quite
Absorbed. Inquisitive the reverie
Reflected in the wide-eyed, languid glance
Bestowed upon Andrei, and more than once.

35

Already it was night. Andrei had come
Back to his home, considerably unsure.
"'O nightingale of mine',"* began to hum,
And agitatedly a solid hour

Ходил один по комнате своей...
Не много было складу в этом пенье —
И пес его, весьма разумный скот,
Глядел на барина, разиня рот.

36

Увы! всем людям, видно, суждено
Узнать, как говорится, «жизни бремя».
Мы ничего пока не скажем... Но
Посмотрим, что-то нам откроет время?
Когда на свет выходит лист — давно
В земле нагретой созревало семя...
Тоскливая, мечтательная лень
Андреем овладела в этот день.

37

С начала самого любовь должна
Расти неслышно, как во сне глубоком
Дитя растет... огласка ей вредна:
Как юный гриб, открытый зорким оком,
Замрет, завянет, пропадет она...
Потом — ее вы можете с потоком
Сравнить, с огнем, и с лавой, и с грозой,
И вообще со всякой чепухой.

38

Но первый страх и трепет сердца, стук
Его внезапный, первое страданье
Отрадно-грустное, как первый звук
Печальной песни, первое желанье,
Когда в огне нежданных слез и мук
С испугом просыпается сознанье
И вся душа заражена тоской...
Как это всё прекрасно, Боже мой!

39

Андрей к соседям стал ходить. Они
Его ласкали; малый был он смирный,
Им по плечу; радушьем искони
Славяне славятся; к их жизни мирной
Привык он скоро сам; летели дни;
Он рано приходил, глотал их жирный
Обед, пил жидкий чай, а вечерком,
Пока супруг за ломберным столом

Paced up and down his solitary room.
The meaning of his song was quite obscure.
His dog, an animal most sensible,
His master watched with drooping mandible.

36

It is the fate of everyone, alas,
The heavy burden of their life to feel.
Enough of that for now. Meanwhile let us
Observe what time will in the end reveal.
When leaves begin to burst, the seed long has
Been germinating hidden in the soil...
An agonizing languor on this day
Was wholly in possession of Andrei.

37

From earliest beginnings true love should
Mature unheard, just as in a deep sleep
A child matures. Proclaimed love is no good.
Just as, by keen eyes found, a new-grown cep
Will wither soon, die back and fade.
Or else love can be likened to the sweep
Of thunderstorm, of lava and of flame,
Or any other junk you care to name.

38

But the first fear, first tremor of the heart,
First pounding, first consolatory pain,
Like when the first notes of a sad song start,
Like the first stirrings of desire when,
Consumed by fires of unexpected hurt
The consciousness with fear wakes up again,
When all the soul with languor is infected...
Good Heavens! How all this is really splendid!

39

Andrei began to visit neighbours. They
Made much of him – he was a splendid fellow,
And suited them. For ever and for aye
The Slavs have been reputed for their mellow
Approach to life, which very soon Andrei
Decided it advisable to follow.
At dinner, tea or later in the day,
When at a game of cards his host held sway,

40

Сражался, с ней сидел он по часам...
И говорил охотно, с убежденьем
И даже с жаром. Часто был он сам
Проникнут добродушным удивленьем:
Кто вдруг освободил его? речам
Дал звук и силу? Впрочем, «откровеньем»
Она не величала тех речей...
Язык новейший незнаком был ей,

41

Нет, — но при нем овладевало вдруг
Ее душой веселое вниманье...
Андрей стал нужен ей, как добрый друг,
Как брат... Он понимал ее мечтанье,
Он разделять умел ее досуг
И вызывать малейшее желанье...
Она могла болтать, молчать при нем...
Им было хорошо, тепло вдвоем.

42

И стал он тих и кроток, как дитя
В обновке: наслаждался без оглядки;
Андрей себя не вопрошал, хотя
В нем изредка пугливые догадки
Рождались... Он душил их, жил шутя.
Так первые таинственные взятки,
С стыдливостью соединив расчет,
Чиновник бессознательно берет.

43

Они гуляли много по лугам
И в роще (муж, кряхтя, тащился следом),
Читали Пушкина по вечерам,
Играли в шахматы перед обедом,
Иль, волю дав лукавым языкам,
Смеялись потихоньку над соседом...
Иль иногда рассказывал Андрей
О службе занимательной своей.

44

Тогда, как струйки мелкие реки
У камышей, на солнце, в неглубоких
Местах, иль как те светлые кружки
В тени густых дубов и лип широких,

40

Andrei would sit with Dunya endlessly,
And speak with willingness and approbation,
And even warmly, quite surprised how frequently
Kind-heartedness became his inclination.
Who caused this change and made him speak so boldly?
However, Dunya thought that "revelation"
Was not what she his rhetoric would call.
She did not know the latest term at all.

41

But in his presence she would be possessed
By rapt attentiveness and heartfelt cheer.
Andrei became the friend considered best,
A brother who her waking dreams could share,
A partner for her in her hours of rest
Who could call forth her very least desire.
With him she could both chatter and be silent;
Their mutual life was always warm and pleasant.

42

He soon was like an infant newly dressed,
Submitting meekly to his new enjoyment,
Asked nothing of himself, although he guessed
That he would soon be facing anxious moments.
He stayed light-hearted, all such thoughts suppressed.
Just so the first of many secret payments,
Combining bashfulness and fiddled books,
Unthinkingly a bent official takes.

43

They very often strolled across the mead,
And (followed by her husband) in a glade,
Would of an evening Pushkin's poems read –
Or games of chess before their dinner played,
Or, giving crafty spitefulness its head,
A mocking portrait of a neighbour made.
Andrei on some occasions grew discursive
On how he had enjoyed the civil service.

44

As rivers start their course with little springs,
In shallows, in the sunshine, in the rushes,
Or like those lighted places, forest rings
Among the oaks and limes and spreading bushes

Когда затихнет ветер, а листки
Едва трепещут на сучках высоких, —
По тонким губкам Дуни молодой
Улыбки пробегали чередой.

45

Они смеялись часто... Но потом
Весьма грустить и горевать умели
И в небо возноситься... Под окном
Они тогда задумчиво сидели,
Мечтали, жили, думали вдвоём
И молча содрогались и бледнели —
И тихо воцарялся в их сердцах
Так называемый «священный страх».

46

Смешно глядеть на круглую луну;
Смешно вздыхать — и часто, цепенея
От холода, ночную тишину
«Пить, жадно пить», блаженствуя, немея...
Зевать и прозаическому сну
Противиться, затем, что с эмпирея
Слетают поэтические сны...
Но кто ж не грешен с этой стороны?

47

Да, много так погибло вечеров
Для них; но то, что в них тогда звучало,
То был любви невольный, первый зов...
Но то, что сердце в небесах искало,
Что выразить не находили слов, —
Так близко, рядом, под боком дышало...
Блаженство не в эфире... Впрочем, кровь
Заговорит, когда молчит любовь.

48

Проворно зреет запрещённый плод.
Андрей стал грустен, молчалив и странен
(Влюблённые — весьма смешной народ!),
И смысл его речей бывал туманен...
Известно: труден каждый переход.
Наш бедный друг был прямо в сердце ранен...
Она с ним часто ссорилась... Она
Была сама смертельно влюблена.

To which the dying wind a stillness brings
And barely rustles leaves in topmost branches,
Across Avdotya's slender-featured face
In swift succession smiles began to race.

45

They often laughed, but then they would grow sad,
And to indulge their grief they never failed,
And pensively beneath the window sat,
And to the heights of heaven they appealed.
They thought, they lived, they dreamt as a duet,
And shivered in their silences, and paled.
And in their hearts a sacred fear, so called,
Without their noticing had taken hold.

46

It's comical to watch the ring-shaped moon,
And comical to sigh, and, often numb
With cold, the night-time silence to drink in
And, wordless, to its blissfulness succumb,
To fight prosaic sleepiness's yawn
Because poetic dreaminess will come,
Descending earthwards from the empyrean...
But who on that account is without sin?

47

Yes, many evenings thus were dissipated,
But that which Dunya and Andrei had heard
Was the first sign which true love indicated...
But that for which they could not find a word,
That for which they Heaven supplicated,
Was deep within their inner being stirred.
The ether holds no bliss, but blood will speak
Whenever love's loquaciousness grows weak.

48

Forbidden fruit will rapidly mature.
Andrei grew sad, and taciturn, and crazy
(To be in love is comical for sure!)
The meaning of his words was sometimes hazy.
One knows – transition loses its allure.
His wounded heart made our poor friend uneasy.
She often used to quarrel with him. She
Herself was just as much in love as he.

49

Но мы сказать не смеем, сколько дней,
Недель, годов, десятков лет волненья
Такие продолжаться в нем и в ней
Могли бы, если б случай, — без сомненья,
Первейший друг неопытных людей, —
Не прекратил напрасного томленья...
Однажды муж уехал, а жена
Осталась дома, как всегда, одна.

50

Работу на колени уронив,
Тихонько на груди скрестивши руки
И голову немножко наклонив,
Она сидит под обаяньем скуки.
И взор ее спокоен и ленив,
И на губах давно затихли звуки...
А сердце — то расширится, то вновь
Задремлет... По щекам играет кровь.

51

Но мысли не высокой предана
Ее душа; напротив, просто «вздором»,
Как люди говорят, она полна...
Улыбкой грустной, беспокойным взором,
Которого вчера понять она
Еще не смела, длинным разговором
И тем, что выразить нельзя пером...
Знакомый шаг раздался под окном.

52

И вдруг — сам бес не скажет почему —
Ей стало страшно, страшно до рыданий.
Боялась она, что ли, дать ему
В ее чертах найти следы мечтаний
Недавних... Но в таинственную тьму
Чужой души мы наших изысканий
Не будем простирать. Прекрасный пол,
Источник наших благ и наших зол,

53

Не всем дается в руки словно клад,
Зарытый хитрой ведьмой. Молчаливо
Она вскочила, через сени в сад
Бежит... в ней сердце бьется торопливо...

49

We dare not say how many days on end,
How many decades agitated thoughts
Would have continued troubling both their minds
If happenstance, which is, without a doubt,
Of inexperienced lovers the best friend,
Their futile agony did not cut short.
One day her husband left, and when he'd gone,
His wife, as ever, stayed at home alone.

50

Embroidery and frame she casts aside,
Her arms across her breast are held.
Her face averted, head a little bowed,
By tedium's fascination she is filled,
Her gaze with tranquil indolence endowed –
And on her lips all sound is long-since stilled.
As for her heart, it first expands, then sleeps,
A flush of colour into both cheeks creeps.

51

Not prone to lofty thinking was her soul,
But rather to the "trivia" of creation.
As people tend to put it, it was full
(That is, sad smiles of anxious contemplation,
Which even yesterday Avdotya still
Had dared not fathom, or lengthy conversation –
In short, what's not to be by pen expounded).
Beneath the window well-known steps resounded.

52

And suddenly – the Devil can't say why –
She grew so frightened tears ran down her face.
She feared, it seems, her features would betray
To him of recent waking dreams the trace.
But our investigations will not stray
Into an alien soul's most secret place.
The fairer of the sexes always should
Be seen as source of all our ills and good.

53

Not everyone will find the treasure store
The sorceress has buried cunningly.
Avdotya rose, and through the garden door
She ran. Her heart was beating rapidly.

Но, как испуганная лань, назад
Приходит любопытно, боязливо,
И слушает, и смотрит, и стрелка
Не видит, — так, на цыпочках, слегка,

54

Она дошла до комнаты своей...
И с легкой, замирающей улыбкой,
Вся розовая, к скважине дверей
Нагнула стан затянутый и гибкий.
Концы ее рассыпанных кудрей
Колышатся пленительно на зыбкой
Груди... под черной бровью черный глаз
Сверкает ярко, как живой алмаз...

55

Она глядит — безмолвно ходит он.
Как виден ясно след немой заботы
И грусти на его лице!.. Влюблен
Андрей. На фортепьянах две-три ноты
Небрежно взял он. Слабый, робкий звон
Возник и замер. Вот — ее работы
Рассматривать он начал... Там в угле
Она платок забыла на столе.

56

И жадно вдруг к нему приник Андрей
Губами — крепко, крепко стиснул руки.
Движенья головы его, плечей
Изобличали силу тайной муки...
Дуняша вся затрепетала... В ней,
Как дружные торжественные звуки
Среди равнин печальных и нагих,
Любовь заговорила в этот миг.

57

Ей всё понятно стало. Яркий свет
Вдруг озарил ее рассудок. Страстно
Они друг друга любят... в этом нет
Теперь уже сомнений... Как прекрасно
Блаженства ждать и верить с ранних лет
В любовь, и ждать и верить не напрасно,
И тихо, чуть дыша, себе сказать:
Я счастлив — и не знаю, что желать!

But as, by hounds pursued, a frightened deer
Inquisitively turns back fearfully
And looks and listens, but then fails to see
The hunter – in the same way quietly she

54
Back to her bedroom on her tiptoes went,
And with the faintest smile upon her face,
And blushing deeply to the keyhole bent –
Her body slim and supple at the waist;
Her ringlets, loosened to their full extent,
Danced captivatingly upon her breast.
Beneath dark brows her eyes were limpid pools,
Their brilliance resembling precious jewels.

55
She watches. On he walks, unspeaking, mute.
How clear upon his face are his unease
And melancholia. Andrei is quite
Besotted. Casually he strikes the keys
Of the piano, whence a timid note
Sounds out and dies. Then her embroideries
He scrutinized. A handkerchief of cotton
She's set down in the corner and forgotten.

56
His avid lips to this now pressed Andrei,
And into tight-clenched fists he balled his hands.
His head and shoulder movements both betrayed
The depth and power of his secret wounds.
Avdotya trembled on that very day.
As melodies harmonious can sound
Amid a land monotonous and bleak,
So in Avdotya love began to speak.

57
Now everything was clear to her: her mind
Enlightened suddenly, and passionate
Their mutual love – of that no doubts remained.
How good it is for blissful days to wait,
To love, to trust, and neither do in vain,
To do so from a very early date,
To softly tell yourself beneath your breath
What's happiness – I do not know myself.

58

Как весело гореть таким огнем!
Но тяжело терять напрасно годы,
Жить завтрашним или вчерашним днем,
И счастья ждать, как узники — свободы...
Упорно, как они, мечтать о нем
И в безответных красотах природы
Искать того, чего в ней нет: другой
Души, любимой, преданной, родной.

59

В Дуняше кровь вся к сердцу прилила,
Потом к лицу. Так хорошо, так больно
Ей стало вдруг... бедняжка не могла
Вздохнуть, как бы хотелось ей, довольно
Глубоко... кое-как она дошла
До стула... Слезы сладкие невольно,
Внезапно хлынули ручьем из глаз
Ее... Так плачут в жизни только раз!

60

Она не вспомнила, что никогда
С Андреем ей не жить; что не свободна
Она, что страсти слушаться — беда...
И что такая страсть или бесплодна,
Или преступна... Женщина всегда
В любви так бескорыстно благородна...
И предаются смело, до конца,
Одни простые женские сердца.

61

Дуняша плакала... Но вот Андрей,
Услышав легкий шум её рыданья,
Дверь отворил и с изумленьем к ней
Приближился... вопросы, восклицанья
Его так нежны были, звук речей
Дышал таким избытком состраданья...
Сквозь слезы, не сказавши ничего,
Дуняша посмотрела на него.

62

Что́ было в этом взгляде, Боже мой!
Глубокая, доверчивая нежность,
Любовь, и благодарность, и покой
Блаженства, преданность и безмятежность,

58

To burn with such a fire how great a joy!
But it is hard the years in vain to waste,
To live for days to come, for yesterday,
As convicts freedom, so good fortune taste
And dream about it stubbornly as they
Will surely do – in Nature's boundless grace
To seek for something it does not possess:
Another loving kindred soul, no less.

59

Avdotya's blood then to her heart then rushed,
Then to her face. Her good life had grown tough.
Whatever poor Avdotya might have wished,
The sighs she gave could not be deep enough.
A vacant chair Avdotya somehow reached...
Her tears were sweet, unbidden tears of love
And issued in a torrent from her eyes.
Thus only once in life a person cries.

60

It had escaped her that she with Andrei
Could not together live, nor was she free,
And passion's prompting she must not obey.
Such passion may be fruitless, or may be
Illicit. Women can in every way
In love act nobly and impartially,
And the plain and simple female heart
Will to the very end itself commit.

61

Avdotya wept, and so it was Andrei,
The gentle, subdued sound of sobbing hearing,
Who opened wide the door in some dismay
And went to her. So tender were his queries
And exclamations, full of sympathy,
And an abundance of compassion bearing...
Avdotya wept, but not a word she spoke,
But on Andrei she cast a silent look.

62

Good Heavens! What was hidden in those eyes!
Profundity, and love, and tenderness,
And gratitude, tranquillity and bliss,
Serenity, complete devotedness,

И кроткий блеск веселости немой,
Усталость и стыдливая небрежность,
И томный жар, пылающий едва...
Досадно — недостаточны слова.

63

Андрей не понял ровно ничего,
Но чувствовал, что грудь его готова
Внезапно разорваться, — до того
В ней сердце вдруг забилось. Два-три слова
С усильем произнес он... на него
Дуняша робко посмотрела, снова
Задумалась — и вот, не мысля зла,
Ему тихонько руку подала.

64

Он всё боялся верить... Но потом
Вдруг побледнел... лицо закрыл руками
И тихо наклонился весь в немом
Восторге... Быстро, крупными слезами
Его глаза наполнились... О чем
Он думал... также выразить словами
Нельзя... Нам хорошо, когда в тупик
Приходит описательный язык.

65

Она молчала... и молчал он сам.
О! то, что в это дивное мгновенье
Их полным, замирающим сердцам
Одну давало жизнь, одно биенье, —
Любовь едва решается речам
Себя доверить... Нужно ль объяснение
Того, что несомненней и ясней
(Смотри Шекспира) солнечных лучей?

66

Он руку милую держал в руках
Похолодевших; слабые колени,
Дрожа, под ним сгибались... а в глазах
Полузакрытых пробегали тени.
Он задыхался... Между тем, о страх!
Фаддей (супруг) входил в пустые сени...
Известно вам, читатели-друзья,
Всегда приходят вовремя мужья.

Of muted gaiety the pallid rays,
And weariness and bashful carefreeness,
And fire low-burning, only just alight.
How all this makes my words inadequate!

63

Andrei had next to nothing comprehended,
And felt his breast was ready to explode.
And suddenly his heart within him pounded,
And it was difficult to say a word.
Her timid gaze upon Andrei descended,
And then she once again began to brood.
Lo and behold, without a second thought,
She with her hand Andrei's hand quietly sought.

64

Belief he lacked, but then the colour drained
From out his face, which with his hands he hid.
In mute delight his body he inclined,
And massive were the teardrops he now shed.
Exactly what Andrei had in his mind
Is difficult in simple words to put.
We frequently are perfectly content
When our descriptive skills hit a dead end.

65

She held her peace... He held his peace himself.
Oh! It was that remarkable sensation
Which to their overbrimming faint hearts gave
Vivacity, the thrill of palpitation.
Love scarcely grants to speeches self-belief.
Is there a need for any explanation
Of what is more indubitably clear
Than rays of sunshine (please see your Shakespeare).*

66

Avdotya's hand he held in hands grown cold.
Andrei began to tremble, and his knees
Grew weak and under him began to fold.
A shadow ran across his half-closed eyes.
He gasped for breath. Meanwhile, lo and behold,
Faddei (the husband) in the vacant porch arrives.
You are aware, dear friends who are my readers,
That husbands will appear when they are needed.

67

«Я голоден», — сказал он важно, вдруг
Шагнувши в комнату. Дуняша разом
Исчезла; наш Андрей, наш бедный друг
(Коварный друг!) глядел не то Фоблазом,
Не то Маниловым; один супруг
Приличье сохранил и даже глазом
Не шевельнул, не возопил «о-го!»
Как муж — он не заметил ничего.

68

Андрей пробормотал несвязный вздор,
Болезненно зевнул, стал как-то боком,
Затеял было странный разговор
О Турции, гонимой злобным роком,
И, наконец, поднявши к небу взор,
Ушел. В недоумении глубоком
Воскликнул муж приятелю вослед:
«Куда же вы? Сейчас готов обед».

69

Андрею не до кушанья. Домой
Он прибежал и кинулся на шею
Сперва к хозяйке, старой и кривой,
Потом к оторопелому лакею...
Потом к собаке. С радостью большой
Он дал бы руку своему злодею
Теперь... Он был любим! он был любим!
Кто мог, о небеса, сравниться с ним?

70

Андрей блаженствовал... Но скоро в нем
Другое чувство пробудилось. Странно!
Он поглядел задумчиво кругом...
Ему так грустно стало — несказанно,
Глубоко грустно. Вспомнил он о том,
Что в голове его не раз туманно
Мелькало... но теперь гроза бедой,
Неотразимой, близкой, роковой

71

Ему представилась. Еще вчера
Не разбирал он собственных желаний.
При ней он был так счастлив... и с утра
Тоской немых, несбыточных мечтаний

67

"I'm very hungry," he was heard to say
As he came in, and Dunya in a flash
Went out. And as for our poor friend Andrei,
He was Manilov first, and then Faublas.*
Alone the aforementioned spouse Faddei
Preserved the decencies and did not rush
To judgement, did not yell "Oho!" –
And like all husbands somehow failed to know.

68

Andrei some incoherent rubbish muttered.
He yawned, and with a stance somehow oblique
Conversed – or, rather, somewhat strangely chattered –
About how Fate pursued the luckless Turk.*
At last he left, his gaze to heaven averted.
Perplexed, and left completely in the dark,
The husband yelled as loud as he was able:
"Where are you off to? Dinner's on the table."

69

Andrei did not want food, and so he hied
Him home post-haste. When there, he first embraced
His housekeeper, an ancient crone one-eyed,
And then his servant, whom he left amazed,
And then his dog. Indeed, with what delight
He would his own worst enemy have faced!
He was adored – oh, how he was adored!
Who could, oh Heaven, be with him compared?

70

Such was his bliss, but soon in him awoke
A different feeling, quite incredibly.
Around himself he cast a pensive look.
He had become so sad, ineffably,
Profoundly sad. When he his mind cast back
To what was briefly, indefinably
Glimpsed there. But now the threat that he was under
Was the approaching sound of fatal thunder.

71

He had, as lately as the day before,
His own deep-felt desires not analysed.
She was his bliss, and from an early hour
By muted waking dreams unrealized

Томился... Но теперь — прошла пора
Блаженства безотчетного, страданий
Ребяческих... не возвратится вновь
Прошедшее. Андрей узнал любовь!

72

И всё предвидел он: позор борьбы,
Позор обмана, дни тревог и скуки,
Упрямство непреклонное судьбы,
И горькие томления разлуки,
И страх, и всё, чем прокляты рабы...
И то, что хуже — хуже всякой муки:
Живучесть пошлости. Она сильна;
Ей наша жизнь давно покорена.

73

Он не шутя любил, недаром... Он,
В наш век софизмов, век самолюбивый,
Прямым и добрым малым был рожден.
Ему дала природа не кичливый,
Но ясный ум; он уважал закон
И собственность чужую... Молчаливый,
Растроганный, он медленно лицо
Склонил и тихо вышел на крыльцо.

74

На шаткую ступеньку сел Андрей.
Осенний вечер обагрял сияньем
Кресты да стены белые церквей.
Болтливым, свежим, долгим трепетаньем
В саду трепещут кончики ветвей.
Струями разливается с молчаньем
Вечерним — слабый запах. Кроткий свет
Румянит о́блака свинцовый цвет.

75

Садится солнце. Воздух дивно тих,
И вздрагивает ветер, словно сонный.
Окошки темных домиков на миг
Зарделись и погасли. Отягченный
Росой внезапной, стынет луг. Затих
Весь необъятный мир. И благовонный,
Прозрачный пар понесся в вышину...
И небо ждет холодную луну.

He was tormented. Now the time was o'er
Of bliss irrational and childish agonies.
There was no going back, the past was gone,
Now that Andrei the pangs of love had known.

72

He could foresee the future, the deceit,
The shame of these, the anxious, tedious future,
A stubborn and inexorable Fate,
The bitter consequences of departure,
And everything the life of slaves will blight.
But what is worse, much worse than any torture,
Is vulgarness, a force persistent, strong,
Which has impacted life for far too long.

73

His love was very serious, and he,
In times of sophistry and raw ambition,
Was kindly and straightforward born to be.
He had a modest and unclouded vision.
He valued law and others' property,
Was taciturn and prone to strong emotion.
His gaze was now directed at the floor,
And then he left by way of the front door.

74

There on a shaky step Andrei now perches.
The autumn evening reddens with its glow
The crosses and the whitewashed walls of churches –
A rustling in the garden, long and slow,
A noisy stirring of the topmost branches,
A silence where the scents of evening flow
In streams and where faint glimmers redden
The dark clouds, thunder-filled and leaden.

75

The sun is setting, and the air is still;
As if from sleep, the wind is fitful, sudden;
The little houses' windows, dark and dull,
For one brief transient second flicker, redden;
And on the meadow there descends a chill
As with a sudden dewfall it is burdened.
The world is silent. Mist ascends the heights;
The firmament the frigid moon awaits.

76

Вот замелькали звезды... Боже мой!
Как равнодушна, как нема природа!
Как тягостны стремительной, живой
Душе ее законная свобода,
Ее порядок, вечность и покой!
Но часто после прожитого года
В томительной мучительной борьбе,
Природа, позавидуем тебе!

76

And now the stars begin to shine. Good Lord!
How wordless and indifferent is Nature –
To questings of a living soul how hard
Its rightful independence and its order,
Tranquillity and everlasting word.
But often, after such a year of torture,
Of agonizing struggles battled through,
O Nature, I am envious of you!

Часть вторая

I

Прошло шесть месяцев. Зима лихая
Прошла; вернулась ясная весна,
Среди полей взыграла голубая,
Веселая, свободная волна,
Уже пробилась почка молодая,
И дрогнула немая глубина...
Здоровая земля блестит и дышит,
И млеет и зародышами пышет.

2

А наш Андрей? Наружной перемены
В его судьбе не замечаем мы.
По-прежнему к соседу после сцены
С его женой — в теченье всей зимы
Ходил он... «Те же люди, те же стены.
Всё то же, стало быть...» Вот как умы
Поверхностные судят большей частью...
Но мы глубокомысленны, по счастью.

3

Любовь рождается в одно мгновенье —
И долго развивается потом.
С ней борется лукавое сомненье;
Она растет и крепнет, но с трудом...
И лишь тогда последнее значенье
Ее вполне мы, наконец, поймем,
Когда в себе безжалостно погубим
Упрямый эгоизм... или разлюбим.

Part Two

1

Six months went by. The winter's cold withdrew
To let return the sparkling springtime days.
Throughout the countryside a field of blue,
A sign of joy and liberty arose.
Already everywhere young buds showed through;
The silent subterranean depths unfroze;
The earth revived, and once again drew breath
And thawed, and was ablaze with new-born growth.

2

But what of our Andrei? If there had been
An altered circumstance, we're not aware.
As always, if the pair had had a scene,
He to his neighbour's house would then repair.
All winter long – same people in the main,
Same walls, same everything, I rather fear.
Such is the judgement of a shallow mind,
But happily our thoughts are more profound.

3

Love happens in the twinkling of an eye,
But subsequent development is slow;
Untrustworthy misgivings with it vie,
And make it difficult for it to grow,
And only then what it may signify
We fully, finally will get to know,
When in ourselves we ruthlessly remove
Our stubborn egoism, or cease to love.

4

Андрей был слишком юн и простодушен...
И разлюбить не думал и не мог.
Он чувствовал, что мир его нарушен,
И тайный жар его томил и жег.
Он был судьбе задумчиво послушен,
К себе же строг, неумолимо строг...
Он уважал то, что любил... а ныне
Не верят люди собственной святыне.

5

Сперва знакомцам нашим было ново
Их положенье... но хоть иногда
Признанье было вырваться готово —
Оно не высказалось никогда.
Они как будто дали себе слово
Прошедшее забыть... и навсегда...
И слово то держали свято, твердо
И друг во друга веровали гордо.

6

Но то, над чем не властны мы до гроба:
Улыбка, вздох невольный, взор немой —
Им изменяли часто... Впрочем, оба
Не пользовались слабостью чужой;
И даже подозрительная злоба
В их жизни, детски честной и прямой,
Не замечала пятен... (чтобы чуда
В том не нашли, прибавим мы: покуда).

7

По-прежнему затейливо, проворно
В беседах проходили вечера.
Они смеялись так же непритворно...
Но если муж уехать со двора
Хотел — ему противились упорно,
И раньше говорили: «спать пора»,
И реже предавались тем неясным,
Мечтательным порывам, столь опасным.

8

Всё так... но каждый принимал участье
Во всем, что думал и желал другой.
И не совсем их позабыло счастье:
Так иногда над тучей грозовой,

4

Andrei was far too trusting, far too young...
To be in love was all he contemplated.
The tumult in his mind he felt was wrong,
And secret passions burnt and enervated.
Obediently with Fate he went along.
Himself he always very sternly treated...
He always had respect for what he loved,
But nothing sacrosanct is now believed.

5

At first our friends thought novel their position,
And on the point of being manifest;
Though all appeared prepared for their admission,
It never reached the point of being expressed.
They, as it were, had taken the decision
For ever to eradicate the past.
They faithfully observed their promise. It
Became a matter mutually implicit.

6

But that which is beyond us to the grave,
Involuntary smiles, a sigh, a glance,
Betrayed them frequently, but both were loath
To profit from the other's hesitance,
And even those suspicious of the truth
Could not declare them to be miscreants.
They nothing found remarkable in that –
At least for the time being, we'd like to add.

7

As ever, complicatedly, in haste,
In chattering the evenings went by.
They laughed quite naturally as they conversed,
But if the husband wished to go away,
The company would stubbornly resist,
And "time for bed" would prematurely say –
Less often would to formless dreams succumb,
Which, as we know, can do a lot of harm.

8

And thus it was, but both their part would take
In anything the other wanted different,
And happiness did no exception make
For them. Thus sometimes as the angry elements

Когда шумит сердитое ненастье,
Откроется внезапно золотой
Клочок небес — и луч косой, широкий
Сквозь частый дождь осветит лес далекий.

9

Как выразить их тайную тревогу,
Когда, на время быстрое пеня,
Они шли тихо, нехотя, к порогу
И расставались до другого дня?
Андрей пускался медленно в дорогу
И, голову печально наклоня,
Шагал, шагал так мерно, так уныло...
А сердце в нем тогда рвалось и ныло.

10

Но Боссюэт сказал: «Всему земному
Командуется: марш!» — и человек,
Владыко мира, ничему живому
Сказать не может: стой вот здесь навек!
Через равнины к морю голубому,
Далекому стремятся воды рек...
И мчится жизнь, играя на просторе,
В далекое, таинственное море,

11

Не только кучерам, но всем известно,
Что под гору сдержаться тяжело.
Андрей боролся совестливо, честно;
Но время шло, без остановки шло...
Великодушье часто несовместно
С любовью... Что ж тут делать? И назло
Отличнейшим намереньям, как дети,
Мы падаем в расставленные сети.

12

Андрей любил, но жертвовать собою
Умел; отдался весь — и навсегда.
Он за нее гордился чистотою
Ее души, не ведавшей стыда.
Как? Ей склониться молча головою
Пред кем-нибудь на свете?.. Никогда!
Узнать волненье робости позорной?
Унизиться до радости притворной?

Give warning that a thunderstorm will break,
A golden patch of sky becomes apparent,
And then a ray of sunshine, slanting, broad,
Will through the pouring rain light up a wood.

9

Can one express their masked anxiety
As they, the speed of passing time berating,
Towards the door went slowly, quietly,
Until their next encounter, separating?
Along the road Andrei set off deliberately,
The ground before him sadly contemplating.
Thus gloomily and steadily he went,
And his despondent heart in two was rent.

10

All earth is told to "march", said Bossuet,*
But Man the Ruler fails in his endeavour
To any living thing these words to say:
"This is the place where you will stand for ever!"
Across the plains, towards the deep-blue sea,
The waters of the rivers ever strive,
And life continues in its headlong motion
Towards the enigmatic distant ocean.

11

As people know who try to drive a coach,
It's hard to stop when going down a hill.
Andrei's behaviour always was impeccable,
But time relentlessly was passing still.
Great-heartedness and love are incompatible.
Can anything be done to cure this ill?
Despite our very best intentions, we
Are caught in snares from which we can't break free.

12

Andrei was deep in love, could sacrifice
Himself and felt devoted for all time.
He took a deal of pride in Dunya's grace,
And in her soul, which knew not any shame.
Would she from anyone avert her face?
She never would indulge in such a game.
Would she the thrill of shameful shyness know,
Or lower herself to simulated joy?

13

Предать ее на суд толпы досужной?
Лишиться права презирать судьбу
И сделать из жены, рабы наружной,
Немую, добровольную рабу?
О нет! Душе слабеющей, недужной,
Но давшей слово выдержать борьбу,
Что надо? Добродетель и терпенье?
Нет — гордость и холодное презренье.

14

А если вам даны другие силы,
И сердце ваше, жадное страстей,
Не чувствует того, чем сердцу милы
Дозволенные радости людей,—
Живите на свободе... до могилы
Не признавайте никаких цепей...
Могущество спокойного сознанья
Вас не допустит даже до страданья.

15

Андрей героем не был... и напрасно
Страдать — свободы ради — наш чудак
Не стал бы; но, как честный малый, ясно
Он понимал, что невозможно *так*
Им оставаться; что молчать — опасно;
Что надобно беде помочь... но как?
Об этом часто, долго, принужденно
Он думал и терялся совершенно.

16

Им овладело горькое сомненье...
И в тишине томительной ночей
Бессонных в нем печальное решенье
Созрело, наконец; он должен с ней
Расстаться... с ней... о, новое мученье!
О скорбь! о, безотрадный мрак! Андрей
Предался грусти страшной, безнадежной,
Как будто перед смертью неизбежной.

17

Во всем признаться... не сказавши слова,
Уехать и в почтительном письме
Растолковать... Но женщина готова
Всегда подозревать обман... В уме

13

For her would gossiping be prejudicial?
Should he of scorn for Fate himself deprive
Or make his wife a servant superficial,
A worthless and a voluntary slave?
What does a weak soul need which fails to thrive,
And yet decides the struggle to be crucial?
To be resigned or to be virtuous?
No, to be proud and be contemptuous!

14

If other strengths should chance to be your lot,
And if your heart, in search of passion's heat,
Remains incapable of feeling what
Gives human hearts permissible delight,
Unfettered live! Until your dying day do not
Let chains of any sort your life restrict...
Tranquillity of conscience has the power
Your freedom from all suffering to ensure.

15

Andrei – no hero he – would not in vain
Be put through an ordeal for freedom's sake;
This strange but decent fellow thought it plain
That silence was the worst move they could make,
That things for them could not the same remain,
That somehow they remedial steps must take.
His thoughts on this were frequent, lengthy, forced,
And in confusion frequently were lost.

16

The bitterest doubts of him then took possession,
And, in painful, sleepless silence lost,
He at long last arrived at a decision.
A new ordeal! He realized that they must
Go separate ways – not easy to envision.
Andrei was sad and gloomy and downcast.
He'd lost all hope – his grief was terrible,
Like one who faced a death inevitable.

17

Confess to everything... without a word,
Or leave and then respectfully explain...
But women always seem to be prepared,
To be suspicious of deceit... Again

Несчастного предположенья снова
Мешались, путались... В унылой тьме
Бродил он... Небольшое приключенье
Внезапно разрешило затрудненье

18

В Саратове спокойно, беззаботно,
Помещик одинокий, без детей —
Андрея дядя — здравствовал; но, плотно
Покушавши копченых карасей,
Скончался. Смерть мы все клянем охотно,
А смерти был обязан наш Андрей
Именьем округленным и доходным,
Да, сверх того, предлогом превосходным

19

К отъезду... Пять-шесть дней в тоске понятной
Провел он... Вот однажды за столом,
С беспечностью совсем невероятной,
Играя лихорадочно ножом,
Он к новости довольно неприятной
Соседей приготовил... а потом
Отрывисто, ни на кого не глядя,
Сказал: «Я должен ехать. Умер дядя».

20

Супруг ответствовал одним мычаньем
(Он кушал жирный блин); его жена
На гостя с изумленным восклицаньем
Глядит... Она взволнована, бледна...
Внезапно пораженное страданьем,
В ней сердце дрогнуло... Но вот она
Опомнилась... и, медленно краснея,
С испугом молча слушает Андрея.

21

«Ваш дядюшка скончался?» — «Да-с. Я с детства
Его знавал... я знаю целый свет.
Позвольте...» «Вы теперь насчет наследства?»
«Да-с. — «Ну, ступайте с Богом — мой совет.
Жаль, жаль лишиться вашего соседства...
Но делать нечего. Надолго?» — «Нет...
О нет... я ненадолго... нет...» И трепет
Остановил его смущенный лепет.

Assumptions in the wretch's mind grew blurred,
And he was wandering in dark terrain.
But then an insignificant event
Meant he the awkwardness could circumvent.

18

A landowner, an uncle of Andrei's,
Lived quietly in Saratov, without children,
Enjoyed rude health, but once ate to excess
Some platefuls of his favourite smoked crucians
And passed away. We all tend death to curse,
But our Andrei to death became beholden.
His new estate was large and lucrative,
And gave him an excuse superlative

19

To go. A week in understandable
Distress he spent. Once, while a meal enjoying,
And with an insouciance improbable
With knife and fork was feverishly toying,
A piece of news somewhat unpalatable
For neighbours he prepared, abruptly saying,
And looking anywhere but in their eye:
"I've got to go. My uncle's passed away."

20

The spouse with only mooing sounds replies
While swallowing a blin. His wife her guest
Regards with exclamations of surprise.
Her face is pale – she's obviously distressed.
Then, suddenly beset by agonies,
Her heart begins to flutter in her breast,
But she herself composes, blushing red,
And listens to Andrei with silent dread.

21

"Your uncle's dead?" "He is. Since I was little,
I've known him as I've known more than a few."
"His will is what you want to go and settle?"
"It is." "That's what I think you have to do.
We'll lose a neighbour, and much sorrow it'll
Occasion. Are you going for long?" "Oh, no,
No, I shall not be long away." A tremor
Brought to an end Andrei's embarrassed stammer.

22

Дуняша смотрит на него... Разлуку
Он им пророчит... но на сколько дней?
Зачем он едет? Радость или муку —
Что, что скрывает он? Зачем он с ней
Так холоден? Зачем внезапно руку
По мрачному лицу провел Андрей?
Зачем ее пытающего взора
Он избегал, как бы страшась укора?

23

Она разгневалась. Перед слезами
Всегда сердиты женщины. Слегка
Кусая губы, ласково глазами
Прищурилась она... да бедняка
Насмешками, намеками, словцами
Терзала целый божий день, пока
Он из терпенья вышел не на шутку...
Дуняше стало легче на минутку.

24

Но вечером, когда то раздраженье
Сменила постепенно тишина,
Немую грусть, унылое смущенье,
Усталый взгляд Андрея вдруг она
Заметила... Невольно сожаленье
В ее душе проснулось, и, полна
Раскаянья, Дуняша молчаливо
По комнате прошлась и боязливо

25

К нему подсела. Взор ее приветно
Сиял; лицо дышало добротой.
«Андрей, зачем вы едете?» Заметно
Дрожал неровный голос. Головой
Поник он безнадежно, безответно,
Хотел заговорить, махнул рукой,
Взглянул украдкой на нее... бледнея...
И поняла Дуняша взгляд Андрея.

26

Она сидела молча, замирая,
С закрытыми глазами. Перед ней
Вся будущность угрюмая, пустая,
Мгновенно развернулась... и, со всей

22

Dunyasha looked at him. This separation
Would last, she sought to know, how many days?
Why was he going? Was he dejection or elation
Concealing. Why adopt such frosty ways
With her? Or then again, why did he hasten
To draw his hand across his downcast face?
Why did he fail to meet her searching look,
As if he could not criticism brook?

23

Her anger grew. Before a woman cries,
She's prone to vent her spleen. A gentle touch
Of teeth on lips, a narrowing of eyes,
And she the livelong day attacked the wretch
With jeers, insinuations, sharp asides
And bitter words, as a result of which,
He lost his temper, fit to cause a seizure,
But Dunya by the minute found things easier.

24

But in the evening, when his irritation
Had been replaced by calmness gradually,
Andrei's despondency, his desolation
And weary look she noticed suddenly.
Unbidden feelings of commiseration
Awakened in her. Dunya silently,
A prey to feelings of profound regret,
In timid fashion crossed the room and sat

25

Beside Andrei. Her glance was radiant
And welcoming, her face with kindness stamped.
"Why are you going?" – all too evident
The tremor in her faltering voice. He slumped
And hung his head, was in despair and spent,
Then tried to speak, but gave up the attempt.
He paled, and cast a surreptitious glance,
Which for Dunyasha had significance.

26

With eyes tight shut she wordless, swooning, sat.
The gloomy future which before her lay
Was clear, and, rising to her feet,
Dunyasha put what strength she had in play,

Собравшись силой, медленно вставая,
Она сказала шёпотом: «Андрей,
Я понимаю вас... Вы не лукавы...
Я благодарна вам... Вы правы... правы!»

27

Его рука, дрожа, сыскала руку
Дуняши... Расставаясь навсегда,
В последний раз, на горькую разлуку
Пожал он руку милую тогда.
Не передав изменчивому звуку
Своей тоски — но страха, но стыда
Не чувствуя, — проворными шагами
Он вышел и залился вдруг слезами.

28

О чувство долга! Сколько наслаждений
(Духовных, разумеется) тобой
Дается нам в замену треволнений
Ничтожной, пошлой радости земной!
Но по причине разных затруднений,
По слабости, всё мешкал наш герой,
Пока настал, к тоске дворян уезда
Бобковского, печальный день отъезда.

29

Андрей с утра в унылую тревогу
Весь погрузился; дедовский рыдван,
Кряхтя, придвинул к самому порогу,
Набил и запер толстый чемодан;
Всё бормотал: «Тем лучше; слава Богу», —
И сапоги запихивал в карман...
Людей томит и мучит расставанье,
Как никогда не радует свиданье.

30

Потом он начал ящики пустые
С великим шумом выдвигать; в одном
Из них нашел он ленточки — немые
Свидетели прошедшего... Потом
Он вышел в сад... и листики сырые
Над ним шумели грустно, старый дом
Как будто тоже горевал, забвенье
Предчувствуя да скорое паденье.

And in a whisper told her lover that
She understood him fully now: "Andrei,
There's not an ounce of cunning in your blood.
You're right! You're right. I'm full of gratitude."

27

His trembling hand sought out Dunyasha's hand,
And, as they bade farewell for evermore,
Before that bitter moment had come round,
Andrei had pressed the hand that he adored.
His anguish he did not betray by sound,
And, being of shame and terror unaware,
Andrei with rapid steps made haste to go.
He left – and then the tears began to flow.

28

Oh, sense of duty! Numerous the pleasures,
The spiritual pleasures you create
For our delight, as barter for the pressures
Of earthly entertainments, futile, trite.
But a bout of chronic discomposure
Compelled our hero to procrastinate,
Until Bobkovo saw the fateful day
When finally our hero went away.

29

All day our hero was in deep gloom sunk.
The family coach he to the front porch moved.
He crammed with things, and locked, a massive trunk.
He lugged it to the coach, and wheezed, and puffed,
And muttered: "This is for the best, I think."
His boots into his pockets he then stuffed.
Such partings will make lovers feel dejected
More than they are by happiness affected.

30

Then he began, with an enormous racket,
To pull out empty drawers. He found in one
Some witnesses of times gone by – a packet
Of ribbons. So our hero thereupon
Went walking in the garden. In the thickets
The leaves above his head made plaintive moan.
The old house seemed to grieve, as if foretelling
Oblivion, the moment of its falling.

31

С тяжелым сердцем к доброму соседу
Андрей поплелся; но не тотчас он
К нему пришел и не попал к обеду.
Уже гудел вечерний, тяжкий звон.
«А, здравствуйте! Вы едете?» — «Я еду».
«Когда же?» — «Завтра до зари». — «Резон;
Лошадкам легче, легче; воля ваша...»
Андрей с ним согласился. Где Дуняша?

32

Она сидела в уголку. Смущенье
Изобличали взоры. В темноте
Она казалась бледной. Утомленье
Ее печальной, тихой красоте
Такое придавало выраженье,
Так трогательны были взоры те,
Смягченные недавними слезами,
Что бедный наш Андрей всплеснул руками.

33

С ней говорил он... как обыкновенно
Перед отъездом говорят: о том,
Что никого на свете совершенно
Занять не в состоянии; причем
Они смеялись редко, принужденно
И странно, долго хмурились потом...
Фаддей зевал до слез весьма протяжно
И, кончив, охорашивался важно.

34

Был у Дуняши садик по старинной
Привычке русской. Садиком у нас
В уездах щеголяют. Из гостиной
Вели две-три ступеньки на террас.
Кончался сад довольно темной, длинной
Аллеей... Вечером, и в жаркий час,
И даже ночью по песку дорожки
Бродили часто маленькие ножки.

35

В тот вечер, над землей, до влаги жадной,
Веселая, весенняя гроза
Промчалась шумно... Легкий сон отрадной
Волной струится мягко на глаза

31

Our hero made his way with heavy heart
To see his kindly neighbour, but he failed
To find him, and at dinner took no part.
The bell for evensong already tolled.
"Hello. You're going?" "I am". "When do you start?"
"Before first light." "With that I can't find fault.
The horses find that time of day much easier."
Andrei agreed, but where was our Dunyasha?

32

We find her in the corner. Awkwardness
Was in her glance. The darkness of the night
Made her look pale. Her weariness
Enhanced her beauty, sorrowful and quiet,
And added to it more expressiveness.
Her glance betrayed the pathos of her plight,
And was so softened by the tears she spilled
That our Andrei was with amazement filled.

33

He spoke to her, as usually is done
Before a separation, of things that now
Are probably of interest to none.
And yet they laughed occasionally somehow
(Their laughter was infrequent, lacked all fun).
Long afterwards they spoke with furrowed brow.
Faddei responded with a lengthy yawn,
But that improved his mood to no mean tune.

34

Dunyasha, following an ancient custom,
The garden tended. In the provinces a plot
Like this is prized. Three steps from the guest room
Led to the terrace and beyond to what
Became an avenue's extended gloom,
Where in the evening, when the air was hot,
Or sometimes even in the depths of night,
Along the path there wandered little feet.

35

On evenings, when the thunder clouds come rolling
To threaten moisture for the earth beneath,
And gentle slumber in a wave consoling
Lies on the eyes of everything that breathes,

Всему, что дышит, и в тени прохладной
На каждом новом листике слеза
Прозрачная дрожит, блестит лукаво,
И небо затихает величаво...

36

Во след другим, отсталая, лениво
Несется туча, легкая, как дым.
Кой-где вдали возникнет торопливо
Неясный шум — и, воздухом ночным
Охваченный, исчезнет боязливо.
От сада веет запахом сырым...
И на ступеньках редкие, большие
Еще пестреют капли дождевые.

37

И на террас они пошли все трое...
Вот, помолчавши несколько, супруг
Им объявил, что время не такое,
Чтобы гулять, и возвратился вдруг
В гостиную. Но небо голубое
Им улыбалось ласково. Сам-друг
Они присели на скамейке, рядом —
Меж светлым домиком и темным садом.

38

Всё так очаровательно: молчанье
Кругом, как будто чутко над землей
Поникла ночь и слушает... Мерцанье
Далекой, робкой звездочки... покой
Немеющего воздуха... Желанье
В сердцах их, полных горестью, тоской,
Любовью, загоралось самовластно...
А вот луна блеснула сладострастно...

39

И, словно пробужденные стыдливым,
Медлительным и вкрадчивым лучом,
Заговорили говором сонливым
Верхушки лип, облитые дождем.
Внезапно по дорожкам молчаливым,
В кустах и на песку перед крыльцом
Взыграли тени слабые... Волненье
Скрывая, смотрят оба в отдаленье.

And every leaf in cooling shade unfolding
A trembling teardrop to the world bequeaths,
It glistens slyly, sparkling, transparent.
Majestic silence rules the firmament.

36

Behind the storm, detached and indolent,
A cloud scuds by, like smoke and just as light;
A distant sound arises, indistinct,
Enveloped by the darkness of the night,
Then vanishing, a tremulous descant.
The scents of rain the garden permeate.
From time to time a scatter of raindrops
Makes multicoloured splashes on the steps.

37

They went out to the terrace, all the three,
Where, after a short silence, Dunya's spouse
Declared that this was not the time to be
Outdoors. Forthwith he went back to the house,
And to the guest room. But the grey-blue sky
Bestowed on them a smile which they deemed "nice".
Now on a bench they sat down side by side
Between the house lights and the garden shade.

38

Enchanted silence permeates the air,
As if above the earth the night is watchful
And listening. A timid distant star
Is glowing, and the muted air is peaceful.
Desire within each anguished, grieving heart,
Which full of love is also sorrowful,
Despotic and unchallenged is ignited,
And then the moon voluptuously is lighted.

39

It is as if ingratiating beams
Have stealthily and tardily aroused
The rain-bespattered summits of the limes,
Which to each other talk in language drowsy.
And suddenly a feeble shadow climbs
Up trees and down the sandy garden track.
Our pair to agitation show resistance,
And keep their eyes fixed firmly on the distance.

40

О ночь! о мрак! о тайное свиданье!
Ступаешь робко, трепетной ногой...
Из-за стены лукавое призванье,
Как легкий звон, несется за тобой...
Неровное, горячее дыханье
В тени пахучей, дремлющей, сырой,
Тебе в лицо повеет торопливо...
Но вдаль они глядели молчаливо.

41

Сердца рвались... но ни глаза, ни руки
Встречаться не дерзали... При луне,
Испуганные близостью разлуки,
Они сидят в унылой тишине.
Лишь изредка порывистые муки
Их потрясали смутно, как во сне...
«Так завтра? Точно?» — «Завтра». Понемножку
Дуняша встала, подошла к окошку,

42

Глядит: перед огромным самоваром
Супруг уселся; медленно к губам
Подносит чашку, благовонным паром
Облитую, пыхтит, кряхтит — а сам
Поглядывает исподлобья. «Даром
Простудишься, Дуняша... Полно вам
Ребячиться»,— сказал он равнодушно...
Дуняша засмеялась и послушно

43

Вошла да села молча. «На прощанье,
Андрей Ильич, откушайте чайку.
Позвольте небольшое замечанье...
(Андрей меж тем прижался к уголку.)
Ваш родственник оставил завещанье?»
«Оставил». — «Он... в каком служил полку?»
«В Измайловском». — «Я думал, в Кирасирском.
И жизнь окончил в чине бригадирском?»

44

«Да, кажется...» — «Скажите! Впрочем, что же
Вам горевать? Покойник был и глух,
И стар, и слеп... Там лучше для него же.
Хотите чашечку?» — «Я больше двух

40

Oh, night! Oh, darkness! Oh, that secret meeting!
You tread with caution, with a light footfall.
Behind a wall there is for you a greeting –
It's given slyly, like a tinkling bell.
And passionately warm, uneven breathing,
In shade which in its slumber bears the smell
Of recent rain, envelops you in haste.
But quietly they towards the distance faced.

41

Their hearts were torn apart. They did not dare
Allow their eyes, still less their hands to meet.
The nearness of their parting caused them fear.
Dejectedly they in the moonlight sat,
From time to time tormented by obscure
Attacks of misery, as if by nightmares hit.
"Tomorrow then?" "Tomorrow." Gradually
Dunyasha rose to see what she could see

42

Inside. Her spouse Faddei had found a seat
Before the samovar, and he was now
A cup, emitting fragrant steam and heat,
About to raise. From underneath his brow
He gazed. He wheezed and puffed. "No need
To catch a cold, Dunyasha. That'll do.
Don't play the child," he in a bored voice said.
Dunyasha burst out laughing and obeyed,

43

Came quietly in and said: "Before you leave,
Andrei Ilich, so have some tea, please do,
And then from me a word or two receive."
(Andrei into a corner then withdrew).
"In the bequests of your late relative
Has he left anything at all for you?"
"He has." "I think he was a brigadier
In the Izmailovsky – Or maybe Kirasir."*

44

"I think he was." "Then will you tell me please
Why grieve? The man was old and blind and deaf.
For him it was a merciful release.
Another cup?" "For me two's quite enough."

Не пью».— «Да; как подумаешь, мой Боже,
Что́ наша жизнь? Пух, совершенный пух;
Дрянь, просто дрянь... Что делать? Участь наша...»
«Эх!.. Спой нам лучше песенку, Дуняша.

45

Ну не ломайся... ведь я знаю, рада
Ты петь с утра до вечера». Сперва
Ей овладела страшная досада...
Но вдруг пришли на память ей слова
Старинные... Не поднимая взгляда,
Аккорд она взяла... и голова
Ее склонилась, как осенний колос...
И зазвучал печально-страстный голос:

«Отрава горькая слезы
Последней жжет мои ресницы...
Так после бешеной грозы
Трепещут робкие зарницы.

Тяжелым, безотрадным сном
Заснула страсть... утихли битвы...
Но в сердце сдавленном моем
Покоя нет — и нет молитвы.

А ты, кому в разлучный миг
Я молча сжать не смею руки,
К кому прощальных слов моих
Стремятся трепетные звуки...

Молю тебя — в душе твоей
Не сохраняй воспоминанья,
Не замечай слезы моей
И позабудь мои страданья!»

46

Она с трудом проговорила строки
Последние... потупилась... У ней
Внезапно ярко запылали щеки...
Ей стало страшно смелости своей...
К Андрею наклонился муж: «Уроки
Она, сударь, у всех учителей
В Москве брала... Ну, Дунюшка, другую...
Веселенькую, знаешь, удалую!»

"All right. But how would you respond to this?
Our life is nothing but a heap of fluff
And trash. What can be done? It is our lot—"
"You'd better, Dunya, sing a song and not

45

Put on an act… I know how much you're pleased
To sing from morn till evening." At first
She was by terrible annoyance seized,
But suddenly recalled these ancient words.
Her eyes not having for a moment raised,
She picked out on the keyboard several chords
And bowed her head, like cornstalks bow their ears,
And sang this song, loud, passionate and clear:

"The bitter bane of my last tear
Has set my eyelashes on fire,
Thus after the wild thunder crashes
The timid summer lightning flashes.

In absent-minded torpor dreary
All passion's spent. The strife is o'er.
And in my heart oppressed and weary
I have no peace, I have no prayer.

And as we go our separate ways,
To press your hands I do not dare.
To you I send this parting phrase,
To you these trembling words aspire.

I beg you in your inmost heart
All memories of me forbid.
Ignore my tears as you depart,
And all my sufferings forget."

46

These last words she found hard to speak.
Dunyasha dropped her gaze and suddenly
A blazing colouring suffused her cheek.
Her boldness worried her considerably.
Faddei said to Andrei: "She used to take
Instruction everywhere she possibly
Could find in Moscow. Dunya knows of old
Another ditty, full of cheer, and bold."

47

Она сидит, задумчиво впадая
В упорную, немую тишину.
Часы пробили медленно. Зевая,
Фаддей глядит умильно на жену...
«Что ж? Пой же... Нет? Как хочешь... — и, вставая, —
Пора, — прибавил он, — меня ко сну
Немного клонит. Поздно. Ну, прощайте,
Андрей Ильич... и нас не забывайте».

48

Кому не жаль действительных борений
Души нехитрой, любящей, прямой?
Дуняша не была в числе творений,
Теперь нередких на Руси святой —
Охотниц до «вопросов» и до прений,
Холодных сердцем, пылких головой,
Натянутых, болезненно болтливых
И сверхъестественно самолюбивых...

49

О нет! она страдала. Расставанье
Настало. Тяжело в последний раз
Смотреть в лицо любимое! Прощанье
В передней да заботливый наказ
Себя беречь — обычное желанье, —
Всё сказано, всему конец... Из глаз
Дуняши слезы хлынули... но тупо
Взглянул Андрей — и вышел как-то глупо.

50

А на заре, при вопле двух старушек
Соседок, тронулся рыдван. Андрей
В нем восседал среди шести подушек.
Ну, с Богом! Вот застава! Перед ней
Ряды полуразрушенных избушек;
За ней дорога. Кучер лошадей
Постегивал и горевал, что грязно,
И напевал задумчиво-несвязно...

51

Три года протекло... три длинных года.
Андрей нигде не свил себе гнезда.
Он видел много разного народа
И посетил чужие города...

47

Dunyasha, motionless, lapsed pensively
Into silence obstinate and studied.
Her husband yawned. The time passed very slowly.
Faddei with tenderness his wife regarded.
"What's this? Do sing. You won't? With that I wholly
Agree. I think I need my bed," he added.
"It's late. Farewell. Until we meet again –
May we forever in your thoughts remain."

48

Who does not pity sufferings of the heart,
Of artless, loving, honest souls quiescent?
Dunyasha was in no way of the sort,
In Holy Russia far from obsolescent,
Who have a love for "questions" and debate,
Whose hearts are cold, whose heads are incandescent,
Who upright are and painfully loquacious,
With amour-propre unnaturally outrageous.

49

Not she! She suffers, for the time to part
Has come. It's hard for one last time to gaze
Into the loved one's eye. Then the distraught
Farewells and over-anxious homilies:
"Take care." As always the same thought.
All's said. This is the end. From Dunya's eyes
The teardrops flowed, but, looking blank, Andrei
Departed in a somewhat stolid way.

50

To sounds of neighbours sobbing in the dawn
The heavy coach moves off, and our Andrei
With six or seven cushions makes a throne.
And here's the barrier before which lie
Ramshackle houses semi-broken down,
And then the road. Now see the coachman ply
His whip, and then the mud and grime lament,
And start to hum a tune which he'll invent.

51

Three years went by – a near-infinity.
Andrei could nowhere find to settle down.
Of other folk he saw a great variety,
And found himself in more than one strange town.

Его не слишком тешила свобода,
И вспоминал он родину, когда
Среди толпы веселой, как изгнанник,
Бродил он, добровольный, грустный странник.

52

Он испытал тревожные напасти
И радости скитальца; но в чужой
Земле жил одиноко; старой страсти
Не заменил он прихотью другой.
Он не забыл... забыть не в нашей власти!
В его душе печальной, но живой,
Исполненной неясного стремленья,
Толпами проходили впечатленья...

53

Однажды пред камином на диване
Андрей сидел и думал о былом.
(Он жил тогда в Италии, в Милане.)
Андрей на чай в один «приятный» дом
Был позван и скучал уже заране...
Его хозяйка в комнату с письмом
Вошла... «Рука Дуняши!», — закричал он. —
И вот что, содрогаясь, прочитал он:

«Признайтесь... Вы письма не ждали
Так поздно и в такую даль.
Вам прежних радостей не жаль?
Быть может, новые печали
Сменили прежнюю печаль.
Иль вам наскучили страданья,
И вы живете не спеша,
И жаждет вечного молчанья
Изнеможенная душа?..
Не возмутили б эти строки
Покоя вашего... меня
Простите вы... мы так далеки...
С того мучительного дня —
Вы помните — прошло так много.
Так много времени, что нас...
Что мы... что я не знаю вас...
Меня вы не судите строго —
Во имя прошлого, Андрей,
Подумайте; среди людей
Живете вы... а я, мой Боже!

He did not much enjoy his liberty,
And would recall his home especially when,
An exile in among a merry crowd
And voluntary wanderer, he roved.

52

Anxiety attacks affected him.
He knew a wanderer's joy, but lived alone
In unfamiliar lands. For no mere whim
Would he the passion he once had disown.
Andrei remembers —memories don't grow dim.
His soul was animated, but cast down
And filled with vague and happy aspiration,
And no impressions went by in procession.

53

Once, sitting by the fire on a divan,
Andrei was thinking of the days gone by.
He was at this point living in Milan.
He'd by a "pleasant" house been asked to tea.
Already he was bored well in advance,
Then came a letter via his landlady.
"Dunyasha's handwriting!" at once he cried,
And, shaking with emotion, thus he read:

"This letter you did not expect
So late, and from so far away.
Do former joys on your mind prey
Or can it be some new regret
Replaces those of former days?
Have you enough of suffering borne,
And do you live unhurriedly?
And does your soul for silence yearn,
The silence of eternity?
May this my letter not upset
Your peace of mind, nor on it prey.
So many miles us separate…
When thinking of that awful day,
Remember much has passed since then,
So many hours and days that now…
That we… That I you hardly know.
Do not be quick me to condemn.
For old time's sake, just think, Andrei.
With other people now you stay.
But I by contrast nothing more

Всё там же — и кругом всё то же...
Что? грустно вам? или смешно?
Иль совершенно всё равно?

Андрей, послушайте: когда-то
Мы жили долго вместе... Свято
Я полюбила вас... ко мне
Вы привязались добровольно...
Потом... но мне сознаться больно,
Как мы страдали в тишине.
С тех пор, Андрей, со дня прощаний,
Хотите знать, как я живу?
Как некогда, в часы свиданий,
Я вас опять к себе зову...
Вот — вы со мной сидите рядом,
Не поднимая головы,
И на меня глядите вы
Тем ласковым и добрым взглядом...

Когда расстались вы со мной,
Я не винила вас. Одной
Заботой — точно, непритворно
Вы были заняты. Тогда
Меня щадили вы... Ну да!
Я благодарна вам, бесспорно.
Я верю — грустно было вам;
Не притворялись вы лукаво;
Вы в целый год успели к нам
Привыкнуть; жертва ваша, право,
Достойна громкой похвалы...
Да; без сомненья: люди злы —
Все малодушны, все коварны
И до конца неблагодарны...
Вам должно было ехать... я
Согласна... но как вы спешили!
Нет, нет, меня вы не любили!
Нет, не любили вы меня!

Ах, если надо мной жестоко
Не насмеялись вы сперва...
Андрей, я чувствую, глубоко
Вас оскорбят мои слова;
Но я живу в такой пустыне...
Но я ношу такой венец —
В моей любви, в моей святыне

Than what surrounded me before.
Are you amused or are you sadder
Or do you think it doesn't matter?

Andrei, hear me. We used to live
As neighbours. And for you my love
Was sacred. Of your own free will
You sought my friendship to obtain...
Then – to confess it gives me pain –
In silence how we suffered ill!
From when, Andrei, you left for ever
My story will you seek to know?
As once, when we would meet together,
Once more to me I summon you.
And so you sit here by my side,
Your eyes cast down, your head not raising,
And yet I feel that you are gazing
At me with looks so kind and good.

Since you from me have separated,
I never once have you berated.
With work – I have no cause to doubt it –
You're totally preoccupied.
You tried to let me gently down.
I'm grateful – there's no doubt about it.
You sadness felt, of that I am assured.
You did not cunningly pretend;
Towards us you became inured
The whole year long, but in the end
Your sacrifice the highest praise
Deserves, for mankind's evil ways
Are full of moral turpitude
And endless black ingratitude.
You had to leave, I quite agree,
But with such speed you hurried off...
I never was your one true love –
No, never felt your love for me.

Oh, had you never been so cruel
And laughed at me right from the first...
Andrei, I have to say I feel
You're deeply wounded by my words.
But I in such a desert live,
Am burdened with a heavy crown,
I in my holy shrine of love

Я сомневаюсь, наконец...
Я гибну!.. Крик тоски мятежной
Сорвался с губ моих... Андрей,
Печаль разлуки безнадежной
Сильнее гордости моей...
Я вас люблю... тебя люблю я...
Ты знаешь это... ты... Поверь,
Навек, мучительно тоскуя,
С тобой простилась я теперь.

Я плачу. Да; ты благороден,
Андрей, ты силен и свободен;
Ты позабыть себя готов.
Из видов низких и корыстных
Ты не наложишь ненавистных,
Хоть позолоченных оков.
О да! Когда перед томленьем
Разлуки, в робкой тишине,
С немым и страшным упоеньем
Тебе вверялась я вполне,
Я поняла твое молчанье...
Я покорилась... От тебя
Я приняла тогда страданье,
Как дар, безропотно, любя...
Я не могла тебе не верить —
Тебе не верить, Боже мой!
Когда я вся жила тобой...
Но не хочу я лицемерить:
Потом — казалось мне, что ты...
Пустые женские мечты!
Мне совестно... но в извиненье,
Андрей, ты примешь положенье
Мое... Подумай: на кого
Меня ты здесь оставил? скука,
Тоска... не знаешь ничего...
Наедут гости — что́ за мука!
Соседки-сплетницы; сосед
Молчит, сопит во весь обед,
Глотает, давится насильно
Да к ручке подойдет умильно.
С утра ждешь вечера, свечей...
Занятий нету... нет детей...
Книг нету... душно, страшно душно...
Попросишь мужа — равнодушно
Проговорит он: «Погоди,

Now doubt, when all is said and done.
I'm perishing. That cry of desperation
Was wrenched, Andrei, from out my lips.
The grief of hopeless separation
Will all my foolish pride eclipse.
I should have said I love you truly.
You know that, but you must believe
From you, in dreadful agony,
I now for ever take my leave.

Andrei, you are nobility.
You have your strength and liberty.
Thoughts of self you always hated,
And you would never have a use
For fetters, even if gold-plated.
Before our parting caused distress,
I in the meek and timid silence
With mute and fearful tenderness
Gave absolute obedience.
I all your taciturnity
Had understood. Your suffering
I took to be a gift to me,
And bore it, uncomplaining, loving.
To lose my faith I am not able,
My faith in you, all my belief,
When you were all my love, my life...
But I am not here to dissemble:
And then it all began to seem
Another futile female dream!
I'm sorry, I apologize,
Andrei, can you but recognize
My plight? What could I do? Just think.
When you abandoned me, the tedium
And anguish – you don't know a thing...
The pain when guests decide to come!
Some gossips and a ghastly male
Who keeps on snoring through the meal,
Who gulps and chokes and swallows and
Emotionally will kiss your hand.
From dawn you wish the day were through –
No candles, nothing much to do,
No books, it's stuffy, very close,
And should you choose to ask your spouse,
He takes no interest, says it looks
As if the pedlar will bring books.

Зайдет разносчик»... впереди
Всё то же — то же — до могилы...
О Господи, пошли мне силы!!!
. . . .
Но прежде — прежде жизнь моя
Была спокойна... помню я
Себя веселой, безмятежной
Перед домашним очагом...
Какой любовью кроткой, нежной
Тогда дышало всё кругом!
Как были хлопоты, заботы
Хозяйки, легкие работы
В то время сердцу моему,
Сама не знаю почему,
Невыразимо сладки, милы!..
Но мне прошедшего не жаль, —
Тогда ребяческие силы
Щадила строгая печаль...

О, мне, конечно, в наказанье
За гордость послано страданье...
Иль и за то, что в самый час,
Когда я вас узнала — вас,
Я позабылась малодушно,
Дала вам право над собой
И без борьбы перед судьбой
Склонила голову послушно!..
Тогда я сердца своего
Не понимала... для чего
Никто с суровостью мужчины
Меня не спас... я до кончины
Жила бы в «мирной тишине,
Не зная помыслов опасных...»

Я плачу... плачу... Стыдно мне
Тех горьких слез — и слез напрасных!
Кому я жалуюсь? Зачем,
Зачем я плачу? Перед кем?
Кто может выслушать упреки
Мои?... Быть может, эти строки,
Следы горячих слез моих,
Друзьям покажет он лукаво,
На толки праздные чужих
Людей предаст меня?.. Но, право,
С ума схожу я...

So life goes on at endless length…
Good Lord above, give me some strength!

. . . .
Before all this my life had been,
As I remember, quite serene.
I see that image of myself,
Impassive by the household hearth,
While all around a tender love
Was present in each gentle breath!
How pleasant domesticity
And trivial worries were for me!
And, I really don't know why,
Rejoiced my heart ineffably.
But for the past I am not sorry,
For then my young vivacity
Was spared the bitterness of sorrow,

Oh then, of course, I was repaid
By suffering for the sin of pride,
Or for the fact that at the hour
When you and I became aware,
I weakly let myself be cowed,
And gave you over me a right.
With destiny I did not fight:
Submissively my head I bowed.
My heart I did not understand,
Nor why there was not any man
Whose resolution would me save.
I would until my very grave
Have lived my life in perfect peace.
I weep – my weeping cannot cease.

My tears are bitter, futile tears.
To whom am I complaining. Why?
Before whom is it that I cry?
Who can hear my plaints the better?
Perhaps the contents of my letter,
The remnants of my tearful prose,
He will to his acquaintance show,
To idle chatterers expose
These lines. However it is true
My mind is wandering…

Вот, Андрей
(Теперь мы с вами хладнокровно
Поговорим), как безусловно
Я верю вам. Души моей
Я не скрываю перед вами.
Конечно, знаете вы сами,
Что значит женская печаль...
Я вспомнила, в какую даль
Вас унесло... Мне стало грустно...
И то, что высказать изустно
Я не посмела бы... Меня
Поймете вы! Что делать, я
Не слишком счастлива. Но годы
Пройдут — соста́реюсь... и той
Любви блаженной, той свободы
Мне не захочется самой.

Я перечла свое маранье...
Андрей, не вздумайте в моем
Письме постыдное желанье
Найти... Но, Боже мой! о чем
Могла я к вам писать?.. Мне больно,
Я плачу, жалуюсь невольно...
Но легче мне теперь, ясней...
И сердце после долгой битвы
Желает отдыха, молитвы
И бьется медленней... вольней...

Андрей, прощайте. Дайте руку
Не на свиданье — на разлуку.
Судьба!.. Но если в тишине
Та дружба старая случайно
Еще живет... и если тайно
Хоть изредка... вам обо мне,
О стороне родной, далекой,
Приходят мысли... знайте: там!
Есть сердце, полное глубокой
Печалью, преданное вам.
Среди волнений жизни новой
Об участи моей суровой
Вы позабудете... Но вас
Я буду помнить — вечно... вечно...
И в каждый светлый, тихий час
Благодарить вас бесконечно.
Прощайте, добрый, старый друг...

Andrei,
(We now will speak cold-bloodedly),
You realize I implicitly
Believe you. I will not withhold
From you the workings of my soul.
Of course, you naturally feel
What women's sorrows signify...
Remembering how far away
You now are gone made me feel sad.
What openly I might have said
I did not dare. So then please try
To understand me when I say
I am unhappy. Years will pass –
I'll age, and former liberty
And love, that used to be my love,
No longer will be dear to me.

Do not, Andrei, think you will find
In lines that I have just reread,
Desire of any shameful kind.
But Heavens! What could I have said
To you? I'm weeping, and I'm ill,
I rail, lament against my will!
But things are better now, more clear.
My heart, so long a battleground,
Has slower, freer tempos found,
And seeks for rest, and seeks for prayer.

Farewell. Give me your hand, Andrei,
To mark that you are going away.
O Fate! If in tranquillity
Our love of former years still lives,
And if by chance you sometimes give
A thought or two addressed to me,
Or to the homeland you have left,
Know this: a distant land is where
A heart devoted lives bereft,
Profoundly grieving, full of care.
Among your new life's ebb and flow
My grim fate you will cease to know.
But memories are infinite...
And I at every quiet hour
My gratitude will demonstrate.
My old and kindly friend, goodbye.
How truly bitter is the moment

Какое горькое мгновенье
Мучительно расстаться вдруг...
Но страшно долгое томленье...
От полноты души моей
На жизнь обильную, святую...
И даже — на любовь иную
Благословляю вас, Андрей!»

54

Он жадно пробежал письмо глазами...
Исписанный листок в его руках
Дрожал... Он вышел тихими шагами
С улыбкой невеселой на губах...
Но здесь, читатель, мы простимся с вами,
С Андреем и с Дуняшей. Право, страх
Подумать — как давно, с каким терпеньем
Вы нас дарите вашим снисхожденьем.

55

Что сделалось с героями моими?..
Я видел их... Тому не так давно...
Но то, над чем я даже плакал с ними,
Теперь мне даже несколько смешно...
Смеяться над страданьями чужими
Весьма предосудительно, грешно...
Но если вас не станет мучить совесть,
Когда-нибудь мы кончим эту повесть.

Of separation's agony,
And terrible the lengthy torment!
So from the bottom of my heart,
And wishing you a fruitful life,
And even wishing you new love,
My benediction I impart."

54
He avidly the scribbled letter scanned,
And went out of the room with faltering steps.
The sheet of paper trembled in his hand,
A mirthless smile remained upon his lips.
We say goodbye to you, dear reader, and
Andrei and his Dunyasha too, perhaps.
God knows how long, with what restraint,
To give us your attention you have deigned.

55
So what of Dunya and Andrei became?
I saw them not so very long ago.
But what I used to weep about with them
Appears a little funny to me now.
To find another's suffering a game
Is not a thing I would myself allow,
But, if your conscience doesn't you assail,
We'll find a way of finishing this tale.

A CONVERSATION

A POEM

Один, перед немым и сумрачным дворцом,
Бродил я вечером, исполненный раздумья;
Блестящий пир утих; дремало всё кругом —
И замер громкий смех веселого безумья.
Среди таинственной, великой тишины
Березы гибкие шептали боязливо —
И каменные львы гляделись молчаливо
В стальное зеркало темнеющей волны.

И спящий мир дышал бессмертной красотой.
Но глаз не подымал и проходил я мимо;
О жизни думал я, об Истине святой,
О всем, что на земле навек неразрешимо.
Я небо вопрошал... и тяжко было мне —
И вся душа моя пресытилась тоскою...
А звезды вечные спокойной чередою
Торжественно неслись в туманной вышине.

Июль 1844

I

В пещере мрачной и сырой
Отшельник бледный и худой
Молился. Дряхлой головой
Он наклонялся до земли;
И слезы медленно текли
По сморщенным его щекам,
Текли по трепетным губам
На руки, сжатые крестом.
Таилась в голосе глухом
Полуживого старика

Before a grim and silent edifice, alone
I'd wander of an evening, deep in thoughtfulness;
The dazzling feast was silent and the world slept all around –
No more was heard the sound of cheerful mindlessness.
Amid a silence both mysterious and grave
The slender, supple birches whispered fearfully.
And sculptured lions watched each other wordlessly,
Reflected in the mirror of the darkening wave.

The sleeping world exuded an immortal beauty,
But I did not look up and merely wandered by;
I thought of life and truth, I thought of sacred duty,
Of things insoluble on earth eternally.
I questioned Heaven, and upon me felt a weight,
My heart and soul entire were sated with depression,
And the eternal stars in a serene procession
Majestically moved across the misty height.

July 1844

I

In a dank cavern, far from light,
A hermit, pallid, decrepit,
Is praying. To the earth he bows
His head. A tear then slowly flows,
And from his wrinkled features drips
And flows across his trembling lips,
Then fall on hands held like a cross.
The half-dead sage's muffled voice
Revealed an anguish he no longer
Was able to contain or conquer.

Непобежденная тоска...
Тот голос... много зол и мук
Смягчили прежний, гордый звук...
И после многих тайных битв,
И после многих горьких слез
Слова смиренные молитв
Он, изнывая, произнес.
Бывало, пламенная речь
Звенела, как булатный меч,
Гремела, как набат, когда
Во дни покорности, стыда
Упругой меди тяжкий рев
В народе будит ярый гнев
И мчатся граждане толпой
На грозный, на последний бой.
Теперь же — с бледных губ — едва
Беззвучно падают слова,
Как поздней осенью с вершин
Нагих и трепетных осин
На землю грустной чередой
Ложится листьев легкий рой.

2

И встал старик... Кончался день;
Темнела даль; густела тень;
И вот настал волшебный миг,
Когда прозрачен, чист и тих
Вечерний воздух... ночь близка...
Заря пылает... облака
Блестят и тают... спит река...
И смутный говор мелких волн
Невыразимой неги полн —
И так торжественны леса,
Так бесконечны небеса...

3

И долго — бледный, как мертвец,
Стоял пустынник... наконец,
Он вышел медленно на свет.
И словно дружеский привет,
Знакомый, любящий, родной,
В вершине липы молодой
Внезапно перелетный шум
Промчался... Сумрачен, угрюм,
Стоял старик... но так светло

Much evil and much torment often
That proud voice had been wont to soften;
He after many inner feuds
And many hours of bitter weeping,
Gave voice to meek, submissive words,
And supplication offered, grieving.
Time was when his impassioned word
Resounded like a damask sword,
Or like the sound of the tocsin
When shame and ignominy threaten,
Or like the clash of martial metal
Which puts a nation on its mettle,
When citizens in massed ranks go
To take the battle to the foe.
Now scarcely from his pallid lips
The sound of utterances slips,
As in late autumn from the bare
And trembling aspens earth receives,
Descending sadly through the air,
A fluttering of dying leaves.

2

The sage stood up – the day had ended;
The distance darkened; shadows thickened,
And then there came that magic moment
When evening air is pure and silent,
Transparent, and the night is close,
Clouds gleam and melt, and sunset glows;
The watercourse no longer flows;
The muffled murmur of each ripple
Is mild and inexpressible;
the woods in solemn splendour lie,
And above is endless sky.

3

And paler than the living dead
The hermit stood, and at last made
To move, but slowly, to the light,
When in the forest's lofty height,
From topmost branches of a linden,
There came a sound of greeting, sudden
Familiar, by breezes borne.
The old man stood, morose and stern;
Illuminated was the stream;

Струилась речка... так тепло
Коснулся мягкий ветерок
Его волос... и так глубок
И звучно тих и золотист
Был пышный лес... и каждый лист
Сверкал так радостно, что вдруг
В безумце замер злой недуг —
И озарилися слегка
Немые губы старика
Под длинной белой бородой
Улыбкой грустной, но живой.

4

Но вот раздался шум шагов...
И быстро вышел из кустов
Нежданный гость. Он иногда
С отшельником — по вечерам —
Сходился в прежние года...
Его задумчивым речам
Он с детской жадностью внимал...
С тех пор он вырос — возмужал —
И начал жить... Прошли, как сон,
За днями дни — за годом год...
Завяла жизнь... И вспомнил он
Те встречи — молодость — и вот
Стоит он с пасмурным лицом
Пред изумленным стариком.

5

И на́звал он себя... Узнал
Его пустынник... быстро встал.
Дал гостю руку... Та рука
Дрожала... Голос старика
Погас... Но странник молодой
Поник печально головой,
Пожал болезненно плечом
И тихо вздрогнул... и потом
Взглянул медлительно кругом.
И говорили взоры те
О безотрадной пустоте
Души, погибшей, как и все
Во всей, как водится, красе.

The breeze's touch was soft and warm
Upon his hair – so resonant the hush,
So tinged with gold was every bush,
So full of joy, that in a moment
The madman was no more in torment.
A hint of colour slowly creeps
Into the sage's wordless lips;
Beneath his beard a sad smile plays,
But now the smile revivifies.

4

But now the sound of steps was heard,
And from behind the bushes there appeared
An unexpected visitor.
He sometimes, as the daylight failed,
Had met the aged sage before,
And heard the musings he retailed.
With childish keenness heard them and
Had now grown up, become a man,
Begun to live. So time went by –
One day, another – year by year.
Preoccupied with memory
Of life, of death, he now stood there,
And gloomily the hermit faced,
And left that aged seer amazed.

5

He gave his name, was recognized.
The desert-dweller quietly rose
And gave his guest his hand, a hand
Which shook. The voice of the old man
Grew faint. The wanderer, being young,
His head dejectedly now hung.
He shrugged his shoulders painfully,
And gave a quiet shudder. He
Then looked around unhurriedly
With an expression which betrayed
A soul of joyfulness devoid,
A soul which, as is customary,
Had been destroyed in all its glory.

6

Но понемногу в разговор
Они вступили... Между тем
Настала ночь. Высокий бор
И спит и шепчет. Чуток, нем
Холодный мрак... окружена
Туманом дымчатым луна...
Старик — поникнув на ладонь —
Сидел угрюмый, без речей...
Лишь иногда сверкал огонь
Из-под густых его бровей...
Казалось, он негодовал...
Он так презрительно молчал...
И не сходила до конца
С его печального лица
Усмешка злая... Говорил
Пришлец о том, как он любил,
И как страдал, и как давно
Ему томиться суждено...
И как он пал... Такой рассказ
Слыхали многие не раз —
И сожалели... нет — едва ль!
Не новость на земле печаль.
«Старик, и я, — так кончил он
Рассказ, — ты видишь, побежден.
Как воды малого ручья,
Иссякла молодость моя...
Меня сгубил бесплодный жар
Упорных, мелочных страстей...
Беспечности (завидный дар!)
Не раз в тоске души моей
Просил я... но коварный бог
Пытливый дух во мне зажег —
А силы... силы нé дал он.
Твой взор я понял... я смешон;
К чему волнуюсь я теперь?
За мной навек закрыта дверь.
В тот пестрый, равнодушный мир
Возврата нет... Так пусть же там
Кипит всё тот же наглый пир,
Всё тем же молятся богам,
И, кровью праведной хмельна,
Неправда царствует одна.
Что́ мне до них! Большой ценой
Купил я право никогда

6

The conversation started by degrees...
The day meanwhile had turned to night.
The lofty forest slept. Its trees
Were whispering, the darkness mute
And cold. The moon was lost,
Surrounded by a smoky mist.
The hermit, head upon his palm,
Was sitting wordless and morose –
Just now and then there flashed a flame
From underneath his beetling brows.
It seemed he some resentment felt,
So scornfully he speech withheld.
The smile upon his mournful mien
Was bitter, and had always been.
The new arrival started now
To talk about his love, and how
His suffering had lasted ages
And troubles were his only wages.
The story which the young man told
Had many times been heard of old.
But there were few to sympathize:
Unhappiness is hardly news.
"Old man," the youth concluded, "I
Am vanquished, as you surely see.
Like water in a summer river
I've seen my youthful spirits wither.
I am with fever quite destroyed,
With futile, petty, stubborn passion,
And unconcern (to be enjoyed!)
Is what I crave now in my anguish.
But an insidious deity
A mind inquisitive gave me,
And strength away from me he took.
I grasp your meaning – I'm a joke.
Why am I troubled and confused?
Why this door forever closed?
To normal life there's no way back.
Our motley world can lack all care,
Our feasts may all decorum lack,
But worship with the self-same prayers,
And, tipsy made with righteous blood,
Triumphantly will reign falsehood.
What of these things? I've paid a price
By guaranteeing I will never

Не вспоминать о жизни той.
Но я люблю — любил всегда
Ночного неба мирный блеск
И темных волн ленивый плеск,
Люблю я вечер золотой,
Лесов задумчивый покой
И легкий рой румяных туч,
Луны стыдливый, первый луч,
И первый ропот соловья,
И тишину полей... О! я
Готов остаться навсегда
С тобою здесь...»

СТАРИК

                    В твои года
Любил я накануне битв
Слова задумчивых молитв,
Любил рассказы стариков
О том как били мы врагов;
Любил торжественный покой
Заснувшей рати... За луной
Уходят звезды... вот — восток
Алеет... легкий ветерок
Играет клочьями знамен...
Как птица спугнутая, сон
Слетел с полей... седой туман
Клубится тяжко над рекой.
Грохочет глухо барабан —
Раздался выстрел вестовой —
Проворно строятся полки —
В кустах рассыпались стрелки...
И сходят медленно с холмов
Ряды волнистые врагов.
Любил я блеск и стук мечей,
И лица гордые вождей.
И дружный топот лошадей,
Когда, волнуясь и гремя,
Сверкала конница в дыму,
Визжали ядра... Полно! Я
Старик. Но — помню — как тюрьму,
Я ненавидел города;
И надышаться в те года
Не мог я воздухом лесов,
И был я силен и суров,
И горделив — и, сколько мог,
Я сердце вольное берег.

About my old life reminisce.
But I have always been a lover
Of night time's peaceful, glowing skies,
Of lazy ripples on dark seas.
I love the evening's golden light,
The forest's contemplative quiet,
The russet storm clouds as they stream,
The moon's initial timid beam,
The trilling of the nightingale,
The silent fields. Oh, I'll not fail
To stay for ever with you here.

OLD MAN

I loved, when I was of your years,
The nights preceding martial actions,
The words of pensive supplications,
The stories which old men repeated
Of how we had our foes defeated.
I loved to see the victors rest
In a triumphant sleeping host.
The moon and stars have gone. The east
Is reddening, and a gentle breeze
With scraps of tattered banners plays,
And, as a startled game bird flies,
So sleep is lifted. Dense mist swirls
And settles heavy on the river.
The sound of muffled drumbeats rolls;
A cannon fires the opening salvo;
Battalions form with swift precision;
The skirmishers take up position,
And slowly, from its lofty height,
The enemy descends to fight.
I loved the gleam and clash of swords,
The proud demeanour of the guards,
The clatter of the martial steeds,
The hussars' charge, their weapons gleaming,
On through the gun smoke, wave on wave,
The cannons' roar, the bullets' scream...
But I am old, and so, enough!
I loathed the jail of city life,
And still recall my strength of loathing,
And how I wanted to be breathing
The air of forests in those years
When I had strength and was severe
And proud. As much as it could be,
I kept my heart at liberty.

МОЛОДОЙ ЧЕЛОВЕК

Дивлюсь я, слушая тебя.
Как? Неужели ж помнишь ты
Тревоги молодости?

СТАРИК

Я
Всё помню.

МОЛОДОЙ ЧЕЛОВЕК

Детские мечты?
Восторги пламенные?

СТАРИК

Да.
Ребенок искренний, тогда
Я был глупей тебя — глупей...
Я не шутил душой моей...
И всё, над чем смеешься ты
Так величаво, те «мечты»
В меня вросли так глубоко,
Что мне забыть их нелегко.
Но ты, бесстрастный человек,
Ты успокоился навек.

МОЛОДОЙ ЧЕЛОВЕК

Кто? Я спокоен? Боже мой!
Я гибну в медленном огне...
Да ты смеешься надо мной,
Старик!

СТАРИК

О нет! Но грустно мне.
Кичливой ревностью горя,
Расправив гордо паруса,
Давно ль в далекие моря
Под неродные небеса
Помчался ты? И что ж? о срам!
Едва дохнула по волнам
Гроза — к родимым берегам,
Проворен, жалок, одинок,
Бежит испуганный челнок.
В разгаре юношеских сил
Ты, как старик, и вял и хил...
Но Боже! разве никогда

YOUNG MAN

> I am surprised when you I hear.
> So can it be you have recalled
> The terrors of your early years?

OLD MAN

> I have.

YOUNG MAN

> And, when you were a child,
> Your dreams, delights and ardent pleasures?

OLD MAN

> Young man, I was, by quite a measure,
> A bigger fool than you... a fool.
> I jested not with heart or soul...
> What you regard with such derision,
> So loftily, these so-called visions,
> Within me have been so inbred,
> I cannot ever them forget.
> But you, in whom all passions cease,
> Will always be a man of peace.

YOUNG MAN

> What, me? A man of peace? Good Lord,
> I'm dying in a conflagration.
> But please don't take me at my word,
> Old man!

OLD MAN

> I do! You see my desolation
> Ablaze with nagging jealousy.
> With all your sails set proudly high,
> Set out to find a distant sea
> Beneath an unfamiliar sky?
> But what is this I see? Oh, shame!
> The waves have scarcely seen the storm
> Subside when, altering its course for home,
> A wretched solitary wherry
> Across the waves makes haste in terror.
> So you, who should be strong and hale,
> Are like an ancient, feeble, frail.
> But Heavens! Did you never claim

Не знал ты жажду мыслей, дел,
Тоску глубокого стыда,
И не рыдал и не бледнел?
Любил ли ты кого-нибудь?
Иль никогда немая грудь,
Блаженства горького полна,
Не трепетала, как струна?

МОЛОДОЙ ЧЕЛОВЕК

    А ты любил?

             И вдруг старик
Умолк — и медленно лицом
На руки дряхлые поник.
Когда же голову потом
Он поднял — взор его потух...
Он бледен был, как будто дух
Тревожный, плачущий, немой
Промчался над его душой.
«Я сознаюсь, — так начал он, —
Твой неожиданный приход
Меня смутил. Я потрясен.
Я ждал тебя так долго... вот
Ты появился, наконец,
Печальным гостем предо мной...
Как сына слушает отец,
Тебя я слушал... И тоской
Внезапно стал томиться я...
И странно! прежняя моя
Любовь — и всё, что так давно
В моей груди схоронено,
Воскресло вдруг... пробуждены
Живые звуки старины,
И тени милые толпой
Несутся тихо надо мной.
Я знаю: стыдно старику
Лелеять праздную тоску;
И, как осенняя гроза,
Бесплодна поздняя слеза...
Но близок смерти горький час;
Но, может быть, в последний раз
Я с человеком говорю,
Последним пламенем горю...
О жизнь! О юность! О любовь!
Любовь мучительная!.. Вновь

To nurture hopes of thought or deed,
Or miserable depths of shame?
Did you not pale, or salt tears shed?
Or was your unresponsive breast
Not filled with bliss, albeit bitter,
Or did it like a bowstring quiver?

YOUNG MAN
　　And you have loved?

　　　　　　The aged man
Fell silent, burying his face
In his decrepit, feeble hands.
When he his head thereafter raised,
His eyes, once lustrous, had grown dim,
As if a spirit entered him,
A spirit plangent, anxious, mute,
Which seized possession of his heart.
"I must acknowledge" – thus he started –
"Your coming unexpectedly
Has shaken me and disconcerted.
I'd waited long, and finally
Dejectedly you have appeared,
A lonely, melancholy man.
As if I heard a filial word,
I listened to you and began
To misery to be the prey...
And love remembered, strange to say,
And all that had been in the past
Profoundly buried in my breast
Began at once to reappear.
The sounds of life of yesteryear,
Beloved shadows in a throng
Above, move quietly along.
As an old man, I know I never
In idle misery should revel –
That, like a storm late in the year
Unfruitful are belated tears.
But close the hour of my demise,
And it is possible that this
Will be the last time that I turn
To fellow man, with passions burn...
Oh, life! Oh, youth! Oh, love! Oh, pain!
The agony of love! Again

Хочу — хочу предаться вам,
Хотя б на миг один... а там
Погасну, вспыхнувши едва...
....
Ты говоришь: любил ли я?
Понятны мне слова твои...
Так отвечайте ж за меня,
Вы, ночи дивные мои!
Не ты ль сияла надо мной,
Немая, пышная луна,
Когда в саду, в тени густой
Я ждал и думал: вот она!
И замирал, и каждый звук
Ловил, и сердца мерный стук
Принять, бывало, был готов
За легкий шум ее шагов...
И с той поры так много лет
Прошло; так много, много бед
Я перенес... но до конца —
В пустыне, посреди людей —
Черты любимого лица
Хранил я в памяти моей...
Я вижу, вижу пред собой
Тот образ светлый, молодой...
Воспоминаний жадный рой
Теснится в душу... страстно я
Им отдаюсь... в них ад и рай...
Но ты послушайся меня:
До старых лет не доживай.
Забуду ль я тот дивный час,
Когда, внезапно, в первый раз
Смущенный, стал я перед ней?
Огнем полуденных лучей
Сверкало небо... Под окном,
Полузакрытая плющом,
Сидела девушка... слегка
Пылала смуглая щека,
Касаясь мраморной руки...
И вдоль зардевшейся щеки
На пальцы тонкие волной
Ложился локон золотой.
И взор задумчивый едва
Блуждал... склонялась голова...
Тревожной, страстной тишиной
Дышали томные черты...

I wish most earnestly that I
Could give myself to you, then die
Before the flames within me flare
Or any latent passions stir.*
You ask me: did I ever love?
I understand what your words mean.
On my behalf your answer give.
O nights miraculous of mine,
Above me it was you who glowed,
O moon, in silent majesty,
When in the garden, in the shade,
I waited, thinking: 'Is it she?'
I fainting fell, caught every sound,
And every heartbeat's measured pound
I took for something in its stead –
The sound of her soft footsteps' tread.
And since that time an age has gone,
And I have many sufferings borne,
But have preserved until the end,
In deserts or society,
The features of a well-loved friend
Imprinted on my memory.
I see, I see before myself
That image full of light and youth,
And in my soul there crowds a wealth
Of recollections, equally
The fruits of hell or paradise.
So, 'Spurn old age' is my advice.
There was a wonderful occasion
When, for the first time, in confusion,
Before her gaze I took my place.
The sky with fiery midday rays
Was glowing, and beneath a window,
Which, ivy-covered, lay half hidden,
A maiden sat. Her cheek was dark
(A gentle blush made there its mark),
Her marble hand gracefully touching.
Across her blushing features brushing,
Her tresses in a golden shower
Upon her slender fingers pour.
She pondered, her attention rapt,
And as she mused, her gaze she dropped.
A passionate and anxious quiet
Her weary countenance exuded.
No, never did I see the sight

Нет! ты не видывал такой
Неотразимой красоты!
Я с ней сошелся... Я молчу...
Я не могу, я не хочу
Болтать о том, как я тогда
Был счастлив... Знай же — никогда,
Пока я не расстался с ней,
Не ведал я спокойных дней...
Но страсть узнал я, злую страсть...
Узнал томительную власть
Души надменной, молодой
Над пылкой, преданной душой.
Обнявшись дружно, целый год
Стремились жадно мы вперед,
Как облака перед грозой...
Не признавали мы преград —
И даже к радости былой
Не возвращались мы назад...
Нет! торжествуя без конца,
Мы сами жгли любовь и жизнь —
И наши гордые сердца
Не знали робких укоризн...
Но всё ж я был ее рабом —
Ее щитом, ее мечом...
Ее рабом я был! Она
Была свободна, как волна.
И мне казалось, что меня
Она не любит.. О, как я
Тогда страдал! Но вот идем
Мы летним вечером — вдвоем
Среди темнеющих полей...
Идем мы... Клики журавлей
Внезапно падают с небес —
И рдеет и трепещет лес...
Мне так отрадно... так легко...
Я счастлив... счастлив я вполне...
И так блаженно-глубоко
Вздыхает грудь... И нет во мне
Сомнений... оба мы полны
Такой стыдливой тишины!
Но дух ее был смел и жив
И беспокойно горделив;
Взойдет, бывало, в древний храм
И, наклонясь к немым плитам,
Так страстно плачет... а потом

Of such inimitable beauty!
We soon were close – I say no more.
I do not want, nor yet desire
To talk with everyone of how
I then was happy. But this know:
As long as with her I did stay,
I never knew a happy day.
But I knew passion, passion sour,
I knew the enervating power
A proud and youthful soul exerts
On a devoted ardent heart,
A whole year long, both deep in love,
Together we two onward strove
Like clouds which storms anticipate –
We recognized no earthly bourn,
And even to our joys of late
In no wise sought we to return.
Our celebrations knew no end;
Ourselves, and love, and life we burned.
Our hearts were both too arrogant,
And even mild reproaches spurned.
However, I was still her thrall,
And yet her sword and shield withal.
Her thrall I always was, and she,
Like waves upon the sea, was free,
And did not love me, it now seems.
Oh, how I suffered at those times.
On summer evenings we would walk
Together in the gathering dark
Across the meadows, she and I,
When suddenly the crane's shrill cry
Descended from above our head,
And shades of red the verdure hid.
I was both joyful and at ease;
My happiness was absolute.
So deeply felt was my heart's bliss
That in me vanished every doubt.
We both felt a satiety
Of innocent tranquillity.
But she was bold and spirited,
And, proudly uninhibited,
Would go into an ancient shrine
And, bowing to the wordless stone,
Would weep, then rise and stand with pride
Before the Saviour crucified.

Перед распятым божеством
Надменно встанет — и тогда
Ее глаза таким огнем
Горят, как будто никогда
Их луч, и гордый и живой,
Не отуманился слезой.
Ах! Та любовь, и страсть, и жар,
И светлой мысли дивный дар,
И красота — и всё, что я
Так обожал, — исчезло всё...
Безмолвно приняла земля
Дитя погибшее свое...
И ясен был спокойный лик
Великой матери людей —
И безответно замер крик
Души растерзанной моей...
Кругом — пленительна, пышна,
Сияла ранняя весна,
Лучом играя золотым
Над прахом милым и немым.
В восторгах пламенной борьбы
Ее застал последний час...
И без рыданий, без мольбы
Свободный дух ее погас...
А я! не умер я тогда!
Мне были долгие года
Судьбой лукавой суждены...
Сменили тягостные сны
Тот первый, незабвенный сон...
Как и другие, пощажен
Я не был... дожил до седин...
И вот живу теперь один...
Молюсь...»

МОЛОДОЙ ЧЕЛОВЕК

               Как ты, любил и я...
Но не могу я рассказать,
Как ты, любовь свою... Меня
Ты не захочешь понимать...
Бывало, в мирный час, когда
Над бледным месяцем звезда
Заблещет в ясной вышине,
И в безмятежной тишине
Журчит и плещет водопад,
И тихо спит широкий сад,

And then with flashing fire it seemed
Her burning gaze intensified,
As if her eyes' effulgent gleam,
Vivacious, arrogant, had never
With bitter teardrops misted over.
Ah, love! The ardency of passion,
The gift of clarity and reason,
And beauty – all which I adored
So much was now for ever vanished,
And earth received, without a word,
The corpse of one who, youthful, perished…
The face was tranquil and serene
Of her who is Maternity,
And muted was at last the scream
Of my poor soul in agony…
And all around, enchanting, lavish
A radiant early springtime flourished
And played its beams of burnished gold
On ashes mute, and mild, and cold.
Amid the joys and strife of passion
She entered on her final hour…
There were no tears, no supplication,
And her free spirit was no more…
But as for me, I did not die!
Ahead the decades endless lay,
Ordained for me by cunning Fate…
A heavy weight of dreams replaced
My dream, once new, unprecedented…
To others mercy may be granted,
But not to me – yet I survived
To age. In solitude I live
And pray…"

YOUNG MAN

    I too have loved like you,
But I'm not able to retell
My story in the way you do.
You do not understand me well…
There often was a peaceful hour
When, high above the moon, a star
Would all the heavens start to light.
The waterfall, in restful quiet,
With murmurings would dance and leap,
And spacious gardens quietly sleep;

И в наклоненных берегах
Дремотно нежится река, —
Сижу я с ней... в моих руках
Лежит любимая рука, —
И легкий трепет наших рук,
И нежной речи слабый звук,
Ее доверчивый покой,
И долгий взгляд, и вздох немой —
Всё говорит мне: ты любим.
И что ж! мучительно томим
Тоской безумной, я молчу...
Иль головой к ее плечу
Я наклонюсь... и горячо
На обнаженное плечо
Неистощимой чередой
Слеза струится за слезой...
О чем, скажи мне, плакал я?
Нет! жизнь отравлена моя!
Едва желанное вино
К моим губам поднесено —
И сам я, сам, махнув рукой,
Роняю кубок дорогой.
Когда ж настал прощальный миг —
Я был и сумрачен и тих...
Она рыдала... видит Бог:
Я сам тогда понять не мог:
Зачем я расставался с ней...
Молчал я... в сердце стыла кровь;
Молчал я... но в душе моей
Была не жалость, а любовь.
Старик, поверь — я б не желал
Прожить опять подобный час...
Я беспощадно разрывал
Всё, всё, что́ связывало нас...
Ее, себя терзал я... но
Мне было стыдно и смешно,
Что столько лет я жил шутя,
Любил забывчивый покой
И забавлялся, как дитя,
Своей причудливой мечтой...
Я с ней расстался навсегда —
Бежал, не знаю сам куда...
Следы горячих, горьких слез
Я на губах моих унес...
Я помнил всё: печальный взор

Between its steep and rugged banks
The lazy river onward wends.
I sit with her, and slowly sinks
A hand beloved to my hands –
And of our hands the gentle tremor,
And of our talk the scarce-heard murmur.
Her trusting air of nonchalance,
Her muted sighs, her long-held glance
"You are beloved" seemed to speak.
Yet I was tortured, rendered weak
And silent, by a mindless woe.
And thereupon I'd bow down low,
And on her shoulder place my head,
And then I would hot teardrops shed.
The teardrops flowed, tear after tear,
And fell upon that shoulder bare.
Why did I weep? Give me a reason.
I am infected with a poison.
The cup of wine, so dearly sought,
Had scarcely to my lips been brought
When I disdained the proffered cup
And, with a gesture, let it drop.
And when of parting came the moment,
Morose and calm was I, and distant.
She sobbed – her grief the Lord could see,
But I had no idea why.
I felt the need from her to part;
I held my peace – my blood ran cold,
And there was nothing in my heart
Of love, compassion, mercy mild.
Old man, believe, I did not want
To live through such an hour – no, never.
I ruthlessly dissolved the bond
Of all that had held us together.
Myself – and her – I went on hurting,
But found it shameful and diverting
That I so many years had lived
And jested, loving thoughtless calm.
I like a child had misbehaved,
Enjoying my capricious dream…
I went away from her for ever,
And ran, myself I knew not whither…
Of burning tears the bitter trace
I bore away upon my face…
Remembering all, the doleful look,

И недоконченный укор...
Но всё ж на волю, на простор,
И содрогаясь, и спеша,
Рвалась безумная душа.
И для чего? Но я тогда
Не знал людей... Так иногда
В степи широкой скачешь ты
И топчешь весело цветы,
И мчишься с радостной тоской,
Как будто там, в дали немой,
Где, ярким пламенем горя,
Сверкает пышная заря,
Где тучки светлые легли
Легко — на самый край земли.—
Как будто там найдешь ты всё,
Чем сердце страстное твое
Так безотчетно, так давно,
Так безвозвратно пленено...
И ты примчался... Степь кругом
Всё так же спит ленивым сном...
Томя нетерпеливый взгляд,
Несется тучек длинный ряд,
Лепечет желтая трава
Всё те же смутные слова...
И та же на сердце печаль,
И так же пламенная даль
Куда-то манит... и назад
Поедешь, сам себе не рад.
Но ты задумался?

СТАРИК

Ты прав.
Твой беспокойный, странный нрав
Мне непонятен. Создал Бог
Нас разно... ты в любви не мог
Найти покоя... но любовь
Не благо высшее людей;
Нетерпеливо пышет кровь
В сердцах немыслящих детей...
Они лишь для себя живут;
Когда ж минует та пора,
Приличен мужу долгий труд
На славном поприще Добра.
Ты жил, скиталец молодой;
Ты жил; так стань же предо мной —

The inarticulate rebuke.
And yet my soul demented broke
Away, beginning fearfully
A search for space and liberty.
But why was this? I did not know
The ways of men. As one might go
Full out across the steppe's expanse
And trample merrily on plants.
With joyful languor on you rush
As if there, in the distant hush,
Where with a fiery flame burns bright
The dawn's luxuriating light,
Where lambent clouds find easy berth
Upon the very edge of earth,
As if it's there that you'll find all
To which your heart has been in thrall
So timidly, and for so long,
Bereft of any sense of wrong…
And so you sped. Around, the steppe
Is sleeping with an idle sleep…
Exhausting the impatient eye
A lengthy line of clouds floats by;
The yellow grasses in hushed tones
Keep whispering the same refrains…
The heart feels sorrow just the same,
And distant vistas all aflame
Will tempt you back, but in that case,
Your inner self you cannot face.
But you are lost in thought?

OLD MAN

                          You're right.
Your character is strange, unquiet,
And baffles me. The Lord above
Did not make us the same. In love
You found no peace. But love is not
The greatest joy mankind desires.
Impatient is the ardent blood
In hearts of children immature…
They are themselves their sole existence,
And when that season comes to term,
Mankind should labour with persistence
For Good, and for its glorious realm.
You've lived, a wanderer young and free –
You've lived. Now stand in front of me

На сердце руку положи
И, не лукавствуя, скажи:
Какой ты подвиг совершил?
Какому богу ты служил?

МОЛОДОЙ ЧЕЛОВЕК

Когда бы кто-нибудь другой
Вопрос превыспренний такой
Мне предложил — ему в ответ
Я засмеялся бы... но нет!
Перед тобой раскрыта вся
Душа печальная моя.
Бывало, полный гордых дум,
Руководимый божеством
Каким-то, жизни вечный шум
Внимал я с тайным торжеством...
Я думал: там, в толпе людей,
Я волю дам душе моей;
Среди друзей, среди врагов,
Узнаю сам, кто я таков...
И за тобой, о мой народ,
Пойду я радостно вперед —
И загорится в сердце вновь
Святая, братская любовь.
Но что же! вдруг увидел я,
Что в целом мире для меня
Нет места; что я людям чужд;
Что нет у нас ни тех же нужд,
Ни тех же радостей; что мне
Они то страшны, то вполне
Непостижимы, то смешны...
И, потрясен до глубины
Души, взывал я к ним... но сам
Не верил собственным словам.
Я с ними сблизиться не мог...
И вновь один, среди тревог
Пустых, живу я с давних пор...

СТАРИК

Ты произнес свой приговор.
Ты, как дитя, самолюбив,
Как женщина, нетерпелив,
И добродушно лишь собой
Ты занят; нет любви прямой
И нет возвышенных страстей

And place your hand upon your heart.
Do not to deviousness resort,
But say what feats you have achieved,
Or which the god that you have served.

YOUNG MAN

Were anyone but you to ask
Of me a question so complex,
By way of a reaction I
Would give a jocular reply.
Before you is revealed the whole
Extent of my despondent soul.
Time was when all my thoughts were proud
And guided by divinity.
I heard the noise of life come loud,
Heard it with great solemnity.
Among the throng and press I thought
My soul at liberty I'd set.
And there among both friend and foe
My true identity I'd know.
My fellow men, I'm in your wake;
The onward path of joy I'll take,
And kindled in my soul will be
A love that's sacred, brotherly.
But then I saw all of a sudden
That I was everywhere unbidden.
My fellow men would spurn me there;
The needs they had I did not share,
Nor yet their joys, which were to me,
A source of fear and utterly
Inscrutable, a laughing stock.
And so completely thunderstruck,
To them I cried, but myself I
Considered my own words a lie.
From them I once again withdrew,
Assailed by empty cares anew
Throughout the years of my existence.

OLD MAN

You have yourself pronounced your sentence.
You, like a child, are full of pride,
Like female patience, sorely tried,
Preoccupied with self, kind-hearted,
For you no love can be straightforward.
No elevated passions dwell

В душе мечтательной твоей.
Но вспомни: «там, в толпе людей»,
Встречал ты юношей живых,
Неговорливых и простых?
Встречал ты старцев и мужей,
Достойных, опытных вождей?
И, примиренный, наконец,
С судьбой, ты видел в них залог
Того, что ревностных сердец
Не покидает правый Бог?

МОЛОДОЙ ЧЕЛОВЕК

Встречал я «старцев молодых»,
Людей прекрасных — и пустых;
Встречал я слабых добряков
И вздорных умников — толпой;
Встречал любезных остряков,
Довольных службой и судьбой,
И государственных людей,
Довольных важностью своей.
А вечный раб нужды, забот,
Спешил бессмысленный народ
На шумный, на постыдный торг...
Мечтал неопытный в тиши;
Но глупенький его восторг
Не веселил моей души;
Разочарованного стон
И бесполезен и смешон;
Но вдохновенный взгляд детей
И ненавистней и смешней.
И вот сограждане мои!
Старик, — вот юноши твои!
И всех пугает новизна,
Им недоступна красота...
И даже доблестным страшна
Насмешка праздного шута.
Нет! юношей не видел я...
Нет! нет! ты знаешь: жизнь моя
Прошла, как безотрадный сон...

СТАРИК

Когда бы не был ты влюблен
В игру бесплодную мечты,
Когда бы в Бога верил ты
И страстной, пламенной душой,

Within your visionary soul.
But there among the throng, mark well,
You often met young men of spirit,
Not chatterboxes – men of merit.
You met young men, you met their elders,
Experienced and worthy leaders,
And, reconciled with them at last,
From them you would assurance take
That those who are with ardour blessed,
The Lord will, justly, not forsake.

YOUNG MAN

Young elders with abilities
I thought were mediocrities.
The feeble and the good I've met,
Of useless, brainy types a crowd,
And very pleasant men of wit
Whose fate and service make them proud.
Inspired attention from the young
Makes hate and mockery more strong.
But, slaves to need, the populace
Is always prey to undue haste,
To shameful dealing, full of noise.
Unworldly, deep in meditation,
I was not able to rejoice,
Or share this foolish exultation.
A disillusioned man's complaint
Is comical and has no point,
But juvenile, elated looks
More laughter and more hate provoke.
These are my fellow citizens,
And these your youthful denizens.
By novelty they're terror-stricken,
The Beautiful they cannot master,
And even the most valiant weaken
At sneering from an idle jester.
No, youthful souls I have not seen,
Again I say – my life has been
A joyless dream and nothing more...

OLD MAN

If it could be that you forbore
To be enamoured of a dream,
If you belief in God could claim,
If passion, ardency of soul

Неутомимой до конца,
Искал бы, как воды живой,
Блаженной близости творца,—
Тогда, быть может, на тебя,
Твою настойчивую страсть,
Твой дух ревнивый возлюбя,
Сошла б таинственная власть.
Внезапным ужасом гоним
И гневом праведным томим,
Ты стал бы, сумрачный, немой,
Пред легкомысленной толпой...
И первый крик души твоей
Смутил бы суетных детей...
Толпа не смеет не признать
Великой силы благодать,
И негодующий пророк
Карал бы слабость и порок —
Гремели б страстные слова,
И, как иссохшая трава,
Пылали б от твоих речей
Сердца холодные людей.
Но малодушный ты! Судьбе
Ты покорился без стыда...
Так что ж, скажи, могло тебе
Дать право гордого суда
Над миром? — Нет! не верю я;
Нет! оклеветана толпа
Тобой... но если речь твоя
Не ложь, достойная раба, —
Тогда — Господь отцов моих,
Всесильный! — посети же вновь
Детей забывчивых твоих...
Напрасна кроткая любовь —
Так посели ты в их сердцах
И трепет и великий страх —
Промчись живительной грозой
Над грешной, суетной землей!

МОЛОДОЙ ЧЕЛОВЕК

Не поминай его, старик...
Он так далек... Он так велик —
А мы так малы... Да притом
Он нас забыл давно... О нем
Твердили миру чудеса —
Теперь безмолвны небеса...

You sought, rejecting weariness,
Like living waters of a pool,
The bliss of the Creator's nearness,
On you, perhaps, might then descend,
And on your unrelenting fervour,
A force to calm your jealous mind,
A hitherto mysterious power.
By sudden horror persecuted
And righteous anger enervated,
You would be gloomy, mute and cowed
Before the petty-minded crowd.
And then your soul's initial cry
Would idle children terrify.
The crowd is eager to confess
That mighty power equates to bliss;
And then the prophet's gorge would rise
And banish weaknesses and vice –
And fervent words would then ring out,
And, as dry grasses in a drought,
In every icy human heart,
Your words would cause a fire to start.
How cowardly you are! To Fate
You shamelessly saw fit to yield.
So, tell me, what gives you the right
To sit in judgement on the world?
No! Your assertions I deny.
No, no! The crowd you have maligned.
But if your words are all a lie,
Fit only for a servile mind,
May then my God, my forbears' Lord
Almighty, visit once again
His children, heedless of his word.
A gentle love is all in vain;
Their hearts with trepidation fill,
And mighty dread in them instil –
And, like a storm, refreshing life,
Surmount this world of sin and strife.

YOUNG MAN

Don't mention Him, old man, I pray:
He is so great, so far away
And we so small – moreover He
Of us retains no memory.
His miracles proclaimed His praise,
But there's a silence in the skies...

О, если бы пророк святой
Сказал мне: встань! иди за мной!
Клянусь, пошел бы я, томим
Великой радостью, за ним —
За ним — на гибель, на позор...
И пусть надменный приговор
Толпы рабов, толпы слепой
Гремит над ним и надо мной!
Но где пророки? О старик!
Тебе противен слабый крик
Души печальной и больной...
Ты презираешь глубоко
Мою тоску... Но, Боже мой!
Ты думаешь, что так легко
С надеждами расстался я?
Что равнодушно сам себе
Сказал я: гибнет жизнь моя!
Что грудь усталая — к борьбе
Упрямо, долго не рвалась?
Что за соломинки сто раз
Я не хватался?.. Ах, о чем
Хлопочем мы? Взгляни кругом:
Спокойно, кротко спит земля;
Леса, широкие поля
Озарены — обагрены
Лучами влажными луны...
И вот — мне чудится: ко мне,
Подобно медленной волне,
Торжественно, как дальний звон
Колоколов, со всех сторон,
С недостижимых облаков
И с гор, живущих сотый век,
Несется плавно звучный зов:
Смирись, безумный человек!

СТАРИК

И я тот голос неземной
Не раз — пред утренней зарей
Слыхал и тронутой душой
Стремился трепетно к нему,
К живому Богу моему.
Но в тишине других ночей
Звучал, бывало, громкий зов
В груди встревоженной моей...
И тех простых и гордых слов

If I had heard the prophet say
"Rise up and follow in my way",
I would have followed, that I swear
With weary joy and great good cheer,
Encountering destruction, shame…
So let the sightless crowd proclaim
Its verdict over Him and me!
But where, old man, are now the seers?
To you rebarbative appears
An ailing soul in agony;
You comprehensively despise,
Good Heavens, all my misery.
Do you imagine I with ease
Have let my hopes and dreams just vanish –
That with complete uninterest
I've told myself my life will perish,
That for the strife my weary breast
For many years has naught availed?
A hundred thousand times I've failed
To clutch at straws. What is it that
We agitate ourselves about?
See how the earth now sleeps in peace;
Its broad expanses and the trees
Are turned to crimson, and are lit
By moonbeams with a watery light.
And then I fancy that I hear,
Like waves that roll in, ever near,
A solemn sound, like distant bells,
Which comes from every side and swells,
From high among the banks of cloud,
From ancient mountains' lofty peaks,
A voice, harmonious and loud:
"Abandon madness. Make your peace!"

OLD MAN

These Heaven-sent words have I heard spoken
Before the dawn's new light had broken.
My soul was touched, and I was taken
In fear and trembling, with all speed
To stand before the throne of God.
But, interrupting night-time peace,
I heard a ringing summons loud
Within my agitated breast.
The words I heard were simple, proud.

Я не забыл: «Не унывай,
Трудись и Бога призывай;
И людям верь, и верь уму —
Не покоряйся никому,
Живи для всех и знай: крепка
Твоя непраздная рука».

МОЛОДОЙ ЧЕЛОВЕК

А между тем не ты ли сам
Покинул «бренный» мир?

СТАРИК

                        Страстям
Я предал молодость... оне
Меня сгубили... но клянусь,
Того, что прежде было мне
Святыней, — нет! я не стыжусь!

МОЛОДОЙ ЧЕЛОВЕК

Ты всех моложе нас, старик;
Мне непонятен твой язык.

СТАРИК

Так будь же проклят ты навек,
Больной, бессильный человек, —
За то, что нагло, без стыда
Ты погубил — и навсегда —
Всё, чем жила душа моя
В часы мучительной тоски,
Мои надежды — всё, что я
Любил, как любят старики!
Зачем пришел ты? Без тебя,
Надежды робкие тая
В груди разбитой, но живой,
Я, грешник, здесь, один, в лесах
Мечтал о жизни молодой,
О новых, сильных племенах —
Желал блаженных, ясных дней
Земле возлюбленной своей;
Дерзал молиться в тихий миг
Не за себя — но за других...
Теперь же — страшной темнотой
Весь мир покрылся; надо мной
Гремит уныло близкий гром...
Один, в пыли перед лицом

They stay with me: "Dejection shun,
Appeal to God and labour on.
Believe in man and intellect,
And to no other be subject.
For others live. Your arm is strong,
And know that it can do no wrong."

YOUNG MAN

Is it not so that you, meanwhile,
From this putrescent world resile?

OLD MAN

To passions I gave all my youth,
And they the life within me killed.
By all I held as scared truth
I swear: I don't feel any guilt.

YOUNG MAN

You're younger than us all, old man.
Your words I do not understand.

OLD MAN

So cursed for ever be your failing.
You are bereft of strength, and ailing.
Imprudently, and with no shame,
You've devastated for all time
Beliefs whereby my soul has lived
In moments of grief-stricken torments,
My hopes, and everything I've loved,
As, in their era, did the ancients.
Why have you come? Before you did
My faint and timid hopes I hid.
My spirits broken, but alive,
Alone amidst the trees, contrite,
I visions had of youthful life,
Of races new, in all their might.
I wished that days with radiance blessed
Would visit land I loved the best;
In quiet moments prayers I offered,
Not for myself at all – for others.
But now the world with darkness dread
Is covered, while, above my head,
The mournful thunder crashes near.
In dust and ashes you before,

Твоим, карающий Творец,
Я каюсь, каюсь, наконец, —
Измучен я... обманут я...
Но сжалься — пощади меня —
Мне смерть страшна — я не готов
Идти на твой могучий зов...
А жить...нет! жить еще страшней
В такой невыносимой мгле —
И места нет душе моей
Ни в небесах, ни на земле!

МОЛОДОЙ ЧЕЛОВЕК

Старик, ты прав, но ты жесток.
Послушай: каждый твой упрек
Неотразим... душа моя
Томится гневом и тоской
И замирает, как змея
Под торжествующей пятой...
И стыдно мне: мои глаза
Сжигает едкая слеза...
Но всё ж ты прав: я шут, я раб —
Я, как ребенок, вял и слаб;
Мои мечты еще глупей
Моих младенческих затей...
И не далась мне тайна слов
Живых — властительных речей;
Не долетает слабый зов
До невнимающих ушей...
Вокруг меня толпа шумит,
Толпа не чувствует тоски —
И недоверчиво глядит
На слезы глупые мои...
Нет! полно! нет — перед тобой
Клянусь я в этот страшный миг,
Клянусь я небом и землей,
Клянусь позором слез моих —
Я не снесу моих цепей,
Родимый край, тебя, друзей.
Без сожаленья, навсегда
Покину... и пойду тогда,
И безнадежен и суров,
Искать неведомых богов,
Скитаться с жадностью немой
Среди чужих, в земле чужой,
Где никому не дорог я,

The bringer of my punishment,
I finally repent, repent.
I am deceived, in agony.
But have compassion, pity me.
Death frightens me – I'm not prepared
To answer to its mighty word.
But yet more terrifying is life
In mist where few can bear to go.
My soul is homeless, cannot live
In heaven or on earth below!

YOUNG MAN

Old man, you're right, although too harsh.
I cannot counter your reproach.
Mark this: my soul is full of wrath,
And, wearied with its share of grief,
Is like a serpent feigning death,
An overweening heel beneath.
I have a sense of shame – my eyes
By bitter tears are cauterized...
You're right: I'm servile, and a joke,
And like a child am feeble, weak;
More idiotic then my dreams
Than all my adolescent schemes...
I did not have the gift of speech:
My words lack power, my words don't live.
Their puny call will only reach
To ears which no attention give...
A noisy crowd encircles me,
A crowd which has no sense of care,
Which contemplates mistrustfully
My every idiotic tear.
No! No! Enough. Before your eyes
At this most dreadful time I swear
By everything in earth and skies,
I swear by every shameful tear
I will not cast away my chains,
My native land, or you, or friends
For evermore, without regret.
I'll go, and then my course I'll set.
Despairing, with a heart of stone,
I'll go in search of gods unknown;
With muted eagerness I'll roam
'Mid foreigners, and far from home.
To no one there will I be dear,

Но где вольна душа моя,
Где я бестрепетно могу
Ответить вызовом врагу —
И, наконец, назло судьбе,
Погибнуть в радостной борьбе!

СТАРИК

Бежать ты хочешь? Но куда?
Зачем? К кому?

МОЛОДОЙ ЧЕЛОВЕК

     Старик, когда
Ты так усердно расточал
Упреки — помнишь? — я молчал;
Теперь я спрашиваю вас,
О, предки наши! что для нас
Вы сделали? Скажите нам:
«Вот, нашим доблестным трудам
Благодаря, — смотрите — вот
Насколько вырос наш народ...
Вот несомненный, яркий след
Великих, истинных побед!»
Что ж? отвечайте нам!.. Увы!
Как ваши внуки, на покой
Бессмысленный спешили вы
С работы трудной — но пустой...
И мы не лучше вас — о нет!
Нам то же предстоит... Смотри:
Над дальним лесом слабый свет,
Предвестник утренней зари,
Мерцает... близок ясный день —
Редеет сумрачная тень...
Но не дождаться нам с тобой
Денницы пышной, золотой,
И в час, когда могучий луч
Из-за громадных синих туч
Блеснет над радостной землей, —
Великий, бесконечный крик
Победы, жизни молодой
Не долетит до нас, старик...
Не пережив унылой тьмы,
С тобой в могилу ляжем мы —
Замрет упорная тоска;
Но будет нам земля тяжка...
Нам даже слава не далась...

But there my soul will be the freer,
And there I will unflinchingly
Be ready for the enemy,
And finally, in spite of fate,
Will perish in a joyful fight.

OLD MAN

But whither is it you will run?
And why? To whom?

YOUNG MAN

               Dear elder, when
I bore the brunt of your rebuke –
Do you recall? I did not speak.
And now to you I put this question:
O forebears! Have you ever done
A thing for us? I beg you tell us:
"Because our deeds were valorous,
It's evident to what great measure
Our native race has grown in stature,
The consequence, without a doubt
Of triumphs genuine and great."
So tell me why – alas the day –
You sought to find a senseless rest
And your descendants led away
From labour hard, but meaningless.
And we are not your betters, no.
The same awaits us. Cast your eye
To where on distant trees a glow
Means dawn's first heralds fill the sky
And light of day will soon flood in
As shadows of the night grow thin.
But neither you nor I will stay
To see the start of golden day,
When out of cloudy banks of blue
The sun's strong beams come bursting through
And strike the celebrating earth.
The infinite and hearty cheer
Of victory, of life, of youth,
Both you and I will fail to hear.
The gloomy dark we'll not survive.
Our common future is the grave,
And stubborn grief will there decay.
But earth will on us heavy weigh.
And even fame is not for us,

И наш потомок — мимо нас
Пройдет с поднятой головой,
Неблагодарный и немой.

Он торопливо встал... Рукой
Лицо закрыл старик седой;
И, думой тягостной томим,
Сидит он грустно-недвижим...
Но где же странник? Он исчез...
Шумит сурово темный лес;
И тучи ходят — и страшна
Пустынной ночи тишина.

And those who follow us will pass
Us by with heads held high and mute
To show us their ingratitude.

The grizzled seer rose up in haste
And with his hand concealed his face,
And, burdened with his heavy thought,
He sat unmoved, with sadness fraught.
But the wanderer, what of him?
He's vanished in the forest grim,
The clouds roll in and fill with terror
The night-time silence of the desert.

THE LANDOWNER

1

За чайным столиком, весной,
Под липками, часу в десятом,
Сидел помещик столбовой,
Покрытый стеганым халатом.
Он кушал молча, не спеша;
Курил, поглядывал беспечно...
И наслаждалась бесконечно
Его дворянская душа.
На голове его курчавой
Торчит ермолка; пес лягавой,
Угрюмый старец, под столом
Сидит и жмурится. Кругом
Всё тихо... Сохнет воздух... Жгучий
Почуя жар, перепела
Кричат... Ползет обоз скрипучий
По длинной улице села...

2

Помещик этот благородный,
Степенный, мирный семьянин,
Притом хозяин превосходный,
Был настоящий славянин.
Он с детства не носил подтяжек;
Любил простор, любил покой
И лень; но странен был покрой
Его затейливых фуражек.
Любил он жирные блины,
Боялся чёрта да жены;
Любил он, скушав пять арбузов,
Ругнуть и немцев и французов.
Читал лишь изредка, с трудом,
Служил в архиве казначейства,
И был, как следует, отцом
Необозримого семейства.

1

Beneath the springtime limes, at tea,
Between the hours of nine and ten,
A landowner of quality
Sat in his quilted dressing gown,
Unhurriedly and quietly eating.
He smoked, and looked round casually,
And took his pleasure endlessly:
This testified to noble breeding.
Atop the curls which crowned his head
A skullcap perched. A hound, long-haired,
A surly elder, sat and frowned
Beneath the table. All around
Was quiet… The air is dry. The quails
Cry out, anticipating heat…
A creaking train of waggons crawls
Along the lengthy village street.

2

A moderate man of lineage noble,
A peaceful family, phlegmatic,
As master, excellent and able –
A Slav, in short, and most authentic.
From childhood on he wore no straps,
Loved peacefulness and loved the open –
And idleness. Somewhat misshapen
And oddly striking were his caps.
A greasy blin was his first love.
He feared the Devil, and his wife.
Five watermelons he would scoff,
And then all foreigners slag off.
Occasional reading made him tired.
He worked in services financial
And had, as is expected, sired
A clutch of children quite substantial.

3

Он отдыхал. Его жена
Отправилась на богомолье...
Известно: в наши времена
Супругу без жены — раздолье.
И думал он: «В деревне рай!
Погода нынче — просто чудо!
А между тем зайти не худо
В конюшню да в сенной сарай».
Помещик подошел к калитке.
Через дорожку, в серой свитке,
В платочке красном набочóк,
Шла девка с кузовом в лесок...
Как человек давно женатый,
Слегка прищелкнув языком,
С улыбкой мирно-плутоватой
Он погрозил ей кулаком.

4

Потом с задумчивым вниманьем
Смотрел — как боров о забор
С эгоистическим стараньем,
Зажмурив глазки, спину тер...
Потом, коротенькие ручки
Сложив умильно на брюшке,
Помещик подошел к реке...
На волны сонные, на тучки,
На небо синее взглянул,
Весьма чувствительно вздохнул —
И, палку вынув из забора,
Стал в воду посылать Трезора...
Меж тем с каким-то мужиком
Он побеседовал приветно
О том, что просто с каждым днем
Мы развиваемся заметно.

5

Потом он с бабой поболтал...
(До баб он был немножко падок.)
Зашел в конюшню, посвистал
И хлебцем покормил лошадок...
Увидел в поле двух коров
Чужих... разгневался немало;
Велел во чтó бы то ни стало
Сыскать ослушных мужиков.

3

He was relaxing, and his wife
Away to be a pilgrim went…
It is a well-known fact of life:
A wifeless husband is content.
"The country is its own reward,"
He thought, "such is the weather now!
It's an idea meanwhile to go
To see my barn or stable yard."
Our hero went up to the gate.
A girl dressed in a short grey coat,
Her headscarf red and slightly skewed,
With basket went from path to wood.
A man long used to wedlock, he
His tongue with irritation clicked,
And, smiling disingenuously,
Would willingly her ears have boxed.

4

And then, with pensive concentration,
A boar beside the fence he watched.
With egocentric dedication
It made sure that its back was scratched.
Then, placing short and stubby fingers
With satisfaction on his front,
Our hero to the river went.
His gaze on sleepy ripples lingered,
On clouds, and on the clear blue sky.
He gave a sentimental sigh,
Then took a paling from the fence,
Trésor into the water sent,
And with a peasant whom he met
Began to chat most affably
About the fact that day by day
We all mature perceptibly.

5

He with a peasant woman talked
(To women he was always drawn),
Then, whistling, to his stables walked
To feed his horses with their corn.
He noticed in his field there were
Two cows – not his – which made him cross.
He told his men, whate'er the cost,
To apprehend the trespassers,

Красноречиво, важно, долго
Им толковал о чувстве долга,
Потом побил их — но слегка...
Легка боярская рука...
Пришел в ужасное волненье,
Клялся, что будущей зимой
Всё с молотка продаст именье, —
И медленно пошел домой.

6

В саду ему попались дети,
Кричат: «Папа́! готов обед...»
«Меня погубят дети эти, —
Он запищал, — во цвете лет!
Адам Адамыч! Вам не стыдно?
Как вы балуете детей!
Помилуйте! Да что́ вы?» Сей
Адам Адамыч, очевидно, ,
Был иностранный человек...
Но для того ли целый век
Он изучал Санхоньятона,
Зубрил «Республику» Платона
И тиснул длинную статью
О божествах самофракийских,
Чтоб жизнь убогую свою
Влачить среди дворян российских?

7

Он из себя был худ и мал;
Любил почтительные жесты —
И в переписке состоял
С родителем своей невесты.
Он был с чувствительной душой
Рожден; и в старческие годы
При зрелище красот природы
Вздыхал, качая головой.
Но плохо шли его делишки,
Носил он черные манишки,
Короткий безобразный фрак,
Исподтишка курил табак...
Он улыбался принужденно,
Когда начнут хвалить детей,
И кашлял, кланяясь смиренно,
При виде барынь и гостей.

To whom he said with eloquence
Of duty they should have a sense.
And then he beat them – not too hard...
Quite mild the hand of Russian lords.
By now in something of a huff,
He swore that when the winter came,
His whole estate would be sold off –
Then slowly made his way back home.

6

He met his children in the garden,
Who cried: "Papa, it's dinner time..."
He gave a squawk: "I fear such children
Will kill me when I'm in my prime!
Have you, Adamych, got no shame?
These kids are being indulged too much."
It was quite clear Adam Adamych*
Was bearer of a foreign name
And had his roots in alien soil.
Had he invested all that toil
In studying old texts Phoenician
Or learning classics, ancient, Grecian,
Or publishing a lengthy piece
On goddesses from Samothrace,
So he could spend his life's poor lease
Among the Russian gentry class?

7

He was a scrawny man, and slight,
And reverential gestures loved.
He often would epistles write
To relatives of his betrothed.
In him was sentiment inbred,
And now that he was growing old,
When Nature's beauty he beheld,
He'd give a sigh and shake his head.
For him now things were looking bad.
Black cuffs on both his sleeves he had,
And wore a frock coat short and tight.
He smoked tobacco on the quiet...
His smile was neither warm nor broad
When people praised the "little pests".
He coughed when he to ladies bowed,
On seeing them or other guests.

8

Но Бог с ним! Тихими шагами
Вернулся под родимый кров
Помещик... Он моргал глазами,
Он был и гневен и суров.
Вошел он в сени молчаливо,
И лани вспуганной быстрей
Вскочил оборванный лакей
Подобострастно-торопливо.
Мной воспеваемый предмет
Стремится важно в кабинет.
Мамзель-француженка в гостиной,
С улыбочкой, с ужимкой чинной
Пред ним присела... Посмотрел
Он на нее лукаво — кошкой...
Подумал: «Эдакий пострел!»
И деликатно шаркнул ножкой.

9

И гнев исчез его, как пар,
Как пыль, как женские страданья,
Как дым, как юношеский жар,
Как радость первого свиданья.
Исчез! Сменила тишина
Порывы дум степных и рьяных...
И на щеках его румяных
Улыбка прежняя видна.
Я мог бы, пользуясь свободой
Рассказа, с морем и с природой
Сравнить героя моего,
Но мне теперь не до того...
Пора вперед! Читатель милый,
Ваш незатейливый поэт
Намерен описать унылый
Славяно-русский кабинет.

10

Все стены на манер беседки
Расписаны. Под потолком
Висят запачканные клетки:
Одна с симбирским соловьем,
С чижами две. Вот — стол огромный
На толстых ножках; по стенам
Изображенья сочных дам
С улыбкой сладостной и томной

8

Enough of him! Our hero slowly
Returned beneath his native roof.
His eyes were blinking rapidly,
And he seemed angry and aloof.
He went indoors in total silence
And quicker than a frightened deer.
A tattered manservant appeared,
Obsequious, his manner urgent.
The subject of my story then
Retreated quickly to his den,
And in the drawing room meanwhile,
Mademoiselle with lofty smile
Sat down beside him, made him think,
As he observed her like a cat,
"She really is a little minx",
And delicately scuffed his foot.

9

His anger disappeared like vapour,
Like dust, like female devastation,
Like smoke, like adolescent fervour,
Or at a happy assignation.
It disappeared, and, in its place,
A hush, instead of outbursts wild.
His cheeks were pink, his former smile
Was visible upon his face.
It would be thought a liberty,
Reserved to writers such as me,
Should I my landowner compare
With Nature – but I won't go there.
I must move on, my reader dear!
Your poet in straightforward fashion
Intends now to describe the drear
Slavonic study of a Russian.

10

The walls are like an arbour painted.
Beneath the ceiling, hanging down,
Bespattered cages are suspended.
A nightingale is housed in one;
A massive table with big feet,
And on the walls some juicy ladies
In portraiture are there displayed.
Their smiles are languid, sickly sweet;

И с подписью: «La Charité,
La Nuit, le Jour, la Vanité...»
На полке чучело кукушки,
На креслах шитые подушки,
Сундук окованный в угле,
На зеркале слой липкой пыли,
Тарелка с дыней на столе
И под окошком три бутыли.

II

Вот — кипы пестрые бумаг,
Записок, счетов, приказаний
И рапортов... Я сам не враг
Степных присылок — и посланий.
А вот и ширмы... наконец,
Вот шкаф просторный, шишковатый...
На нем безносый, бородатый
Белеет гипсовый мудрец.
Увы! Бессильно негодуя,
На лик задумчивый гляжу я...
Быть может, этот истукан —
Эсхил, Сократ, Аристофан...
И перед ним уже седьмое
Колено тучных добряков
Растет и множится в покое
Среди не чуждых им клопов!

12

Помещик мой достойно, важно,
Глубокомысленно курил...
Курил... и вдруг зевнул протяжно,
Привстал и хрипло возопил:
«Эй — Васька!.. Васька! Васька! Васька!!!»
Явился Васька. «Тарантас
Вели мне заложить». — «Сейчас».
«А. что? починена коляска?»
«Починена-с». — «Починена?..
Нет — лучше тарантас». — «Жена, —
Подумал он, — вернется к ночи,
Рассердится... Но нету мочи,
Как дома скучно. Еду — да!
Да, чёрт возьми — да!» Но, читатель,
Угодно ль вам узнать, куда
Спешит почтенный мой приятель?

They're captioned "*Nuit*" or "*Charité*",
Or "*Jour*", or even "*Vanité*".*
And on the shelf a model cuckoo;
An armchair with embroidered cushions;
A corner with an iron-bound trunk;
A mirror with a layer of silt;
A table with a melon chunk;
Three bottles on a window sill.

11

Assorted papers in a pile,
Accounts and statements of procurement,
Reports... Myself, I'm not hostile
To local letters of endearment.
And finally, we find a screen,
And then a cupboard, fairly spacious.
Upon it, bearded and sagacious,
But noseless, stands a figurine.
With impotent distaste, alas,
I gaze upon that pensive face.
It may be Aristophanes,
Or Aeschylus, or Socrates...
Before it are the generations
Of worthy fellows, stout and good,
And non-stop silent replications
Of bedbugs using them as food.

12

My landowner liked solemnly
His pipe in pensive mode to smoke.
He'd smoke, and then yawn suddenly,
Get to his feet and hoarsely croak:
"Hey, Vaska, Vaska, Vaska – fetch
And harness up the tarantas."
"At once." "And tell me has
The work been done on the calèche?"
"It has." "But no, I'd rather have
The tarantas. My better half
Is due home by tonight," he thought.
"She won't be pleased. There's nothing for it,
I'm bored at home and so I'm going.
Yes, dammit, going." But, as you read,
Would you be helped at all by knowing
In detail where he's going at speed?

13

Так знайте ж! от его села
Верстах в пятнадцати, не боле,
Под самым городом жила
Помещица — в тепле да в холе,
Вдова. Таких немного вдов.
Ее супруг, корнет гусарский,
[Соскучившись на службе царской]
Завел охоту, рысаков,
Друзей, собак... Обеды, балы
Давал, выписывал журналы...
И разорился б, наконец,
Мой тороватый молодец,
Да в цвете лет погиб на «садке»,
Слетев торжественно с седла,
И в исступленном беспорядке
Оставил все свои дела.

14

С его-то вдовушкой любезной
Помещик был весьма знаком.
Ее сравнил остряк уездный
С свежепросольным огурцом.
Теперь ей — что ж! о том ни слова —
Лет под сорок... но как она
Еще свежа, полна, пышна
И не по-нашему здорова!
Какие плечи! Что за стан!
А груди — целый океан!
Румянец яркий, русый волос,
Немножко резкий, звонкий голос,
Победоносный, светлый взор —
Всё в ней дышало дивной силой...
Такая барыня — не вздор
В наш век болезненный и хилый!

15

Не вздор! И был ей свыше дан
Великий дар: пленять соседей,
От образованных дворян
До «степняков» и до «медведей».
Она была ловка, хитра,
И только с виду добродушна...
Но восхитительно радушна
С гостями — нынче, как вчера.

13

Some way away, let it be known,
Eleven miles, or thereabouts,
On the approaches to the town
A female landlord had her house.
A widow (lots of those around) –
Her spouse a junior hussar,
Who'd tired of service to the Tsar,
Liked hunting, so bred hunting hounds,
Liked organizing balls the most,
Subscribed to journals through the post.
Behaviour over-generous
And likely to be ruinous.
When youthful vigour in him breathed,
He fell, while hunting, from the saddle.
The only things that he bequeathed
Were papers in a total muddle.

14

So with this little widow fair
Our landowner was well acquainted.
Thus her would local wags compare:
"A cucumber fresh marinated."
She now – we'd better keep this quiet –
Was nearly forty, but looked splendid,
Luxuriant and fresh, full-bodied,
Not in the least what we call "fit".
She had such shoulders, such a waist,
And like an ocean was her breast!
Her voice was somewhat shrill in tone;
Her cheeks were pink, her hair light-brown,
Triumphant, luminous her eyes,
And everything her strength betokened.
A girl like that is deemed a prize
In times which are by sickness weakened!

15

A prize! To her the gods had given
The gift her neighbours to attract,
From educated noblemen,
To "bears" and what we call *"stepniaks"*.*
She was skilful, she was sly,
And, superficially, was kind.
With guests her joy was unconfined,
As much today as yesterday.

Пред ней весь дом дрожал. Не мало
Она любила власть. Бывало,
Ей покорялся сам корнет...
И дочь ее в семнадцать лет
Ходила с четырьмя косами
И в панталончиках. Не раз
Своими белыми руками
Она наказывала вас,

16

О безответные творенья,
Служанки барышень и бар,
. . . .
. . . .
О вы, которым два целковых
Дается в год на башмаки,
И вы, небритые полки
Угрюмых, медленных дворовых!
Зато на двести верст кругом
Она гремела... с ней знаком
Был губернатор... кавалеры
Ее хвалили за манеры
Столичные, за голосок
(Она подчас певала «Тройку»),
За беспощадный язычок
И за прекрасную настойку.

17

Притом любезная вдова
Владела языком французским,
Хоть иностранные слова
У ней звучали чем-то русским.
Во дни рождений, именин
К ней дружно гости наезжали
И заживались и вкушали
От разных мяс и разных вин.
Когда ж являлась до жаркого
Бутылка теплого донского —
Все гости, кроме дев и дам,
Приподнимались по чинам
И кланялись хозяйке, — хором
«Всего... всего» желали ей...
А дети вместе с гувернером
Шли к ручке маменьки своей.

She made things quake – to no mean tune
She loved to be in charge, and soon
The cornet too was gripped by fear…
Her daughter, in her eighteenth year,
Arranged her hair in four long strands,
And bloomers sported. More than once
The widow used her snow-white hands
Her own rough justice to dispense.

16

On you, most timid of creations,
You lackeys and you serving maids,
Or those of even humbler station
Whom every nobleman upbraids,*
O ye, to whom two roubles given
For shoes is deemed to be enough,
And ye, battalions unshaven
Of slow and surly household serfs!
For miles around she would raise hell,
The local governor knew her well,
While all the local gentlemen
Thought her a metropolitan,
And would extol her singing voice
(Of 'Troika'* she gave fine renditions).
Her language tended to be choice –
Her drinks to be in top condition.

17

And so it was our widow merry
In speaking French was very fluent,
Although the words she spoke were very
Affected by a Russian accent.
When there were birthday celebrations,
The guests would come to her to dine,
Enjoy themselves and drink the wine,
And many other consumations.
Before the meat, wine from the Don
Was served and tasted, whereupon
The guests, though not of course the ladies,
Stood up according to their status.
Their hostess they saluted – *tutti*,
And wished her every warmest wish.
Her children, meanwhile, and their tutor,
Lined up their mother's hand to kiss.

18

А по зимам она давала
Большие балы... Господа!
Хотите вы картиной бала
Заняться? Отвечаю: да,
За вас. Во времена былые,
Когда среди родных полей
Я цвел — и нравились моей
Душе красавицы степные,
Я, каюсь, — я скитался сам
По вечерам да по балам,
Завитый, в радужном жилете,
И барышень «имел в предмете».
И память верная моя
Рядком проводит предо мною
Те дни, когда, бывало, я
Сиял уездною звездою...

19

Ах! этому — давно, давно...
Я был тогда влюблен и молод,
Теперь же... впрочем, всё равно!
Приятен жар — полезен холод.
Итак, на бале мы. Паркет
Отлично вылощен. Рядами
Теснятся свечи за свечами,
Но мутен их дрожащий свет.
Вдоль желтых стен, довольно темных,
Недвижно — в чепчиках огромных —
Уселись маменьки. Одна
Любезной важности полна,
Другая молча дует губы...
Невыносимо душен жар;
Смычки визжат, и воют трубы
И пляшет двадцать восемь пар.

20

Какое пестрое собранье
Помещичьих одежд и лиц!
Но я намерен описанье
Начать — как следует — с девиц.
Вот — чисто русская красотка,
Одета плохо, тяжела
И неловка, но весела,
Добра, болтлива, как трещотка,

18

In winter she was wont to give
Some splendid balls. Friends, do you want
Me such an evening to describe?
I with a "yes" to you respond.
I flourished once in times of old
Around my native fields and pastures,
A time when I would be in raptures
When local beauties I beheld,
When of an evening I would roam
Round local balls, to which I'd come
In coloured waistcoat, hair in curls,
To target all the local girls.
And so my trusty memory
Displays before me, line by line,
The days on which it happened I
Would like a star provincial shine.

19

Oh, that was very long ago,
And I was deep in love, and youthful,
But now... Do I really want to know?
The heat has charms, the cold its uses.
We are, then, at the ball. The floor
Is highly polished. There in huddles
Stand endless rows and rows of candles.
Their light is flickering, and poor.
Along the walls of yellow matt,
Immobile all the mothers sit
In massive bonnets. One of them
Is affable and yet is solemn.
Another quietly sucks in air,
So stuffy is the atmosphere.
The fiddles screech, a trumpet blares,
The floor is thronged with thirty pairs.

20

How colourful is this collection
Of landowners, their clothes and faces!
But I will start now my depiction
Quite properly, with the fair sex.
So here's a purely Russian belle,
Who's ponderous and badly dressed,
Lacks nimbleness, but does have zest,
Is kind, and babbles like a rill,

И пляшет, пляшет от души.
За ней — «созревшая в тиши
Деревни» — длинная, худая
Стоит Коринна молодая...
Ее печально-страстный взор
То вдруг погаснет, то заблещет...
Она вздыхает, скажет вздор
И вся «глубоко» затрепещет.

21

Не заговаривал никто
С Коринной... сам ее родитель
Боялся дочки... Но зато
Чудак застенчивый, учитель
Уездный, бледный человек,
Ее преследовал стихами
И предлагал ей со слезами
«Всего себя... на целый век...»
Клялся, что любит беспорочно,
Но пел и плакал он заочно,
И говорил ей сей Парис
В посланьях: «ты» — на деле «вы-с».
О жалкий, слабый род! О время
Полупорывов, долгих дум
И робких дел! О век! о племя
Без веры в собственный свой ум!

22

О!!!.. Но — богиня песнопений,
О муза! — публика моя
Терпеть не может рассуждений...
К рассказу возвращаюсь я.
Отдельно каждую девицу
Вам описать — не моему
Дано перу... а потому
Вообразите вереницу
Широких лиц, больших носов,
Улыбок томных, башмаков
Козлиных, лент и платьев белых,
Турбанов, перьев, плеч дебелых,
Зеленых, серых, карих глаз,
Румяных губ и... и так дале —
Заставьте барынь кушать квас —
И знайте: вы на русском бале.

And dances, dances to exhaustion.
Then one "in countryfied seclusion
Matured", who is both long and thin,
And young, and modelled on Corinne.*
Her sorrowful and passionate eye
Is dimmed and lit alternately.
She talks a lot of rubbish, sighs,
And revels in "profundities".

21

Corinne by everyone was shunned.
Her mother and her father feared
Their daughter. On the other hand
A local fellow, shy and weird,
A timid teacher, loitering palely,
Bombarded her with reams of verse,
And offered her, in floods of tears
Himself entire, eternally.
He swore no love could purer be,
But none but he his tears could see.
And when he wrote, this Paris *fou*
Used "thou", whereas he would use "you"
In normal speech. Oh, nation feeble,
Oh, home of thoughts and long outbursts,
And lack of deeds. Oh, age! Oh, people,
Who its intelligence mistrusts.

22

O goddess! O thou Muse sublime!
For reasoning my audience
Declares it has not got the time.
And so my story I commence.
Describing girls in quick succession
Is hardly suited to my pen,
But if you just imagine then
Of faces broad a long procession,
Plus languid smiles and lengthy noses,
And many pairs of goatskin shoes,
White dresses by the score, and ribbons,
And plumpish shoulders, feathers, turbans,
And eyes of colours most diverse,
And lips of rosy hue, and all...
Compel the ladies to drink kvass,
And there, you're at a Russian ball!

23

Но вот — среди толпы густой
Мелькает быстро перед вами
Ребенок робкий и немой
С большими грустными глазами.
Ребенок... Ей пятнадцать лет.
Но за собой она невольно
Влечет вас... за нее вам больно
И страшно... Бледный, томный цвет
Лица — печальный след сомнений
Тревожных, ранних размышлений,
Тоски, неопытных страстей,
И взгляд внимательный — всё в ней
Вам говорит о самовластной
Душе... Ребенок бедный мой!
Ты будешь женщиной несчастной...
Но я не плачу над тобой...

24

О нет! пускай твои желанья,
Твои стыдливые мечты
В суровом холоде страданья
Погибнут... не погибнешь ты.
Без одобренья, без участья,
Среди невежд осуждена
Ты долго жить...но ты сильна,
А сильному не нужно счастья.
О нем не думай... но судьбе
Не покоряйся; знай: в борьбе
С людьми таится наслажденье
Неистощимое — презренье.
Как яд целительный, оно
И жжет и заживляет рану
Души... Но мне пора давно
Вернуться к моему «роману».

25

Вот перед вами в вырезном
Зеленом фраке — шут нахальный,
Болтун и некогда «бель-ом»,
Стоит законодатель бальный.
Он ездит только в «высший свет».
А вот — неистово развязный,
Довольно злой, довольно грязный
Остряк; вот парень средних лет,

23

And where there's least room to be had,
A child appears quite rapidly,
A child whose eyes are large and sad,
Who moves in silence, timidly.
Just fifteen summers has she seen,
But she will take you in her wake...
You're worried, fearful for her sake...
Her countenance is weary, wan,
Betraying mournful hesitation,
And youthful, anxious contemplation,
And inexperienced passions, languor.
She has an eager look and manner,
Which indicates a soul self-willed.
A hapless woman you will be,
My wretched and unlucky child.
But I'm not weeping over thee.

24

Oh, no! So may your every wish,
Your modest, bashful, waking dreams,
In suffering's harsh climate perish.
You will not die in such extremes.
When none approve and none take heed,
You are condemned to live among
Know-nothings, but you are so strong
Of happiness you have no need.
Think not of it, but don't submit
To fickle Fate, for in the fight
With people can be found content,
Of which one never tires. Contempt
Will like a toxic unguent burn,
But get the wounded soul to heal.
And so it's high time to return
And end my novelistic spiel.

25

And now before you see him come –
In green tailcoat – a brass-necked clown,
A loudmouth and one-time *bel homme*,
Who now in ballrooms sets the tone.
Society's alone his stage.
And here's a wit, insouciant,
But grubby and malevolent.
And there's a man of middle age,

В венгерке, в галстуке широком,
Глаза навыкат, ходит боком,
Хрипит и красен, как пион.
Вот этот черненький — шпион
И шулер — впрочем, малый знатный,
Угодник дамский, балагур...
А вот помещик благодатный
Из непосредственных натур.

26

Вот старичок благообразный,
Известный взяточник, а вот
Светило мира, барин праздный,
Оратор, агроном и мот,
Чудак для собственной потехи
Лечивший собственных людей...
Ну, словом — множество гостей.
Варенье, чернослив, орехи,
Изюм, конфекты, крендельки
На блюдцах носят казачки...
И, несмотря на пот обильный,
Все гости тянут чай фамильный.
Крик, хохот, топот, говор, звон
Стаканов, рюмок, шпор и чашек...
А сверху, с хор, из-за колонн
Глазеют кучи замарашек.

27

Об офицерах, господа,
Мы потолкуем осторожно...
(Не то рассердятся — беда!)
Но перечесть их... Это можно.
Чувствительный артиллерист,
Путеец маленький, невзрачный,
И пехотинец с виду мрачный,
И пламенный кавалерист —
Все тут как тут... Но вы, кутилы,
Которым барышни не милы,
Гроза почтенных становых,
Владельцы троек удалых,
И покровители цыганок —
Вас не видать на тех балах,
Как не видать помадных банок
На ваших окнах и столах!

With round his neck a broad cravat;
With hussar jacket, crab-like gait,
He snuffles and is red as beet.
And this dark fellow is a cheat
And spy, and yet considered splendid,
A clown, and something of a lecher.
And there's a noble, gracious, landed,
And of the most straightforward nature.

26

And here's a handsome-looking elder,
Well known for taking bribes, and this
A luminary, *barin*,* idle,
A spendthrift and agronomist,
Who for his own peculiar reasons,
On servants would his home cures test...
In short – a multitude of guests.
Dried plums, and jam, and pies, and raisins,
And a variety of nuts
Borne in by pageboys on large plates...
And, despite their perspiration,
The guests take tea in celebration.
There's stamping, clatter, raillery,
The clink of glasses, cups and spurs,
While, from the upper gallery,
Come glances from a bunch of whores.

27

We must take care when we discuss
The officers, and must remember
That they could well get cross, alas.
But let us now go through their number...
One sensitive artificer,
A small and ugly engineer,
A gloomy-looking grenadier,
A dashing lancer officer –
All here, but you of wilder spirit,
For whom the fair sex has no merit,
The scourge of all the local forces,
Who speed along behind three horses,
Enjoy protecting Gypsy maids –
We miss your presence at these balls,
And on your tables miss pomade
(And miss it from your window sills).

28

Превозносимый всем уездом
Дом обольстительной вдовы
Бывал обрадован приездом
Гостей нежданных из Москвы.
Чиновник, на пути в отцовский
Далекий, незабвенный кров
(Спасаясь зайцем от долгов),
Заедет... умница московский,
Мясистый, пухлый, с кадыком,
Длинноволосый, в кучерском
Кафтане, бредит о чертогах
Князей старинных, о . . . . . .
От шапки-мурмолки своей
Ждет избавленья, возрожденья;
Ест редьку, западных людей
Бранит — и пишет донесенья.

29

Бывало, в хлебосольный дом
Из дальней северной столицы
Примчится борзый лев; и львом
Весьма любуются девицы.
В деревне лев, глядишь, ручной
Зверек — предобрый; жмурит глазки;
И терпеливо сносит ласки
Гостеприимности степной.
В деревне — водятся должишки
За ним... играет он в картишки...
Не платит... но как разговор
Его любезен, жив, остер!
Как он волочится небрежно!
Как он насмешливо влюблен!
И как забудет безмятежно
Всё, чем на миг был увлечен!

30

Но мой помещик? Не пора ли
К нему вернуться, наконец?
Пока мы с вами поболтали,
Читатель, — староста, кузнец,
Садовники, покинув тачки,
Кондитор, ключник, повара,
Мальчишки, девки, кучера,
Столяр, кухарки, даже прачки —

28

Extolled throughout the whole *uezd*,*
The house of the seductive widow
Was with the coming very pleased
Of unexpected guests from Moscow:
A functionary in headlong flight
To refuge find in his estate,
And to avoid a pile of debt –
A very clever Muscovite.
Obese and prominent of throat,
Long-haired, and in a coachman's coat,
He loves to talk of palaces,
Of ancient princes and princesses.
Through hats much liked by Slavophiles*
He seeks redemption and salvation,
Eats radishes, the West reviles,
And likes to write denunciations.

29

A "lion" hastens to this home,
Where folk are so hospitable,
A lion of a species whom
Girls flatter in the capital.
In country circles he, you see
Is tame, and kind, and bats his eyes,
And patiently gives his replies
To local hospitality.
In country circles he incurs
Big losses when he plays at cards.
He doesn't pay up – he is broke,
But talks with zest and likes a joke.
How careless is his hot pursuit,
And his *amour insouciant*!*
How rapidly he will refute
What had his interest – for an instant!

30

What of our hero? Is it not
Time to return to him forthwith?
While we were busy with our chat,
Dear reader, bailiff and blacksmith,
And gardeners without their barrows,
And coachmen, and the caterer,
Young boys and girls, the housekeeper,
The laundress and the carpenter –

Вся дворня, словом, целый час
Справляла «ветхий тарантас».
И вот, надев армяк верблюжий,
На козла лезет кучер дюжий;
фалетор сел; раздался крик
Ребят; победоносно взвился
Проворный кнут — и шестерик
Перед крыльцом остановился.

31

Выходит барин... целый дом
За ним идет благоговея.
Безмолвно — в шляпах с галуном,
Надетых криво, два лакея
Ведут его... Приятель наш
Детей целует, на подножку
Заносит ногу, понемножку,
Кряхтя, садится в экипаж,
И под его дворянским телом,
Довольно плотным и дебелым,
Скрипят рессоры. «Взят тюфяк
На всякий случай! Ты, дурак,
Смотри, под горку тише... Что вы
Мне в ноги положили? стой!
Где ларчик?» — «Здесь». — «А! Ну, готовы?
Пошел!.. Я к вечеру домой».

32

Уехал барин. Слава Богу!
Какой веселый, дружный гам,
Какую шумную тревогу
Все подняли! Спешит Адам
Адамыч в комнатку... гитару
(Подарок будущей жены)
Снимает тихо со стены,
Садится, скверную сигару
С улыбкой курит... и не раз
Из голубых немецких глаз
Слеза бежит... и край любимый
Он видит снова — край родимый,
Далекий, милый... и, пока
Еще не высохли те слезы,
В убитом сердце старика
Взыграли радостные грезы.

In short, the household, hours on end
Put in, the ancient coach to mend.
At last we see the coachman stout
Get ready in his camel coat.
Postilion placed; the children shriek;
Triumphantly the whip is up,
The tarantas, or "coach and six",
Before the house comes to a stop.

31

Out comes the *barin*. His household
Come after him with reverence,
And then, with hats with braids of gold
Worn crooked, come two manservants.
The children in his entourage
Are kissed. The *barin* puts his foot
Onto the step and takes his seat
And settles puffing in his carriage.
Beneath this gentleman's large weight
Of solid flesh – or solid fat –
The springs are groaning. "We have brought
A mattress with us. Idiot!
Make sure on hills you take it steady.
What's this you're putting at my feet?
A little chest? Are you quite ready?
Then off we go! Back home tonight!"

32

Off drove the *barin*, thank the Lord.
What happy and harmonious bedlam!
What noise and general uproar
Was raised! Then in came rushing Adam
Adamovich, who straightway lifted
Down from the wall his old guitar
(A present his betrothed had gifted),
Sat down and lit a cheap cigar.
He smokes and smiles, and more than once
From German eyes a teardrop runs.
He sees a land to which he's drawn,
He sees the land where he was born,
A distant, pleasant land. Meanwhile
The old man's tears had not yet dried,
But in his devastated soul
Consoling fancies had appeared.

33

Помещик едет. Легкий сон,
Надежный друг людей дородных,
Им овладел... не видит он
Равнин окрестных плодородных.
О Русь! Люблю твои поля.
Когда под ярким солнцем лета
Светла, роскошна, вся согрета,
Блестит и нежится земля...
Люблю бродить в лугу росистом
Весной, когда веселым свистом
И влажным запахом полна
Степей живая тишина...
Но дворянин мой хладнокровно
Поля родные проезжал;
Он межевал их полюбовно,
Но без любви воспоминал

34

О них... Привычка! То ли дело,
Когда в деревню как-нибудь
Мы попадем, бывало... Смело,
Легко, беспечно дышит грудь...
И дорога нам воля наша,
Природа — дивно хороша,
И в каждом юноше душа
Кипит, как праздничная чаша!
Так что ж? Ужели ж те года
Прошли навек и без следа?
Нет! Нет! Мы сбросим наши цепи,
Вернемся снова к вам, о степи!
И вот — за бешеных коней
Отдав полцарства, даже царство —
Летим за тридевять полей
В сороковое государство!..

35

Раскинувшись на пуховых
Подушках, спит самодовольно
Помещик. Кучер пристяжных
Стегает беспощадно. Больно
Смотреть на тощих лошадей.
Фалетор на кобыле тряской
Весь бледный прыгает. Со связкой
В руках храпит себе лакей.

33

On goes our hero. A light snooze,
The trusty friend of the inane,
Possessed him. Did he somehow lose
A sight of the surrounding plain?
I love your open fields, O Russia,
When under the bright rain of summer,
The fertile earth is bright and lusher,
Luxuriantly basking, warmer.
I love to wander in the spring
In meadows where the sweet birds sing,
And cheerfully a dewy fragrance
Pervades the steppe lands' living silence.
Our hero quite dispassionately
Across his native pastures passed,
Divided them quite happily,
But thought of them with some disgust.

34

Sheer habit! On the other hand
If in the country we should be,
We breathe more nonchalantly and
More boldly and more easily.
Our freedom is most dear to us,
And Nature seems miraculous.
In every youthful soul emotions
Are brimming over like libations.
But what is this? Is it the case
These years have vanished without trace?
No, no, we will throw off our chains,
And our beloved steppes regain,
And for some speedy horses yield,
A half a kingdom, or a whole.*
We'll fly beyond the farthest field
To find the earth's most distant pole.

35

The landowner on downy cushions
Sleeps sprawled, the picture of content.
Meanwhile the horses from the coachman,
"Reminders" get without relent.
To witness this is most unpleasant.
Postilion on knock-kneed mare
Is pale, as on he trots. A snore
Is given by a sleeping servant

Бойка дорога. Все ракиты,
Как зимним инеем, покрыты
Тончайшей пылью. Жарко. Вдруг
(Могу ль изобразить испуг
Помещика?) на повороте
Ось пополам — и тарантас
(Прошу довериться работе
Домашней...) набок...Вот те раз!

36

Поднявшись медленно с дороги,
Без шапки, трепетной рукой
Ощупал спину, нос и ноги
Мой перепуганный герой.
Все цело... Кучер боязливо
Привстал... и никаких речей
Не произнес... Один лакей
Засуетился торопливо —
То вскочит сам на облучок,
То вдруг возьмется за задок,
То шляпу двинет на затылок...
Но как ни ловок он и пылок —
Напрасно всё... Что делать! Сам
Помещик вовсе растерялся,
Не верил собственным глазам
И, как ребенок, улыбался.

37

«Ах, чёрт возьми! Ну, что там?» — «Ось
Сломалась». Барин для порядка
Ее потрогал. «Да; хоть брось.
Ох, эта бестия Филатка!
(Филаткой звался старый плут
Каретник.) До деревни сколько?»
«Да будет верст пяточек». — «Только?
Скачи за кузнецом... да кнут
Возьми...» Но взоры в отдаленье
Вперило хитрое творенье,
Лакей... и вдруг он крикнул: «Э!
К нам едет барыня...» — «Где? где?
Какая барыня?» — «Полями.
Знать, она взяли... Точно так»
«Не может быть!» — «Смотрите сами:
Оне-с...» — «Ну, ну, молчи, дурак!»

With bundle. Rough the road, and dust
Has covered all the trees like frost.
It's hot. A bend. The axle sheers
(Shall I depict our hero's fears?),
Is split in half, two pieces left.
As a result, the tarantas
(I hope you trust domestic craft)
Is leaning on its side, alas.

36

He slowly from the road arose,
And found he was without his cap.
He felt his back, his legs, his nose,
And was intact, despite this flap.
Meanwhile the coachman, fearfully
Got to his feet, said not a word;
Another flunkey then was stirred
Enough to bustle hastily:
He tries to jump onto the box,
Then grabs the carriage by the back,
Then shifts his hat back on his crown.
But all his efforts are in vain.
Our hero can do nothing: he
Has lost his head, is growing wild,
Does not believe what he can see,
And takes to smiling, like a child.

37

"What is it, dammit?" "Axle's snapped."
The landowner the axle felt
For form's sake. "Yes. Now get it scrapped.
This coachman is a swinish dolt!"
(Filatka was the name he bore.)
"Next village?" "Two miles, maybe three."
"That doesn't sound a lot to me –
Go fetch the smith, and make damn sure
You take your whip." A flunkey cried
As he a distant prospect spied:
"A lady's coming. Just look there!"
"What is this lady? Who and where?"
"The track across the fields she took.
I'm speaking nothing but the truth."
"That cannot be." "Just take a look:
It's *her*!" "You fool, just shut your mouth."

38

Действительно: в кибитке длинной,
Подушками, пуховиком
Набитой доверху, в старинной
Измятой шляпке, с казачком,
С собачкой, с девкой в казакине
Суконном, едет на семи
Крестьянских клячах «chère amie».
Своей любезной половине
Приятель наш едва ли рад...
Он бросился вперед, назад...
Им овладело беспокойство,
Весьма естественное свойство
Иных мужей при виде жен...
Кибитка стала... дыбом волос
На нем поднялся... слышит он
Супруги дребезжащий голос:

39

«Сергей Петрович, это вы?»
«Я, матушка». — «Ах, мой спаситель!
Куда ж вы ехали?» Увы!
Разочарованный сожитель
Молчит уныло. «Верно, к той
Вдове? Уж эта мне вострушка!
Да говорите ж!.. К ней, Петрушка?»
Лакей проворно головой
Кивнул. «Ах, старый греховодник!
Вот я молилась — вас угодник
И наказал... Ну, как я зла!
А я вам просвиру везла!..
Неблагодарный! Отлучиться
Нельзя мне на денек, ей-ей...
Подвинься, Аннушка... Садиться
Извольте к нам — да поскорей».

40

Покорный строгому веленью,
Садится муж. В его груди
Нет места даже сожаленью...
Всё замерло. Но впереди
Беду предвидит он. Подруга
Его когда-то молода
Была, но даже в те года
Не думала, что друг для друга

38

It was his *chère amie** indeed,
In a kibitka filled with cushions.
She lay upon a feather bed,
And wore a hat well out of fashion.
With her, a girl in coat of cloth,
A pageboy and a little dog,
A team of seven peasant nags.
To meet up with his better half
Our man felt far from truly glad.
He rushed about this way and that,
Possessed by some anxiety –
A very natural quality
In certain husbands when they see
Their wives. The carriage stopped. His hair
Rose up on end especially
When came the treble of his "*Chère*".

39

"Can it be you, Sergei Petrovich?"
"It can, my dearest." "Oh, my saviour.
Where were you bound?" A query which
Her somewhat soured cohabiter
Reduced to silence. "To that widow?
Of this I'm sure, I hate that floozie.
So tell me, am I right, Petrushka?"
Immediately the flunkey nodded.
"You reprobate, who loves to sin!
I asked my saint to discipline
You, but you make me still see red.
I've brought you some communion bread.
Ungrateful man! Out of my sight
You for a day I can't allow.
Come hither, Annushka, and sit
Yourself beside us both – and now!"

40

To this command her spouse submits,
And takes his seat. He cannot nurse
Within his inner heart regrets.
The world is dead, but there is worse,
He thinks, to come. His lawful wife
Had once upon a time been young,
But even then she did not think
That man and wife were made to live

Супруги созданы... нет! муж
Устроен для жены. К тому ж
Неравный бой недолго длился:
Сергей Петрович покорился.
Теперь везет его домой
Она для грозного расчета...
Так ястреб ловкий и лихой
Уносит селезня с болота.

41

Вот тут-то я б заметить мог,
Как всё на свете ненадежно!
Бог случая, лукавый бог,
Играет нами... Что возможно
Вчера — сегодня навсегда
Недостижимо... Да мы сами
Непостоянны... за мечтами
Гоняемся... Но, господа,
Хоть я воображаю живо,
Как вы следите терпеливо
И добросовестно за ним,
За бедным витязем моим, —
Однако кончить не пора ли?
Боюсь, приелись вам стихи...
За чистоту моей морали
Простите мне мои грехи.

42

Я прав. Мои слова — не фраза
Пустая, нет! С *своей* женой —
Заметьте — под конец рассказа
Соединяется герой.
Закон приличья, в том свидетель
Читатель каждый — сей закон
Священный строго соблюден,
И торжествует добродетель.
Но весело сказать себе
Конец мучительной гоньбе
За рифмами... придумать строчку
Последнюю, поставить точку,
Подняться медленно, легко
Вздохнуть, с чернилами проститься —
И перед вами глубоко,
О мой читатель, поклониться!

For one another. Oh dear, no!
The man was for his wife, and so
This feud unequal did not drag.
Sergei then hoisted the white flag.
And now he's being transported back
For settlement of their accounts.
Just so a swift and agile hawk
Will on a swimming mallard pounce.

41

Here I an observation could
Attempt on how all things are fallible.
The god of chance, that crafty god
Deceives us. Things once possible
Forever and a day are gone.
And we ourselves lack constancy
And like pursuing every fancy.
But listen to me, gentlemen,
Though I imagine vividly
How you all follow patiently,
And do so as your conscience leads,
My hapless knight and all his deeds.
But now it's time to end. I'm sure,
Before my verse drives you half-witted,
Because my morals are so pure,
Forgive the sins I have committed.

42

My words amount to more than zero.
My tale concludes, let it be noted,
By telling how our errant hero
And lawful wife are reunited.
Propriety, as will bear witness
My readers, who this claim accept,
Is sacred, has been strictly kept,
And virtue demonstrates its fitness.
But I am happy to attest
The end of this uneasy quest
For rhymes, to thankfully dream up
A final line and a full stop,
To stand up slowly with a sigh,
And to my inkwell bid adieu.
So now, my dearest readers, I
Will bid a fond farewell to you.

THE VILLAGE PRIEST

A NARRATIVE POEM

Смиренный сочинитель сказки сей
В иных местах поделал варианты
Для дам, известных строгостью своей,
Но любящих подобные куранты.

1

Бывало, я писал стихи — для славы,
И те стихи, в невинности моей,
В божий мир пускал не без приправы
«Глубоких и значительных» идей...
Теперь пишу для собственной забавы
Без прежних притязаний и затей —
И подражать намерен я свирепо
Всем... я на днях читал Pucelle и Верро.

2

Хоть стих иной не слишком выйдет верен,
Не стану я копаться над стихом;
К чему, скажите мне на милость? Скверен
Мой слог — зато как вольно под пером
Кипят слова... внимайте ж! я намерен —
Предупредив читательниц о том —
Предаться (грязная во мне природа!)
Похабностям различнейшего рода.

3

Читатели найдутся. Не бесплодной,
Не суетной работой занят я.
Меня прочтет Панаев благородный
И Веверов любезная семья;
Белинский посвятит мне час свободный,
И Комаров понюхает меня...
Языков сам столь важный столь приятный
Меня почтит улыбкой благодатной.

The humble author of this piece of fun
In several places has made variants
For ladies who for strictness are well known,
But love analogous experience.

I

I once wrote verse in hope of recognition;
Those self-same verses, in my innocence,
I sent into the world with some addition
Of concepts of profound significance.
To entertain myself is now my mission,
To jettison conceits and all pretence;
I now intend to copy vehemently –
I read *Pucelle* and *Beppo* recently.*

2

Although some things go haywire with my verse,
I will not let it make me feel alarmed.
Why should I? Tell me, please. My style gets worse,
But how the words beneath my pen have swarmed!
So listen when I say that I propose,
Ensuring lady readers are forewarned,
To give myself (I am by nature crude)
To themes as various as they are rude.

3

I will find readers, for not pointlessly
Nor fruitlessly do I exert my brain –
Panayev* will peruse my poetry,
And so will Vever's* much respected clan.
Belinsky* will devote free hours to me,
And Komarov* will sniff me if he can;
Yazykov,* so congenial and important,
Will honour me with smiles benevolent.

4

Итак, друзья, я жил тогда на даче,
В чухонской деревушке, с давних пор
Любимой немцами... Такой удаче
Смеетесь вы... Что делать! Мой позор
Я сам глубоко чувствовал, тем паче,
Что ничего внимательный мой взор
Не мог открыть в числе супруг и дочек,
Похожего на лакомый кусочек.

5

Вокруг меня — всё жил народ известный:
Столичных немцев цвет и сок. Во мне
При виде каждой рожи глупо-честной
Кипела желчь. Как русский — не вполне
Люблю я Честность... Немок пол прелестный
Я жаловал когда-то... но оне
На уксусе настоенные розы...
И холодны, как ранние морозы.

6

И я скучал, зевал и падал духом.
Соседом у меня в деревне той
Был — кто же? поп, покрытый жирным пухом,
С намасленной, коротенькой косой,
С засаленным и ненасытным брюхом.
Попов я презираю всей душой...
Но иногда — томим несносной скукой —
Травил его моей легавой сукой.

7

Но поп — не поп без попадьи трупёрдой,
Откормленной, дебелой... Признаюсь,
Я человек и грешный и нетвердый
И всякому соблазну поддаюсь.
Перед иной красавицею гордой
Склоняюсь я — но всё ж я не стыжусь
Вам объявить (известно, люди слабы...):
Люблю я мясо доброй русской бабы.

8

А моего соседушки супруга
Была ходячий пуховик — ей-ей...
У вашего чувствительного друга
Явилось тотчас множество затей;

4

A dacha was where I preferred to hide,
A Finnish village dacha, at that time
With Germans popular. You may deride
Success, but what am I to do? My shame
I deeply felt, and it was magnified
By failure to spot anything sublime
Among the serried ranks of wives and daughters,
Not anything you'd call a tasty morsel.*

5

Renowned were those who lived round and about,
The cream of Germans metropolitan.
The sight of every stupid, honest snout
Upset my spleen. We Russians are not keen
On honesty, though in my time I've sought
Out German girls, who turned out to have been
As vinegary as roses dipped in brine,
And colder than a frost in early June.

6

And I was bored, depressed and prone to yawn;
Who was it in the village lived quite near?
None other than a priest with greasy down,
A short pigtail with something oily smeared,
And gut insatiable and grubby brown.
With scorn for priests I heartily concur...
But on occasions, when with boredom faced,
My hunting hound and I would him have chased.

7

No priest's a priest without a female weighty,
Well fed, well rounded – and, I have to say,
I am a sinner who neglects his duty
And to temptation frequently gives way.
I'm partial both to haughtiness and beauty –
I won't, however, countenance delay
In telling you (it's known that we are weak)
A meaty Russian woman's what I seek.

8

The legal consort of my neighbour-priest
Was like a feather mattress automated!
But as for me, born sentimentalist,
I lots of hanky-panky formulated...

Сошелся я с попом — и спился с круга
Любезный поп по милости моей;
И вот — пока сожитель не проспится,
В блаженстве я тону, как говорится.

9

Так что ж?.. скажите мне, какое право
Имеем мы смеяться над таким
Блаженством? Люди неразумны, право.
В ребяческие годы мы хотим
Любви «святой, возвышенной» — направо,
Налево мы бросаемся... кутим...
Потом, угомонившись понемногу,
Кого-нибудь ебем — и слава Богу!

10

Но Пифагор, Сенека и Булгарин
И прочие философы толпой
Кричат, что человек неблагодарен,
Забывчив... вообще подлец большой...
Действительно: как сущий русский барин,
Я начал над злосчастной попадьей
Подтрунивать... и на мою победу
Сам намекал почтенному соседу.

11

Но мой сосед был человек беспечный.
Он сытый стол и доброе вино
Предпочитал «любови скоротечной»,
Храпел — как нам храпеть не суждено.
Уж я хотел, томим бесчеловечной
Веселостью, во всем сознаться... но
Внезапная случилась остановка:
Друзья... к попу приехала золовка.

12

Сестра моей любовницы дебелой —
В разгаре жизни пышной, молодой,
О Господи! — была подобна спелой,
Душистой дыне, на степи родной
Созревшей в жаркий день. Оторопелый,
Я на нее глядел — и всей душой,
Любуясь этим телом полным, сочным,
Я предавался замыслам порочным.

Together priest and I did not desist
From drink, and I my chance awaited;
And long before the hapless spouse came round,
I, as they say, in blissful pleasure drowned.

9

So then, what right have we, please tell me, do,
Such blissful pleasure ludicrous to deem?
Irrational are humans, it is true;
As youths, of sacred love we sometimes dream,
Of love that's elevated through and through,
But often choose the opposite extreme...
And then we start to weary bit by bit,
And screw someone, and thank the Lord for it.

10

Pythagoras, Seneca and Bulgarin,*
And hosts of other celebrated thinkers,
Proclaim that men are basically uncaring,
Are thoughtless and, in other words, are stinkers.
I started, as a proper Russian *barin*,
To treat the hapless wife with mocking banter...
And to my conquest I made reference,
Although I held the priest in reverence.

11

The priest, however, was not prone to stress;
Good wine and groaning table he preferred
To love intrigues that all too quickly pass.
He snored as not a soul had ever snored.
I wanted, tired by cruel happiness,
To be quite frank about what had occurred,
Then mercifully came about a stop:
The carriage of her sister trundled up.

12

The sister of my plump beloved one
Was in her salad days and full of pep –
Good Lord, she seemed just like a ripe melon,
Most fragrant fruit of this its native steppe.
Whenever days were hot, I gazed upon
Her avidly, and felt the rise of sap.
I found her body full, voluptuous,
And gave myself to plans nefarious.

13

Стан девственный, под черными бровями
Глаза большие, звонкий голосок,
За молодыми, влажными губами
Жемчужины — не зубки, свежих щек
Румянец, ямки на щеках, местами
Под белой, тонкой кожицей жирок —
Всё в ней дышало силой и здоровьем...
Здоровьем, правда, несколько коровьим.

14

Я некогда любил всё «неземное»,
Теперь — напротив — более всего
Меня пленяет смелое, живое,
Веселое... земное существо.
Таилось что-то сладострастно-злое
В улыбке милой Саши... Сверх того,
Короткий нос с открытыми ноздрями
Не даром обожаем блядунами.

15

Я начал волочиться так ужасно,
Как никогда — ни прежде, ни потом
Не волочился... даже слишком страстно.
Она дичилась долго — но с трудом
Всего достигнешь... и пошли прекрасно
Мои делишки... вот — я стал о том
Мечтать: когда и как?.. Вопрос понятный,
Естественный... и очень деликатный.

16

Уж мне случалось, пользуясь молчаньем,
К ее лицу придвинуться слегка
И чувствовать, как под моим лобзаньем
Краснея, разгоралася щека...
И губы сохли... трепетным дыханьем
Менялись мы так медленно... пока...
Но тут я, против воли, небольшую —
Увы! — поставить должен запятую.

17

Все женщины в любви чертовски чутки...
(Оно понятно: женщина — раба.)
И попадья злодейка наши шутки
Пронюхала, как ни была глупа.

13

A figure maidenly beneath black brows,
Her eyes were large, and resonant her voice;
Behind moist lips her teeth in pearly rows,
While rosy cheeks set off a dimpled face.
Her fine and white translucent skin allowed
The outline of the flesh beneath to trace;
Robustness, health were in her every breath,
But there was something bovine in that health.

14

I once all things "unearthly" venerated,
But now above all other things I love
Those feelings which with joy are animated,
Those things audacious, bold and of this earth.
In Sasha's smile was something calculated,
Both sensual and sweet, while over and above
All that, her nose was short, her nostrils flared
(A feature long by whoremongers adored).

15

I started to chase skirt in shocking fashion,
As never in my life before had done,
And did it with a little too much passion.
She kept away, but with hard work you'll gain
The thing you seek. The plans I'd put in action
Went excellently. And now I had begun
To wonder: when and where, which I would rate
As questions natural and delicate.

16

It happened, of her silence making use,
That moves in her direction I could make,
And feel how, in responding to my kiss,
Her lips went dry and blushes burned her cheeks...
Our trembling breaths in one we sought to fuse...
But here I really ought to make a break
(Although this is against my will, alas,
And at this point a final full stop place).

17

All women are as sensitive as hell
In love, although they are the slaves of men.
The priest's wife, who is villain of our tale,
Had not a great deal in the way of brains,

Она почла, не тратив ни минутки,
За нужное — уведомить попа...
Но как она надулась — правый Боже!
Ей поп сказал: «Ебёт её, так что же?..»

18

Но с той поры не знали мы покоя
От попадьи... Теперь, читатель мой,
Ввести я должен нового героя.
И впрямь: он был недюжинный «герой»,
«До тонкости» постигший тайны «строя»,
«Кадетина», «служака затяжной»
(Так лестно выражался сам Паскевич
О нем) — поручик Пантелей Чубкевич.

19

Его никто не вздумал бы Ловласом
Назвать... огромный грушевидный нос
Торчал среди лица, вином и квасом
Раздутого... он был и рыж и кос —
И говорил глухим и сиплым басом:
Ну, словом: настоящий малоросс!
Я б мог сказать, что был он глуп как мерин,
Но лошадь обижать я не намерен.

20

Его-то к нам коварная судьбина
Примчала... я, признаться вам, о нем
Не думал — или думал: «Вот скотина!»
Но как-то раз к соседу вечерком
Я завернул... о гнусная картина!
Поручик между Сашей и попом
Сидит... перед огромным самоваром —
И весь пылает непристойным жаром.

21

Перед святыней сана мы немеем...
А поп — сановник, я согласен; но...
Сановник этот сильно — под шефеем...
(Как слово чисто русское, должно
«Шефе» склоняться)... попадья с злодеем
Поручиком, я вижу, заодно...
И нежится — и даже строит глазки,
И расточает «родственные» ласки.

But did, however, have a sense of smell,
And to her husband thought she'd spill the beans.
How very proud of this she was, good God!
The priest replied: "He's screwing her – so what?"

18

But from that moment on we got no peace
From Mrs Priest. And now, my reader gentle,
The time has come for me to introduce
A type of hero new, exceptional,
An expert in the drill square's mysteries,
A "veteran cadet", who "lacked potential".
How flattering were the terms used by Paskevich*
About Lieutenant Pantelei Chubkevich.

19

No one would think to call him a Lovelace…*
A huge proboscis rather like a pear
Adorned a face made red by wine and kvass.
He had a cross-eyed look and reddish hair,
And had a voice you'd call a muffled bass.
In short, he was Ukrainian *tout pur*,*
And stupid as a gelding, one might say –
But that's unfair to horses anyway.

20

His visit was decreed by Fate malign…
I rarely thought of him, I must agree,
Or if I did, I thought: "The man's a swine!"
But, seeking once my neighbour's company,
I called, and oh, how loathsome was the scene!
Chubkevich, priest and Sasha taking tea.
He by a massive samovar was seated,
And most improperly was overheated.

21

Faced with high office we are often mute
(And priests are high officials, I agree);
This one was firmly underneath the foot
("*Chevet*" is thought the Russian word to be).
Against me were two people in cahoots,
The pair of them together I could see…
She loved it, and was even making eyes,
And more than sisterly was her embrace.

22

И под шумок их речи голосистой
На цыпочках подкрался сзади я...
А Саша разливает чай душистый,
Молчит — и вдруг увидела меня...
И радостью блаженной, страстной, чистой
Ее глаза сверкнули... О друзья!
Тот милый взгляд проник мне прямо в душу...
И я сказал: «Сорву ж я эту грушу!»

23

Не сватался поручик безобразный
Пока за Сашей... да... но стороной
Он толковал о том, что к «жизни праздной
Он чувствует влеченье... что с женой
Он был бы счастлив!..» Что ж? он не приказный
Какой-нибудь!.. Притом поручик мой,
У «батюшки» спросив благословенья,
Вполне достиг его благоволенья.

24

«Но погоди ж, — я думал, — друг любезный!
О попадья плутовка! погоди!
Мы с Сашей вам дадим урок полезный —
Жениться вздумал!!.. Время впереди,
Но всё же мешкать нечего над бездной.»
Я к Саше подошел... В моей груди
Кипела кровь... поближе я придвинул
Мой стул и сел... Поручик рот разинул.

25

Но я, не прерывая разговора,
Глядел на Сашу, как голодный волк...
И вдруг поднялся... «Что это? так скоро!
Куда спешите?» — Мягкую, как шелк,
Я ручку сжал. «Вы не боитесь вора?..
Сегодня ночью... — «Что-с?» — но я умолк —
Ее лицо внезапно покраснело...
И я пошел и думал: ладно дело!

26

А вот и ночь... торжественным молчаньем
Исполнен чуткий воздух... мрак и свет
Слилися в небе... Долгим трепетаньем
Трепещут листья... Суета сует!

22

The noise of chattering enabled me
On tiptoe to sneak up on them behind,
While Sasha poured out cups of fragrant tea,
Said nothing – but was suddenly not blind...
With passionate and blissful ecstasy
Her eyes began to flash... Oh how, my friends,
Her glances to my heart directly went!
And I declared: "This is the fruit I want."

23

Chubkevich was not affianced to Sasha...
So much was very true. Yet on the side
He spoke of how he liked a life of leisure,
And how he would be happy with a bride.
So what was this? He was no mere pen-pusher!
What's more, the bold lieutenant would decide
To ask the father to pronounce him blessed.
The priest in full complied with his request.

24

"Dear friend, I beg you, not so fast," I thought.
"You crafty priest's wife, please hang on a minute,
Myself and Sasha want you to be taught
A lesson. Marriage? Time is infinite,
But trembling on the edge avails us naught."
Sasha I approached. My breast and all within it
Were seething. Then I nearer to her moved
My chair, and left Chubkevich open-mouthed.

25

But I, not interrupting any chat,
At Sasha like a hungry wolf now gazed.
I suddenly stood up. "You're going? Why's that?"
Her little hand as soft as silk I squeezed.
"Will you be scared of thieves tonight, or not?"
"Explain yourself." But I by now had ceased.
A modest blush across her features spread...
I left and told myself: "I've got this made!"

26

And so night falls and silence fills the ether.
Majestic silence. Mingled in the sky
Are light and darkness, while the leaves all quiver,
Their tremors long. Oh, height of vanity!

К чему мне хлопотать над описаньем?
Какой же я неопытный «поэт»!
Скажу без вычур — ночь была такая,
Какой хотел я: тёмная, глухая

27

Пробила полночь... Время... Торопливо
Прошел я в сад к соседу... под окном
Я стукнул... растворилось боязливо
Окошко... Саша в платьице ночном,
Вся бледная, склонилась молчаливо
Ко мне...— «Я вас пришел просить»...— «О чем?
Так поздно... ах! Зачем вы здесь? скажите?
Как сердце бьется — Боже... нет! Уйдите»...

28

«Зачем я здесь? О Саша! как безумный
Я вас люблю»... — «Ах, нет — я не должна
Вас слушать»... — «Дайте ж руку»... Ветер шумный
Промчался по березам. — Как она
Затрепетала вдруг!!.. Благоразумный
Я человек — но плоть во мне сильна,
А потому внезапно, словно кошка,
Я по стене... вскарабкался в окошко.

29

«Я закричу», — твердила Саша... (Страстно
Люблю я женский крик — и майонез.)
Бедняжка перетрусилась ужасно —
А я, злодей! развратник!.. лез да лез.
«Я разбужу сестру — весь дом»... — «Напрасно»...
(Она кричала — шёпотом.) — «Вы бес!»
«Мой ангел, Саша, как тебе не стыдно
Меня бояться?... право, мне обидно».

30

Она твердила: «Боже мой... о Боже!»
Вздыхала — не противилась, но всем
Дрожала телом. Добродетель всё же
Не вздор — по крайней мере не совсем.
Так думал я. Но «девственное ложе»,
Гляжу, во тьме белеет... О зачем
Соблазны так невыразимо сладки!!!
Я Сашу посадил на край кроватки.

Why do I strive this picture to deliver?
How inexperienced a bard am I!
I tell you straight, for me the night was right,
A motionless, impenetrable night.

27

The midnight saw me enter hastily
My neighbour's garden, signal I was there.
A window was thrown open cautiously,
And there was Sasha in her night attire.
Her face was pale. She bent down silently.
"I've come to ask…" "What is it you desire
So late at night? Why are you here, please say.
My heart is pounding. No! Please go away."

28

"What brings me here? Because I've lost my mind
With love, O Sasha." "No, it cannot be
That I should hear…" "Give me your hand." The wind
Was whistling through the trees, then suddenly
She started trembling. I'm a rational kind,
But urges of the flesh are strong in me.
And cat-like, and without much more ado,
I climbed the wall, and to her window flew.

29

"I'll scream," repeated Sasha (how I love
Like mayonnaise to hear a woman scream!)
The wretched girl completely lost her nerve,
But, villain that I am, I climb and climb.
"I'll wake my sister." "That will nothing serve."
She quietly screamed: "You fiend! This is a dream!"
"My angel Sasha, are you not ashamed
To be afraid of me? I feel defamed…"

30

She then repeated: "Oh, Good Lord! Good Lord!"
And sighed, did not resist, but gave a shiver.
They say that virtue is its own reward…
Indeed, it sometimes is, but hardly ever.
That's what I thought, but then I peered
And saw the maiden's bed, all white. Oh, never
Can I resist temptation's honeyed taste!
And so I Sasha on the bed's edge placed.

31

К ее ногам прилег я, как котенок...
Она меня бранит, а я молчок —
И робко, как наказанный ребенок,
То ручку, то холодный локоток
Целую, то колено... Ситец тонок —
А поцелуй горяч... И голосок
Ее погас, и ручки стали влажны,
Приподнялось и горло — признак важный!

32

И близок миг... над жадными губами
Едва висит на ветке пышный плод...
Подымется ли шорох за дверями,
Она сама рукой зажмет мне рот...
И слушает... И крупными слезами
Сверкает взор испуганный... И вот
Она ко мне припала, замирая.
На грудь... и, головы не подымая,

33

Мне шепчет: «Друг, ты женишься?» Рекою
Ужаснейшие клятвы полились.
«Обманешь... бросишь»... — «Солнцем и луною
Клянусь тебе, о Саша!»... Расплелись
Ее густые волосы... змеею
Согнулся тонкой стан... — «Ах, да... женись»...
И запрокинулась назад головка...
И... мой рассказ мне продолжать неловко.

34

Читатель милый! Смелый сочинитель
Вас переносит в небо. В этот час
Плачевный ангел, Сашин попечитель,
Сидел один и думал: «Вот-те раз!»
И вдруг к нему подходит Искуситель:
«Что, батюшка? Надули, видно, вас?»
Тот отвечал, сконфузившись: «Нисколько!
Ну смейся! зубоскал!.. подлец — и только».

35

Сойдем на землю. На земле всё было
Готово... то есть — кончено... вполне.
Бедняжка то вздыхала — так уныло...
То страстно прижималася ко мне,

31

I lay before her like a little kitten;
She criticized me, but I held my peace,
And meekly, like a child who had been beaten,
I kissed a hand, an elbow, cold as ice,
A knee, a covering of flimsy cotton.
My kisses burned, she quieted her voice;
Her hands were moist, and prominent her throat.
This always is significant – take note!

32

Above my hungry lips – the moment nears –
The fruit clings to the branch, alluring, lush;
A rustling can be heard behind the doors;
My mouth she closes with her hand, says: "Hush!"
And listens, and meanwhile enormous tears
Well up, and make her frightened glances flash,
And going limp, she fell upon my breast,
And thus, her head not raising, came to rest.

33

She whispers: "I'm your wife." Without a break,
A torrent of the filthiest abuse
Began. "You'll cheat, abandon…" I will take
A solemn oath, my Sasha." Now, hair loose,
She curled her supple waist up like a snake.
"Oh, take me as your wife, do not refuse…"
As she said this, her little head fell backward,
And… going on with this is rather awkward.

34

My dearest reader, now you will be taken
From earth to heaven. It was at this hour
With bitter tears an angel, Sasha's patron,
Sat all alone and thought: "Well, there you are!"
Then suddenly he was approached by Satan:
"You've obviously been cheated, my good sir."
The flustered angel said: "Not in the least.
And you can laugh – you're nothing but a beast."

35

So back to earth, where all had been prepared,
That is to say, was over finally.
The wretched woman sighed, and now despaired,
Now pressed herself with feeling up to me,

То тихо плакала... В ней сердце ныло.
Я плакал сам — и в грустной тишине,
Склоняясь над обманутым ребенком,
Я прикасался к трепетным ручонкам.

36

«Прости меня,» — шептал я со слезами, —
«Прости меня...» — «Господь тебе судья...» —
«Так я прощен?!» (Поручика с рогами
Поздравил я.) — Ликуй, душа моя!
Ликуй — но вдруг... о ужас!! перед нами
В дверях — с свечой — явилась попадья!!
Со времени татарского нашествья
Такого не случалось происшествья!

37

При виде раздраженной Гермионы
Сестрица с визгом спрятала лицо
В постель.. Я растерялся... Панталоны
Найти не мог... отчаянно в кольцо
Свернулся — жду... И крики, вопли, стоны,
Как град — и град в куриное яйцо, —
Посыпались... В жару негодованья
Все женщины — приятные созданья.

38

«Антон Ильич! Сюда!.. Содом-Гоморра!
Вот до чего дошла ты, наконец,
Развратница! Наделать мне позора
Приехала... А вы, сударь, — подлец!
И что ты за красавица — умора!..
И тот, кому ты нравишься, — глупец,
Картежник, вор, грабитель и мошенник!»
Тут в комнату ввалился сам священник,

39

«А! ты! Ну полюбуйся — посмотри-ка,
Козел ленивый — что? что, старый гусь?
Не верил мне? Не верил? ась?.. Поди-ка
Теперь — ее сосватай... Я стыжусь
Сказать, как я застала их... улика,
Чай, на лицо» (... in naturalibus —
Подумал я), — «измята вся постелька!»
Служитель алтарей был пьян как стелька.

Now quietly wept. No joy in her heart stirred.
I wept myself, and sadly, silently,
I stooped, and still before the child dissembled,
And lightly touched her hands, so that they trembled.

36

"I beg forgiveness," through my tears I breathed.
"Forgiveness can come only from the Lord."
"So I'm forgiven?" The cuckold soon received
My plaudits. Now you can rejoice, dear heart.
"Rejoice!" But then the Father's wife arrived
And blocked the door. A candle she had brought.
But never since the Tatar horde's invasion
Had anything resembled this occasion.

37

On seeing a very angry Hermione,*
My Sasha made an effort to conceal
Her face. My trousers had embarrassingly gone;
I desperately curled into a ball;
I waited, hearing cries, a shriek, a groan,
Which fell like egg-sized hailstones in a squall.
When she is fired by righteous indignation,
A woman is a wonderful creation.

38

"Anton Ilich! Oh, Sodom and Gomorrah!
So you have come to this, immoral cow!
She's come here to present me with this horror.
And you, my man, are lower than the low.
You call yourself a beauty – you're in error,
And as for lover-boy, he's rather slow,
A card sharp, who has many people fleeced."
That moment saw the entry of the priest.

39

"All right! So feast your eyes on this, will you?
You indolent old goat, you ancient goose!
You thought I'd got it wrong, did you? Go through
With giving her away. I shall refuse
To say what was the scene, but here's a clue:
Some tea – and us *in naturalibus*.*
The crumpled bed compounding our disgrace."
The Father was completely off his face.

40

Он улыбнулся слабо... взор лукавый
Провел кругом... слегка махнул рукой
И пал к ногам супруги величавой,
Как юный дуб, низринутый грозой...
Как смелый витязь падает со славой
За край — хотя подлейший, но родной, —
Так пал он, поп достойный, но с избытком
Предавшийся крепительным напиткам.

41

Смутилась попадья... И в самом деле
Пренеприятный случай! Я меж тем
Спокойно восседаю на постеле.
«Извольте ж убираться вон...» — «Зачем?»
— «Уйдете вы?»...— «На будущей неделе.
Мне хорошо; вот видите ль: я ем
Всегда — пока я сыт; и ем я много»...
Но Саша мне шепнула: «ради Бога!..»

42

Я тотчас встал. «А страшно мне с сестрицей
Оставить вас»...— «Не бойтесь... я сильней»...
«Эге! такой решительной девицей
Я вас не знал... но вы в любви моей
Не сомневайтесь, ангелочек». Птицей
Я полетел домой... и у дверей
Я попадью таким окинул взглядом,
Что, верно, жизнь ей показалась адом.

43

Как человек, который «взнес повинность»,
Я спал, как спит наевшийся порок
И как не спит голодная невинность.
Довольно... может быть, я вас увлек
На миг — и вам понравилась «картинность»
Рассказа — но пора... с усталых ног
Сбиваю пыль: дошел я до развязки
Моей весьма не многосложной сказки.

44

Что ж сделалось с попом и с попадьею?
Да ничего. А Саша, господа,
Вступила в брак с чиновником. Зимою
Я был у них... обедал — точно, да.

40

He smiled, but faintly, and then cast around
A cunning glance, and gestured with his arm
Before his spouse fell prostrate on the ground,
As would an oak tree toppled by the storm,
As would a gallant knight with glory downed,
Defending lands unpleasant he called "home".
So fell the priest, who'd had more than enough
Of strengthening, intoxicating stuff.

41

The priest's good wife was flustered, and indeed
This all was most unpleasant. Meanwhile I,
Without undue concern, sat up in bed.
"I must insist you leave at once." "But why?"
"When will you leave?" "This coming week," I said.
"I'm happy here. You see, I always try
To eat my fill, and then some more partake."
But Sasha whispered: "Oh, for Heaven's sake!"

42

I rose at once and said I was afraid
To leave her with her sister. "Have no fear,
I'm stronger." "And a more decisive bride
I've never known. But do not doubt, my dear,
"My love…" And swift as any bird I made
My homeward way, just pausing by the door
To cast such looks upon the priest's good wife –
She no doubt thought how hellish is this life.

43

Like someone who to charges "guilty" pleads,
I slept, as does a vice that overeats,
Or hungry innocence which no sleep needs.
Enough! Perhaps your pleasure is complete,
Albeit briefly. Maybe you were pleased
My tale was picturesque. From weary feet
I brush the dust, and now to end I'm able
My most uncomplicated modern fable.

44

What happened to the wife and to the priest?
Not much. My Sasha, gentlemen, became
The wife of an official. This winter past
I dined with them, and honestly can claim

Она слывет прекраснейшей женою
И недурна... толстеет — вот беда!
Живут они на Воскресенской, в пятом
Этаже, в нумере пятьсот двадцатом.

She for a splendid wife has long since passed.
Though looking good, she's stout, which is a shame!
They live on Voskresenskaya,* fifth floor –
The number of their flat is five two four.

Note on the Text

All five poems can be found in Volume 1 (1978) of the 30-volume edition of Turgenev's *Complete Works*. This edition can also be found online at https://rvb.ru/turgenev/tocvol_01.htm. The notes by M.P. Alekseyev form the basis of many of the notes in this translation.

Notes

p. 3, *Epigraph to Parasha*: A line from 'Meditation' ('Duma'), an 1839 poem by Mikhail Lermontov (1814–41).

p. 5, *Tatyana*: The heroine of Pushkin's novel in verse *Eugene Onegin* (1832), which was a major influence on Turgenev's poem.

p. 11, *Marlinsky's works*: Marlinksy was the pen name of Alexander Bestuzhev (1797–1837), a second-rate author, enormously popular in his day, but vastly inferior to Pushkin.

p. 13, *Parasha*: Affectionate form of the name Praskovya. Parashas play a part in two major narrative poems by Pushkin: *The Little House in Kolomna* (1833) and *The Bronze Horseman* (1837).

p. 19, *Comm'ça*: "Like that" (French).

p. 35, *poshlost*: A word made popular by Pushkin and Gogol, and often said to be untranslatable. It implies flashy vulgarity. "Naffness" might be a modern, if colloquial, equivalent.

p. 55, *The deeds... past*: From Pushkin's 1820 narrative poem *Ruslan and Lyudmila* (1, l. 1).

p. 57, *Un-Corsair-like*: A reference to Byron's poem *The Corsair* (1814).

p. 61, *"Dvoryanskaya"*: The name of the street, ironically, is "Noble Street".

p. 63, *Avdotya*: An affectionate form of the name Yevdokiya, as are Dunya and Dunyasha.

p. 69, *A well-known piece... Beethoven*: A reference to the funeral march which forms the second movement of Beethoven's Third Symphony ("The Eroica", 1803).

p. 69, *O nightingale of mine*: A romance composed in 1825 by Alexander Alyabyev (1787–1851) to words by Anton Delvig (1798–1831).

p. 83, *please see your Shakespeare*: An oblique reference to *Hamlet*, Act II, Sc. 2, ll. 116–19: "Doubt thou the stars are fire, / Doubt that the sun doth move, / Doubt truth to be a liar, / But never doubt I love."

p. 85, *Manilov... Faublas*: Respectively the ultra-sentimental landowner in Chapter 3 of Nikolai Gogol's (1809–52) *Dead Souls* (1842) and the hero of the novel usually referred to as *The Amours of the Chevalier Faublas* (1787–90) by Jean-Baptiste Louvet de Couvrai (1760–97). The title is self-explanatory. The name is used by several nineteenth-century Russian authors, most pertinently by Pushkin in the first chapter of *Eugene Onegin*, as a byword for aristocratic debauchery. A Russian translation by Alexander Levanda (1765–1812) appeared 1792–96, but Turgenev, like most upper-class Russians, almost certainly read the work in the original French.

p. 85, *how Fate pursued the luckless Turk*: In the middle of the nineteenth century, Turkey was experiencing a deep internal crisis caused by the beginning of the collapse of the feudal Ottoman Empire.

p. 95, *Bossuet*: The French theologian and orator Jacques-Bénigne Bossuet (1627–1704). A copy of his *Discours sur l'histoire universelle* (*Discourse on Universal History*, 1681) was in Turgenev's library. This six-word summary of his views (four words in the original Russian) is, to say the least, inadequate.

p. 109, *Izmailovsky... Kirasir*: An elite-guards regiment founded in 1730. Kirasir is the Russian version of "cuirassier", a member of a particular type of cavalry regiment.

p. 143, *Or any latent passions stir*: A gap in the original has been filled by the translator.

p. 175, *Adam Adamych*: Adam Adamovich (or Adamych) Vralman is a German tutor in Denis Fonvizin's (1745–92) celebrated comedy *The Minor* (1782).

p. 179, *"Nuit"... "Vanité"*: "Night"... "Charity"... "Day"... "Vanity" (French).

p. 181, *stepniaks*: Provincial noblemen.

p. 183, *Whom every nobleman upbraids*: Two lines are missing from the original and, in the absence of a manuscript, can only be guessed at, as the translator has done here.

p. 183, *'Troika'*: Probably a reference to an 1825 poem by Fyodor Glinka (1786–1880), set to music by Alexei Verstovsky (1799–1862) in 1828.

p. 187, *Corinne*: The intellectual heroine of Madame de Staël's (1766–1817) novel *Corinne, ou l'Italie* (1807).

p. 191, *barin*: A landowner or gentleman, a man deserving of respect.

p. 193, *uezd*: Russian for "district".

p. 193, *hats much liked by Slavophiles*: This, and the reference in the same stanza to "prominent of throat" were clear allusions to the Slavophile Konstantin Aksakov (1817–60). The whole of stanza 28 was omitted, at Turgenev's insistence, from an 1857 publication of the poem. In the sixth chapter of his *Memoirs of a Hunter*, 'The Smallholder Ovsyannikov', Turgenev again makes fun of clothing affected by the Slavophiles.

p. 193, *amour insouciant*: "Frivolous love" (French).

p. 197, *A half a kingdom, or a whole*: An allusion to the famous words pronounced by Richard III in Act 5 Sc. 4 (l. 7) of Shakespeare's play ("A horse!

A horse! My kingdom for a horse!"), which had been translated into Russian by Yakov Bryansky (1790–1853) in 1833.

p. 201, *chère amie*: "Dear friend" (French).

p. 207, *Pucelle... Beppo*: A reference to *La Pucelle d'Orléans* (*The Maid of Orléans*), a satirical poem by Voltaire (1694–1778), banned in his lifetime and not published until 1899, and to *Beppo* (1817), a long poem by Lord Byron, written, like *The Village Priest*, in *ottava rima*.

p. 207, *Panayev*: Ivan Panayev (1812–62) was a Russian writer, literary critic, journalist and magazine publisher.

p. 207, *Vever's*: M.N. Vever and other members of her family were acquaintances of the Turgenev family in Oryol.

p. 207, *Belinsky*: The influential literary critic Vissarion Belinsky (1811–48). His review of *Parasha* brought Turgenev to public notice. Turgenev dedicated *Fathers and Children* to his memory.

p. 207, *Komarov*: The engineer Alexander Komarov (1814–62), a member of the Belinsky circle.

p. 207, *Yazykov*: Mikhail Yazykov (1811–85), a Petersburg friend of Belinsky.

p. 209, *A dacha... tasty morsel*: The original Stanza 4, in which Turgenev made mild fun of village priests, was deleted by him.

p. 211, *Bulgarin*: The notorious novelist, journalist and police spy Faddei Bulgarin (1789–1859).

p. 215, *Paskevich*: Field Marshal Ivan Paskevich (1782–1856).

p. 215, *Lovelace*: The villainous libertine in Samuel Richardson's (1689–1761) novel *Clarissa* (1748). Turgenev would have known the famous 1786 French translation by Pierre Le Tourneur (1737–88), which was the basis of an unfinished Russian translation in 1791–92.

p. 215, *tout pur*: "All pure" (French).

p. 223, *Hermione*: The daughter of Menelaus and Helen of Troy, rival of Andromache, widow of Hector. The immediate source of this reference would be Jean Racine's (1639–99) tragedy *Andromaque* (1667).

p. 223, *in naturalibus*: "In Nature's attire" (Latin) – that is, naked.

p. 227, *Voskresenskaya*: A square in the centre of Moscow, now Revolution Square.

Extra Material

on

Ivan Turgenev's

Parasha
and
Other Poems

Ivan Turgenev's Life

Ivan Sergeyevich Turgenev was born in the Russian city of Oryol on 9th November 1818 (all dates in this section follow the Gregorian calendar). His mother, the wealthy Varvara Petrovna Lutovinova, according to many reports was an extremely capricious and cruel woman. Her baronial estate of Spasskoye contained twenty villages, and she had control of five thousand serfs; she is reported to have had some of her serfs deported to Siberia because they did not take their hats off in her presence, and to have regularly inflicted corporal punishments on them. She came into her inheritance at the age of twenty-six, and three years later married a twenty-three-year-old army officer, Sergei Turgenev, from an ancient family of aristocrats who had fallen on hard times: he possessed only one village and had just a hundred and thirty serfs. He married her presumably for her money: he seems to have taken very little interest in her afterwards, spending his time in numerous affairs with women, mainly serf girls at Spasskoye and his own estate, Turgenevo.

Ivan Turgenev had an older brother, Nikolai, who was born in 1816, and a younger brother, Sergei, who was born in 1821; very little is known about this last child, but it appears he was partially paralysed, epileptic and mentally retarded; he died in his teens.

Varvara Petrovna's already unpleasant personality became, *Childhood* it seems, progressively worse as a result of her husband's philandering, and Ivan recounted later that he and Nikolai had been whipped and beaten almost daily during their childhoods, frequently as a result of a whim on their mother's part.

As in most Russian upper-class families of the time, French was spoken as the language of preference; indeed, Russian was considered among this class to be a barbaric language.

Therefore Turgenev was from an early age fluent in French, and also acquired a good knowledge of German from private tutors. Fortunately for his career as a writer in Russian, his parents almost totally ignored their sons, leaving Ivan ample time to roam around the locality getting to know the peasants and play with their children. It was from them that Turgenev learnt spoken Russian: he later claimed that he was taught to read and write Russian by his father's valet.

Move to Moscow By 1827 the whole family had moved to Moscow, where the boys were enrolled at a private academy. However, after a couple of years, Nikolai was transferred to the Military Officer Training School in Petersburg, and Ivan was brought back home to have his education completed by tutors who would prepare him for the university entrance exams. By the age of eleven, Turgenev was being given lessons in French, German, Maths and Philosophy, and already trying his hand at writing poetry and dramas in the "sublime" style of pre-Pushkin Russian authors.

University and Ill Turgenev entered Moscow University in 1833, but lasted
Health there only one term. Just before entering university, he had been bedridden for some months by an unknown illness, probably of a hypochondriac nature, and having missed too much time from his initial term he was transferred in autumn 1835 to the Philological Faculty of Petersburg University. On 11th September of that year, when Turgenev was only sixteen, his father died.

Although intending to become a university academic, probably in Philosophy, he was already writing Romantic poetic dramas in the manner of Byron. When he sent one of them to a leading literary magazine, it was rejected, but with some encouraging words from the editor, and in 1838 he did have two poems published in this periodical. As part of his studies, he had now begun to learn English, and he attempted to translate extracts from *King Lear*, *Othello* and Byron's *Manfred*. Besides English, Turgenev was devoting a great deal of his time to studying Latin and Ancient Greek. He also took private lessons in painting and drawing, and became an accomplished artist and caricaturist.

Stay in Berlin Turgenev graduated from the Faculty of History and Philology in June 1837. His mother thought that the true fount of all learning was outside Russia, so in May 1838 she sent him to do extra study in the subject at the University of

Berlin. On the crossing from Stettin to Berlin the ferry caught fire, and Turgenev offered some of the sailors large bribes to let him embark on a lifeboat before anybody else, including women and children – an incident that was to haunt and embarrass him for the rest of his life.

In Berlin he devoted himself intensively to the study of Philosophy, History, Latin and Greek. He fell under the spell of Hegel's philosophy, and soon became involved in the seething discussion groups regularly held by the students. There were a large number of young Russians studying in Germany: the vast majority of these were social progressives who wanted a total transformation of the social and political situation at home – often by violent revolutionary means, including assassination. Among the people he met in Berlin was Mikhail Bakunin, one of the founders of the Russian anarchist movement. Although Turgenev held intense philosophical discussions with him, and was at first attracted by Bakunin's charismatic personality, he managed to keep his distance intellectually and maintain a moderate stance in regard to the methods of achieving social change. Some contemporary critics claimed that the figure of Rudin, the eponymous hero of Turgenev's first novel, was a portrait – in fact, a caricature – of Mikhail Bakunin.

In the spring of 1841 Turgenev returned to Russia. In the *Return to Russia* meantime, his mother's mansion at Spasskoye had been burnt down by a fire, apparently caused by a peasant woman performing a propitiatory ritual with hot coals. Only one wing was left, and Turgenev had to be content with one room there until the end of the summer. In the winter of that year, his elder brother Nikolai married one of his mother's parlour maids. Varvara Petrovna immediately stopped his allowance, and Nikolai was forced to resign his officer's commission in the army and get a lowly job in the civil service. She severed all contact with him for many years. Ivan enrolled again at Petersburg University and began to study for a Master's in Philosophy which would have enabled him to gain a university post. He moved into his brother's flat and, after a period of intense studies, passed the exams successfully in June 1842. He then travelled to Moscow to apply for the vacant Chair of Philosophy at Moscow University.

However, he never submitted this application, as Turgenev's *Love Life* personal life underwent a dramatic change. In May 1842 he had had a brief affair with a sempstress employed by his mother. She became pregnant by him, and his mother threw them out of the house. He found a room for her in Moscow, and settled an allowance on her. She soon bore him a daughter who was given the humble peasant name of Pelageya. At the same time, Turgenev met in Moscow Bakunin's sister Tatyana, who was even more imbued with Hegelian ideals than her brother. She claimed that, though she loved Turgenev, she simply wanted to be his "sister" and his "friend". This Platonic relation lasted for two years, by which time it seems Turgenev had become thoroughly disillusioned with Tatyana, Bakunin, Hegelianism and philosophy in general.

Parasha and the Birth of a Literary Career

Turgenev gave up any ambition of becoming an academic, and took a civil-service job at the Home Office. But he also began now to devote more time to writing, and one of his first mature works was a long narrative poem entitled *Parasha*. The poem, written in clear and simple language, in imitation of Pushkin, tells the tale of a love affair among ordinary peasant folk. The Romantic subjects and flowery style of his younger years had been left behind – as it turned out, for ever. *Parasha* was published in 1843 at the author's own expense, and the renowned critic Belinsky described it as one of the most remarkable productions of the year. Following this, Turgenev and Belinsky became close friends, and the critic introduced the author into the literary circles of Petersburg and Moscow.

Reprimanded by his office superiors for being often late for work or not turning up at all, Turgenev decided to resign his job and devote himself entirely to literature. His mother, in disgust, cut off his allowance and all contact with him for several years. During this period, Turgenev had to live on practically nothing, in unheated rooms, even during the Russian winter.

Pauline Viardot

In 1843 occurred an event that was to prove the decisive turning point of Turgenev's life, and that caused him to spend much of the rest of his life outside Russia. The world-renowned Spanish opera singer Pauline Viardot, née García, visited Petersburg to sing at its opera houses. She was married to Louis Viardot, a man twenty years older than herself. Turgenev met her for the first time in November 1843, and became immediately infatuated with her. This passion was to remain with him for the rest of his life, making it difficult for him to form a stable relationship with any other woman. During Pauline's first visit to Russia, Turgenev had only a brief contact with her, as she was constantly monopolized by her many other long-standing admirers. Turgenev was able to see Pauline again when she came back to sing in Petersburg the following year, but he was once more almost ignored by her, though he inveigled himself into a long and animated conversation with her husband.

In February 1845 Turgenev went abroad, allegedly to consult *Travels Abroad* an eminent oculist, but in fact to follow the Viardots to Paris, having received an invitation from Pauline to spend a short time at her country chateau of Courtavenel. He was by now writing affectionate letters to her; her letters to him were far more intermittent and reserved.

Turgenev spent much of the next few years abroad. While in France in 1845, he began to write, from his own experiences, stories of Russian peasant life, portraying the cruelty suffered by serfs from their landowners. These sketches, for the most part originally printed in Russian literary journals, were finally collected and published in volume form in August 1852 as *Memoirs of a Hunter*.

Turgenev once again saw Pauline singing in Petersburg in 1846, and then left Russia with the Viardots in early 1847. From then on, for the rest of his life, he would spend long periods of time with Pauline and her husband in France, Germany and Britain, always remaining on friendly terms with her husband. There is little evidence as to whether Pauline and Ivan ever consummated their relationship. Paul, the child born to Pauline in 1857, may well have been Turgenev's son, although she frequently had other lovers.

Turgenev was in Paris for the latter part of the 1848 revolution. The first upheaval had seen the monarchy being overthrown and replaced by a bourgeois government. Afterwards there had been further turmoil on the streets when the workers, in their turn, tried to obtain concessions from the new administration. Turgenev, while declaring at first his full sympathy with those who brought down the monarchy and then with those who tried to establish a more democratic government, was sickened by the needless violence of the intellectual revolutionaries who incited the working classes to man the barricades, leading to many of them being slaughtered by government troops.

In the summer of 1850, Turgenev finally left Paris and went *Return to Russia* back to Russia. In the preceding years he had written most of the sketches for *Memoirs of a Hunter* as well as several plays, which are generally considered to be among his weaker works, with the exception of *A Month in the Country*. The play, heavily cut by the censor, was published in a drastically altered version in January 1855 and premiered in its fuller, uncensored version in Moscow only in 1872.

While Turgenev was in France, his mother had repeatedly appealed to him to return home, and when he refused, she had devised a vicious way of punishing him, forcing his daughter Pelageya, now seven years old, to work in the kitchen with the other servants. When he returned home and discovered the situation, Turgenev immediately withdrew Pelageya from Spasskoye, and wrote to Pauline Viardot asking whether the singer could accept his daughter into her family. Pauline accepted, and Pelageya was dispatched to France, promptly renamed Paulinette, provided with tutors and brought up as a French lady.

Mother's Death and Inheritance   Varvara Petrovna became suddenly ill and died on 10th December 1850. The estates and wealth were divided between Ivan and his elder brother Nikolai, leaving the writer with the whole of Spasskoye. Proving the sincerity of his democratic ideals, he emancipated all his serfs and gave them reasonable financial severance payments – a move that was considered revolutionary at the time. If they wished to remain on his land they could pay him a moderate rent and farm it for their own profit, rather than having to turn over most of their produce to him.

Imprisonment and Exile   In March 1852 the famous writer Gogol had died, and Turgenev published a brief obituary in the press. Although by the end of his life Gogol had become profoundly reactionary and Turgenev's article contained nothing of a political nature, but simply spoke glowingly of his works, the Tsarist government reacted angrily and sentenced Turgenev to a month in prison. At the end of that term, he was sent back to Spasskoye for a two-year period of house arrest. Turgenev spent this time writing, reading and hunting on his estate. In April 1853, he wrote to the Crown Prince Alexander acknowledging his guilt and asking for permission to leave the estate in order to consult doctors. The permission was finally granted by the Tsar in November that year, meaning that Turgenev had only served sixteen months of his sentence. However, he was kept under police surveillance until 1856.

In August 1852 *Memoirs of a Hunter* had appeared in volume form, and it was an instant success. One alarmed aristocrat described it as "an incendiary work", and the Tsar, Nicholas I, dismissed the censor who had authorized its publication.

First Novel   Turgenev now began to experiment with longer forms, such as novellas and novels. On 17th June 1855, he sat down to write his first novel, *Rudin*, and completed it in only seven weeks. It was published, with considerable additions, in the January and February 1856 issues of the literary journal *Sovremennik* (*The Contemporary*).

In 1856 Turgenev spent the summer at Spasskoye, then travelled to France to be with the Viardots. His time there was embittered by the realization that Pauline was having an affair with the artist Ary Scheffer. Possibly as a result of Viardot's unfaithfulness, Turgenev was often ill with what appears to be some kind of psychosomatic illness, of which a major symptom was agonizing pains in his bladder. He suffered from this illness for many years afterwards, and there is speculation he may have become impotent as a result of it. He and Pauline had a big argument towards the end of 1856, and his affliction became even worse, plaguing him for another sixteen months or so. Turgenev lost his interest in writing and was plunged into despair, possibly suffering a mild nervous breakdown. He spent most of this period lodging in Paris, with occasional visits to Germany, Britain and Italy. On a visit to London in May 1857, he had repeated contact with such luminaries as Disraeli, Thackeray, Macaulay and Carlyle: by this time his English was competent enough for him to engage in long conversations on literature and politics with those he met there.

Illness and Despair

In October 1856 Turgenev began to write *Home of the Gentry*. Owing to his mental and physical sufferings, work proceeded very slowly, and the novel was completed only in the autumn of 1858. It was published in January 1859 in *Sovremennik* and was an immediate success. On a brief return to Russia, Turgenev found himself lionized in literary society.

In June 1858, Viardot's lover, Ary Scheffer, died suddenly. Although Turgenev wrote to her a couple of times soon afterwards expressing his condolences, he did not send her any more letters until April 1859, just before he returned to France, perhaps because relationships between them had greatly deteriorated. Even when he did return, he saw little of Viardot, and she kept him at a distance.

During this period, Turgenev was able to begin a new novel, *On the Eve*, which was almost finished by the time he went back to Russia in October 1859. It was published in the January and February 1860 editions of the periodical *Russkiy Vestnik* (*Russian Herald*). Generally approved by the critics for its style, the novel was criticized by some for the absence of any social

On the Eve

viewpoint and for not attempting to stimulate readers to improve the social conditions surrounding them.

Fathers and Children and the Critical Backlash

Between May 1860 and May 1861, Turgenev spent most of his time in France, except a brief visit to Britain and a few weeks on the Isle of Wight in August 1860. It was here that, as he swam off the beach at Ventnor, the first idea for his next novel, *Fathers and Children*, occurred to him. He swiftly set about drawing up the characters, and then working out a detailed story around this germ of an idea. The first draft of the novel was completed at Spasskoye on 11th August 1861; then, in September that year, on his return to Paris he began revising it extensively. Published in Russia in February 1862, *Fathers and Children* unleashed a torrent of abuse from all sides that Turgenev simply had not anticipated. The right-wing press vilified him for daring to take the radical and free-thinking younger generation as its heroes, while the radicals saw the representatives of this generation in the novel, particularly the young doctor Bazarov, as caricatures of themselves. Incidentally, Bazarov describes himself as a "nihilist", a word which, although not unknown in Russian before, was popularized by Turgenev with this novel: following its publication, many of the younger generation ostentatiously adopted this label for themselves. In Turgenev's usage, it implies not so much somebody who believes in nothing, but a person who takes none of the commonly accepted beliefs on trust, subjecting everything to analysis by intensive reasoning. Years later, Turgenev wrote to a correspondent that he regretted giving what he called the "reactionary rabble" this word to beat the younger generation with.

Move to Baden-Baden

Viardot and her husband had in the meantime moved to a villa near the fashionable German spa town of Baden-Baden, so in 1863 Turgenev settled in this town too, living there until 1871, with the exception of a few brief visits back to Russia. In the spring of 1862, Viardot had resumed contact with him, possibly because she wanted him to help her select a number of Russian poems she could set to music and use his influence to sell them for her in Russia.

Problems with Russian Authorities

At this time, Turgenev was still under suspicion from the Russian authorities. On a visit to England in May 1862, he had met up with a number of Russian radicals based in London, and discussed their ideas with them. This became known in Russia, and he was summoned back there to be tried for his association with these people or face the risk of having all his property confiscated. He wrote a letter to the Tsar in person, in which he said that he had never expressed his political opinions by violent means, but had explained them in all moderation in his works. Back in Russia, in September 1863 he appeared before a court consisting of members of the Senate, and all charges were immediately dropped. Herzen and Bakunin, however, two of the revolutionaries based in London, in their publications accused Turgenev of having compromised himself by writing to the Tsar, and have betrayed his old ideals. To make up for the contempt with which he was regarded by some of his Russian contemporaries, Turgenev became acquainted with famous French authors such as Gustave Flaubert, whom he first met in January 1863.

In 1862, Turgenev had started drafting detailed plans and *Smoke* character sketches for another novel, *Smoke*. He began writing it in November 1865, and finished it in January 1866. After lengthy discussions with the editorial board of the *Russian Herald* as to the work's political and moral content, the book was published in March 1867. *Smoke* takes place largely outside Russia, and one of its major characters, a Russian called Potugin, who is vaguely reminiscent of Turgenev, is a passionate Westernizer contemptuous of the Russian mentality. Not surprisingly, this provoked a storm in Russia, where the press accused Turgenev of a total lack of patriotism.

The Franco-Prussian War of 1870–71, and the resulting growth *Move to England* of aggressive anti-French feelings in Germany, meant that Pauline Viardot, whose husband was French, no longer felt safe living there. The family moved to England in the autumn of 1870, and settled there till the end of the war. Turgenev, although as a Russian he had no reason to feel unsafe in Germany, faithfully followed them to London in November 1870, where he stayed for almost a year. He spent what Henry James – whom he met in Paris four years later – called a "lugubrious" winter in London.

While in England Turgenev was introduced into the leading artistic circles. There he met, among other literary figures, Tennyson, Dante Gabriel Rossetti and Ford Madox Brown, and struck up a close friendship with George Eliot. Although there is no record that he ever spoke to Dickens, it is likely that he met him, since he attended three of his public readings and was enthralled by them. Turgenev's English was by now excellent, and he was invited to Edinburgh to give an address in English at the Walter Scott centenary celebrations in August 1871. While there he went grouse-shooting on the Scottish moors, where he met the poet Robert Browning.

Move to Paris

Turgenev followed the Viardots on their return to Paris in October 1871 and, apart from a few brief spells in Russia, he spent four years living as a guest in the various houses occupied by Pauline and her husband. In 1875, he and the Viardots purchased a large country estate at Bougival, near Saint-Germain-en-Laye, a forty-five-minute ride from Paris. He built himself a Swiss-style chalet on the estate, very close to the manor house where Pauline lived, and it was here at Bougival that he spent the last years of his life. Turgenev now established a very close friendship with Flaubert, and also had frequent contact with George Sand, Zola, Daudet and, some time later, Maupassant.

Virgin Soil a
Prophetic Novel

Turgenev spent his time not only writing original prose, but also translating into Russian from French, German and English: for instance, his was the first version into Russian of Flaubert's *Trois Contes,* His last novel, *Virgin Soil,* a book that he had been planning, writing and revising for six years, was published in the January and February 1877 issues of the *European Herald*. He told the editor of this periodical that, in this last novel, he intended to put everything that he thought and felt about the situation in Russia, both about the reactionary and revolutionary camps. The novel was fiercely attacked in the Russian press, with many commentators claiming that the author had now been so long out of his country he had no longer any knowledge of Russian life. However, just a month after the novel's publication, fifty-two young people were arrested for just such activities as Turgenev had described in his book and, exactly as he had foretold, they were put on trial. This created great sympathy for the prisoners both at home and abroad, and *Virgin Soil* became a best-seller in Britain, France and America, with one French critic claiming that Turgenev had shown himself to be a true prophet.

Triumphal
Return to Russia

If Turgenev, as a result of the Russian press reaction to his novel, now believed he was despised by the public, including the liberal younger generation, he was mistaken. In January 1879 his brother Nikolai died, and Ivan set off to Russia to oversee the disposal of Nikolai's estate. At a literary gathering, a toast was proposed to him as "the loving instructor of our young people". Turgenev was so staggered at this unexpected reception that he burst into tears. He was invited to meeting after meeting, where he was constantly greeted by thunderous applause, although the authorities still disapproved of him. In Petersburg his hotel was stormed by thousands of people wanting his autograph, or even just a sight of him. He returned to Paris, looking – as friends said – younger and more cheerful. He was now showered with academic honours, including an Honorary Doctorate at Oxford University, for which he travelled to England. The orator at this ceremony declared that his works had led to the emancipation of the Russian serfs.

Turgenev was by now beginning to feel very unwell. He paid *Illness and Death* a final brief visit to Russia in February 1880, and spent one further short period in England in October 1881, where he went partridge-shooting at Newmarket, meeting Anthony Trollope, R.D. Blackmore and other writers.

On 3rd May the following year, he wrote to a friend from Bougival that he had been suffering from some kind of angina connected with gout. His shoulders and back ached, and he often had to lie down for long periods. In January 1883 he was operated in Paris for a small tumour in his abdomen. But his condition continued to worsen: he was in intolerable pain and had become very emaciated. His illness was at last diagnosed as incurable cancer of the spine. By now he was bedridden at Bougival, and on 1st September 1883 he slipped into unconsciousness, dying two days later. His body, unaccompanied by Pauline Viardot, was transported to Petersburg. The funeral service was held in the Cathedral of Our Lady of Kazan, and a vast funeral procession followed the coffin to the Volkovo Cemetery in Petersburg, where Turgenev was buried on 9th October.

Ivan Turgenev's Works

As mentioned before, Turgenev's early works were mainly poems *Juvenilia* in the high-flown classical style of pre-Pushkin Russian writers. However, he swiftly turned against these models, and strove to achieve for his mature writings a limpid idiom, including dialogue based on the everyday language of the Russian peasant. In sharp distinction to many of the writers of the time, who explicitly tried to put forward a progressive social message in their works, Turgenev aimed to achieve total objectivity and impersonality. Whilst depicting the sufferings of the working people around him, he limited himself to describing their lives without passing judgement and leaving the readers to draw their own conclusions.

Plays Turgenev wrote nine plays in all, but the only one to have found a permanent place in the repertoire is *A Month in the Country* (1855). Indeed, after 1857 he virtually abandoned the genre.

A Month in the Turgenev wrote the first version of *A Month in the Country*
Country in 1850. It was originally called *The Student*, then *Two Women*. He sent the manuscript to *Sovremennik*, who agreed to publish it, but the censors demanded drastic cuts, as the speeches of the student Belyayev were too inflammatory, and the motif of a married woman in love with another man was morally impermissible. The censors ordered that she be changed into a widow, and Turgenev reluctantly made the relevant cuts. The play was still turned down, and had to be revised even further. This version was published only in 1855, and does not appear to have ever been staged. It was only with the easing of the political climate under Tsar Alexander II that Turgenev's play was published again in 1869, in a version much closer to his original idea. In the revised text, the widow is once again shown as a wife in love with another man. However, even when it was finally staged in Moscow in 1872, under the title *A Month in the Country*, further revisions had to be made because a few of the speeches were still regarded as too incendiary. The play was not a great success, but in 1879 the renowned young actress Marya Savina chose it for a benefit performance in Petersburg, and asked for just a few short cuts to be made on grounds of length. This time it was a triumph, and immediately entered the repertoire.

A Month in the Country predates Chekhov in its depth of characterization and its skilful depiction of the series of barely perceptible changes that take place over a month in the relationships between the characters, leading, by the end, to their lives being totally altered. The play contrasts two social groups, the old and the young, in what was to become a recurring theme in Turgenev's work: the older gentry living fruitless and frustrated lives, with the younger generation full of hope and idealism – and neither of them attaining happiness.

In the play, Natalya is married to the staid and much older Arkady Islayev, while a "friend of the family", Rakitin, also lives in their country house. Natalya and Arkady are clearly based on Pauline Viardot and her husband, and Turgenev explicitly stated in a letter that Rakitin represented how Turgenev felt about his own situation with regard to them. Natalya falls in love with a young, idealistic, socially progressive student, Belyayev, whom she has engaged as tutor to her son. Vera, her seventeen-year-old ward, instantly falls in love with him too, but Natalya, as a result of her own feelings for him, forces her into marrying the much older and boring Bolshintsov. Belyayev cannot cope with the intensity of the two women's passions and flees. Rakitin, badly hurt by Natalya's lack of feeling for him, withdraws from the scene, leaving her alone with her husband, whom she respects, but does not love. They return to their aimless, idle lives after this month of emotional turmoil.

The title which first established Turgenev's reputation in Russia *Memoirs of a* was *Memoirs of a Hunter* (which has also been translated as *Hunter* *Sketches of a Huntsman* and *Notes of a Sportsman*). This collection of tales of Russian rural life was mostly written in France and Germany, where Turgenev lived at the end of the 1840s and beginning of the 1850s. It consists of twenty-four stories of between 3,000 and 12,000 words in length, most of them originally published as they were written in *Sovremennik* between 1847 and 1851. Twenty-one sketches were published in volume form in 1852; a further story was added in 1872, and another two in 1874. The tales were drawn from Turgenev's own observations of the appalling living conditions of the peasants and the cruelty imposed by the upper classes on their serfs, which he had witnessed when he had roamed round the countryside in his childhood and when, as a youth, he had gone hunting in the locality. The style of the stories, set against lyrical descriptions of nature, is totally impersonal. The reactionary Tsar Nicholas I dismissed the censor who had permitted the volume's publication, but when he died in 1855, the new Tsar, the reforming Alexander II, is said to have read the book and resolved to free the serfs – which finally happened in 1861. The book was a great success and was immediately reprinted.

The Diary of a Superfluous Man (1850) may be considered *The Diary of a* Turgenev's first novella. It was with this work that he introduced *Superfluous Man* into the Russian consciousness the concept of the "superfluous man", which had played such a large part in Russian literature before and was to appear in many subsequent literary incarnations. The term denotes either a person who has the education and abilities to work for society and improve social and political conditions, but who through lack of willpower never manages to achieve anything, or someone who strives to achieve change but is totally ignored by society and so gives up in baffled disillusionment. The story is a personal account written by a young, well-educated man who has learnt from his doctor that he may be dying of an unnamed illness. He has drifted through life without any goal, has never managed to make much use of his education, or fulfil any of his ambitions, or set up any permanent relationship with the opposite sex. Now, as he may be approaching an early death, he is left to reflect on his wasted life.

Mumu   "Mumu' (1854) was based on an incident which had happened at Spasskoye, and the female landowner of the story represents Turgenev's own mother. A hard-working young peasant, being deaf and dumb, has never managed to marry, and the only thing he can find to love is a young puppy that has been abandoned. As he is unable to speak, Mumu is the only name he can give to it. But the landowner complains that the puppy's barking is keeping her awake at night, and the order goes out, via the steward, to kill it. The peasant takes the dog to a river and, uncomplainingly, drowns the only thing ever to have loved him. However, the story ends with him striding away from his owner's control, and readers are left to draw their own conclusions about what his feelings are at this piece of wanton viciousness on her part.

Faust   *Faust* (1856) consists of nine letters from a character called Pavel to his friend Semyon. Pavel recounts how, a few years after his first meeting with her, he sees again Vera, now a married woman. She had been brought up in a very strict manner, and forbidden by her mother to read any books, especially poetry. Pavel, now he has met her again, visits her frequently at home, and tries to interest her in literature by reading her Goethe's *Faust*. Her feelings are so inflamed by this first exposure to literature that she falls in love with Pavel and arranges a tryst with him; however, on the way to her rendezvous, she sees an apparition of her dead mother – possibly caused by her subconscious guilt – falls seriously ill and dies.

Asya   *Asya* (1858) is a novella set in a small village on the Rhine and, unusually for Turgenev, it contains no implicit social message. The unnamed narrator, a middle-aged Russian, recalls events of twenty years before, when he was on holiday in Germany and met a Russian painter called Gagin, who introduces him to Asya, a girl he claims is his sister. The narrator suspects she is his mistress, but later Gagin tells him she is his illegitimate half-sister, whom he has been bringing up since the death of her parents. Although loving Gagin with the feelings of a sister, she falls passionately in love with the narrator, who baulks at the idea of marrying her and decides to give the matter some prolonged thought. By the time he decides in favour of the relationship, Gagin and Asya have returned to Russia, and he accepts that he has missed his chance of happiness. She writes to him reproachfully, telling him that one word of encouragement from him would have been enough to persuade her to marry him. However, his feelings prove shallow: he doesn't suffer long, and he never hears of her again.

First Love (1860) is perhaps the most autobiographical of all Turgenev's works. The author claimed that an identical incident had happened to him in his adolescence at Spasskoye. The hero is a boy who falls in love with the slightly older daughter of a young neighbour. Realizing she does not return his feelings and has a lover, the boy takes a knife to attack his rival. However, on drawing near the girl and her lover, he sees to his dismay that it is his own father. He drops the knife and flees mortified, with bitterness having entered his young soul. *First Love*

In *King Lear of the Steppe* (1870), the narrator is an adult who recalls the time he was an adolescent still living on his mother's estates. The tale's main character is one of her serfs, Kharlov, the "King Lear" of the story. He is a man of gigantic stature and strength, a hard-working peasant farmer who lives in a small house he has built with his own hands. The narrator's mother, Kharlov's owner, had married him off at the age of forty to a seventeen-year-old girl who bore him two daughters but then died. The two girls, out of compassion, were subsequently brought up in the narrator's home, but they became cruel and grasping. One night Kharlov has a dream he interprets as a premonition of his coming death, and immediately draws up a will dividing his estate between his two daughters. Just a few weeks later he is evicted by them, and is given refuge by the narrator's mother. But, driven mad, he climbs up onto the roof of the house he had built, which has now passed into other hands, and begins to tear chunks from it. He falls from the roof to his death. *King Lear of the Steppe*

Based on a chance encounter Turgenev had had with a beautiful young girl in Frankfurt in 1841, *Spring Waters* was published in 1872. As he returns home from a party, the fifty-year-old Dmitry Sanin reflects on the futility of life. He recalls a time in the 1840s, when he once stopped off in Frankfurt. A beautiful young girl, Gemma, rushes from a building and asks him to *Spring Waters* help her brother Emilio, who she thinks is dying but has only fainted. When Sanin revives him, he is welcomed into Gemma's household as Emilio's saviour. Sanin cancels his plans to return to Russia, because he is now in love with Gemma, who is unfortunately engaged to be married to a vile old German shopkeeper. But Gemma returns Sanin's love, breaks off her engagement, and she and Sanin agree to marry. He is about to go back to Russia to sell his lands when he meets an old acquaintance, Polozov, who is married to a wealthy and attractive woman. He convinces Sanin that his wife will buy his lands, but she, simply out of malevolence, seduces him in order to wreck his projected marriage. He becomes totally infatuated with her, and writes Gemma a letter breaking off their liaison. Polozov's wife, having achieved her aim, starts to treat him with cold contempt and then discards him, leaving him desolate and with nothing.

Novels   As well as novellas and short stories, Turgenev wrote six novels. The first four were published in the space of just six years, between 1856 and 1862. Possibly as a consequence of the criticism he had received for these works in the Russian press – especially for the fourth, *Fathers and Children* – his following novel appeared only five years later, and the last one ten years after that.

Rudin   Originally entitled *A Highly Gifted Nature*, Turgenev's first novel, *Rudin* (1856), tells the tale of another "superfluous man". He is a well-educated but impecunious young nobleman, who has been educated at Moscow University, as well as in Heidelberg and Berlin. The setting is the country estate of a wealthy noblewoman, Darya Lasunskaya, in a provincial backwater. The charismatic Rudin, whom nobody knows, is introduced into their circle and totally disrupts the settled life of the household, especially affecting the peace of mind of young Natalya. When he leaves, things return to their normal state, but some of the characters have subtly changed for ever. The unexpected entry of an outsider into a social circle and the turmoil it causes is a leitmotif in Turgenev's writings: other examples are Lavretsky in *Home of the Gentry*, Insarov in *On the Eve*, Bazarov in *Fathers and Children* and Belyayev in *A Month in the Country*. The feckless Rudin now moves into Darya's mansion, sponging off the family, and obviously striking up a liaison with her impressionable young daughter Natalya. This budding romance becomes known to Darya, who strongly disapproves of it. Instead of standing up firmly for their love, however, Rudin declares one must "submit to destiny", leaving Natalya hurt, confused and feeling deceived by him. When Rudin departs from the estate, he sends her a letter confessing that he has always been guilty of such indecision.

The final section of the novel portrays events some two years later. Natalya is now engaged to a staid, worthy local landowner, and Rudin is still drifting around Russia, living at the expense of anybody he can latch on to. There is a very short epilogue which is not entirely convincing, and seems to have been appended as an afterthought: Rudin takes the part of the workers manning the barricades in the Paris Insurrection of 1848, which Turgenev had been witness to. He is shot dead by the soldiers, and even in death his sacrifice appears to have been meaningless, as somebody shouts out: "They've got the Pole!" Perhaps the message of this apparently incongruous ending is that, ironically, the first time this aimless Russian nobleman tries to exert himself to do something useful, he dies, and nobody even realizes that he is Russian, or has any personality of his own. He is still just another "superfluous man".

Although the critics noted the novel's lucid prose style, the press reaction was puzzled; the right-wing journals accused Turgenev of disrespecting the upper classes in his portrayal of them as ineffective drifters and spongers, while the radicals thought that Rudin was a satirical portrait of one of them – well-educated, full of fine words, but ineffectual, and able to make no lasting impact on anything. As mentioned before, it was even claimed that Rudin was a caricature of the revolutionary Bakunin, who became one of the founders of the Russian anarchist movement, and whom Turgenev had met when they were both students in Berlin.

Home of the Gentry is Turgenev's second novel. Turgenev had heard, when he was in Rome in 1857, that the Tsarist government was at last considering the question of the emancipation of the serfs, and decided that he should devote himself entirely to depicting the reality of the social situation in Russia in his writings. Accordingly, he started planning *Home of the Gentry*, which was completed in 1858 and published in early 1859. Whereas in *Rudin* he had been portraying an aimless member of the educated upper classes, in his next novel he depicted what he most valued in Russian life and tradition and, unusually for him, looked quite critically at some aspects of Western culture.

Home of the Gentry

The setting is the country house of a wealthy family in the town of O—— (most probably Oryol, the county town of the region where Turgenev was born). This house, and the family's estate, represent here for Turgenev an oasis of peace and stability amidst the turbulent changes taking place around them. Towards the beginning of the novel, the hero, Lavretsky, comes back to re-establish himself in his real home, his "nest", after years of fruitless strivings away from his roots. We are given a long "pre-history" of the character: his family had used him as an experimental subject for all kinds of advanced educational theories, and so he had fled abroad to escape from them. There he had married a thoroughly vacuous and unscrupulous woman, who soon abandoned what she saw as an uncouth Russian backwoodsman for the greater attractions of the European rakes she encountered. Lavretsky returns to Russia without his wife, embittered but determined to justify his existence by hard work for the social good. He meets again the nineteen-year-old Liza, whom he had known when they were children. They fall in love and, when a false rumour of his wife's death reaches them, they decide to marry. However, they learn that his wife is still alive. Liza is profoundly religious and, believing that she has committed a grave sin in daring to love a married man, she enters a convent to atone. Some years later, Lavretsky visits the convent, although as an outsider he is not allowed to speak to the nuns. Liza passes by just a few feet away from him and, obviously aware of his presence, simply drops her head and clasps her rosary beads tightly to her.

However, Lavretsky, in the epilogue to the novel, seems to have achieved some measure of contentment: he has become a good landowner, and has worked very hard at improving the lot of his peasants. Therefore, he has done something positive with his life, and has to a certain extent re-established contact with his roots and ensconced himself within his Russian family "nest".

The novel was extremely popular in Russia, because it showed the country's traditional values in a positive light. This was acceptable for all sections of Russian society, both the reactionary classes and the progressives who desired political change but believed that the fount of all wisdom was to be found in indigenous rural culture.

On the Eve   The genesis of Turgenev's next novel *On the Eve* (1860) – if we are to believe Turgenev – is very peculiar. While under house arrest at Spasskoye in 1852–53, he was visited by a young local landowner, Vasily Karatayev, an army officer who was shortly due to go abroad with his regiment. Just before he departed, he gave Turgenev a story he had written, based on his own experiences as a student in Moscow, when he'd had an affair with a girl who then left him for a Bulgarian patriot. Karatayev felt he had neither the time nor the talent to work this tale up into a decent artistic work, and asked Turgenev to do so. Turgenev later claimed that Karatayev had died in the Crimean War of 1854–56, and so some years later he had devoted himself to reworking the officer's original sketch.

In the story, Yelena Stakhova, a Russian girl, falls in love with a Bulgarian patriot, Dmitry Insarov, who is an exile in Russia striving to free his country from its Turkish overlords. He and Yelena marry, and leave for Bulgaria together. However, on the way there, he falls seriously ill and dies in Venice. She decides to take on his struggle for Bulgarian freedom and continues to Bulgaria, where she becomes a nurse. After a few letters home, she is never heard of again. There is a brief meditation at the end of the novel on the death of such young, idealistic people. However much Turgenev admired them, he also, with his usual objectivity, seems to have found them slightly naive and perhaps even rather unpleasantly fanatical.

When the work appeared in the *Russian Herald*, the twenty-three-year-old radical critic Nikolai Dobrolyubov issued a long review which, though very warm in praise of the novel's style and Turgenev's sympathy for his characters, took issue with his objectivity and impersonality. He declared that this kind of standpoint was now obsolete and irrelevant, and that writers should take an explicit position as to the necessity of improving the conditions of life around them.

Sometimes erroneously translated as *Fathers and Sons*, *Fathers and Children* (1862) is generally considered to be Turgenev's masterpiece. In this novel he attempts to portray the kind of Russian "new man" who has energy and drive, and is actively striving to alter Russian society. *Fathers and Children*

In a letter to an acquaintance, Countess Lambert, Turgenev claimed that he had the first idea of the novel while walking along the beach at Ventnor on the Isle of Wight, but in a later article, "Concerning *Fathers and Children*', he tells his readers that he thought of it while swimming in the sea off the same town.

Between the writing of *On the Eve* and *Fathers and Children* a vast social change had taken place in Russia: the serfs had at last, in March 1861, been emancipated from their owners. Perhaps buoyed up by this positive trend in Russian social life, Turgenev sat down to write a novel with a central character, Yevgeny Bazarov, who is an idealistic young doctor describing himself as a "nihilist" – a word which, as we have seen before, in this context has a positive connotation, signifying someone who subjects every commonly held viewpoint or belief to profound rational analysis.

The story begins in May 1859. Arkady, a young university student who has just graduated, brings back to his father's estate a university friend, Yevgeny Bazarov, who is a newly qualified doctor and the only son of a family living on a small country estate. Bazarov represents the new young, idealistic, scientific mentality in Russian society. While there, Yevgeny becomes involved in violent arguments both with Arkady's father, who is a well-meaning liberal, and particularly with his uncle who, for all his Western ways, is an inveterate reactionary.

Love interest is provided by the appearance of Anna Odintsova, described as a frivolous woman who spends most of her time reading silly French novels. Bazarov has always scoffed at love as being irrational, but despite that he becomes infatuated with her and has to accept that not everything can be explained scientifically.

After a couple of weeks, Bazarov finally goes back home to his parents. His father is a retired doctor who still occasionally goes out to tend the local peasantry free of charge. Bazarov accompanies his father on some of these missions, and one day, while carrying out an autopsy on a typhus victim without any disinfectant, he accidentally cuts himself and becomes infected with the disease, soon falling ill and dying. His heartbroken parents are depicted as visiting his grave right into their old age, while beautiful but indifferent nature looks on.

The story was met with total incomprehension across the political spectrum, with radical reviewers calling Bazarov a malicious caricature of Dobrolyubov, while the conservative press accused him of prostrating himself to the radicals and grovelling at their feet.

Smoke   Although the idea for his next novel, *Smoke*, may have occurred to Turgenev as early as 1862, shortly after the publication of *Fathers and Children*, he took more than five years to write it, and it was not published until March 1867. He began drafting *Smoke* in Baden-Baden in November 1864, and most of the story takes place there, over less than a fortnight in August 1862, among the large community of wealthy Russians living in the town. The central character, the thirty-year-old Grigory Litvinov, after completing his university education in Western Europe, is awaiting the arrival of his fiancée Tatyana, who is also holidaying in Western Europe, so that they can return to Russia together. However, in Baden-Baden he meets Irina, a woman he had known and been infatuated with some ten years before, now married to another man. Their love affair is rekindled. He breaks off his engagement to Tatyana and begs Irina to run off with him, but she does not have the courage to do so. Litvinov returns to Russia desolate and alone. After several years, he becomes a successful farmer on his estate, meets Tatyana again. She forgives him and they marry.

The title derives from the frequent appearance in the novel of smoke (such as when Litvinov is on the train back to Russia and the smoke from the steam engine is billowing around both sides of his carriage, making the surroundings almost invisible) as a symbol of the confusion and futility of life.

Most of the critics deplored the novel, both for its immorality – a married woman falling in love with an old flame – and for its negative – indeed, almost contemptuous – portrait of the typical Russians who lived abroad.

The background of *Virgin Soil* (1877) is the great movement *Virgin Soil* of young idealistic students, most of them from the educated and moneyed classes, who from the late 1860s through to the early 1870s "went to the people". Living among the peasantry and urban working classes, they shared their work and living conditions – and, of course, tried to imbue them with modern democratic ideals. Especially among the reactionary country people these youths were met with anything from amusement to contempt, and in many cases were actually handed over to the police by them as troublemakers, leading to large-scale trials, with many of the radicals being exiled to Siberia and other remote areas of the Russian Empire.

The story, the most complex and ambitious that Turgenev ever attempted, presents many minor characters and subsidiary plots. Mashurina is a follower of the fanatical and charismatic Vasily Nikolayevich. However, not all his adherents are uncritical of him – for example Nezhdanov, with whom Mashurina is in love, who is too objective and sceptical to follow anybody unquestioningly. The illegitimate and impecunious son of a nobleman, he has to earn his living by tutoring the children of wealthy reactionary members of the aristocracy and high government bureaucrats. Nezhdanov, who is in love with Maryanna, another naive radical, proves to be a "superfluous man" – unsure both of his revolutionary ideals and of his love for Maryanna. He is, more than anything else, an aristocrat who longs to be a peasant, and a poet and dreamer, not a political activist.

Nezhdanov and Maryanna run off together, and are given protection by Solomin, a rural factory manager who, although not a revolutionary, is sympathetic to those who want change. He is the novel's real hero, a hard-working modern man: he has studied science and maths, and lived and worked in Britain. He – like Turgenev – believes in slow and patient change. Nezhdanov, trying to become one of the local peasantry, simply succeeds in drinking himself into stupor in the local pubs and having to be carried back home. Solomin persuades Maryanna that she can be far more useful to the common people, not by trying to spread revolutionary ideals, but by becoming a nurse or teacher to the local children. Humiliated as a result of his failure to communicate with the local working people, and even more depressed when he realizes that he and Maryanna are drifting apart, Nezhdanov writes to Maryanna and Solomin telling them to marry each other, then he shoots himself. Maryanna and Solomin plan to get married and, although we are never told what happens in the end, they presumably devote themselves to the improvement of society in the ways advocated by Solomin. As mentioned before, barely one month after *Virgin Soil* had been published, as Turgenev was being criticized in Russia as out of touch with the present reality of the country, fifty-two young people were arrested – of whom eighteen were women.

Select Bibliography

Biographies:

Magarshack, David, *Turgenev: A Life* (London: Faber and Faber, 1954)

Pritchett, Victor, *The Gentle Barbarian: The Life and Work of Turgenev* (London: Chatto and Windus, 1977)

Schapiro, Leonard, *Turgenev: His Life and Times* (Oxford: OUP, 1978)

Troyat, Henri, *Turgenev*, tr. Nancy Amphoux (London: W.H. Allen, 1989)

Yarmolinsky, Avrahm, *Turgenev: The Man, His Art and His Age* (New York, NY: Orion Press, 1959)

Additional Recommended Background Material:

Andrew, Joe, Offord, Derek and Reid, Robert, eds., *Turgenev and Russian Culture* (Amsterdam and New York, NY: Rodopi, 2008)

Beaumont, Barbara, tr. and ed., *Flaubert and Turgenev: A Friendship in Letters* (London: Athlone Press, 1985)

Costlow, Jane, *Worlds within Worlds: The Novels of Ivan Turgenev* (Princeton, NJ: Princeton University Press, 1990)

Freeborn, Richard, *Turgenev – the Novelist's Novelist: A Study* (Oxford: Oxford University Press, 1963)

Lowe, David, tr., *Turgenev: Letters* (Ann Arbor, MI: Ardis, 1983)

Lowe, David A., ed., *Critical Essays on Ivan Turgenev*, (Boston, MA: G.K. Hall and Co., 1989)

Moser, Charles A., *Ivan Turgenev* (New York, NY, and London: Columbia University Press, 1972)

Waddington, Patrick, *Turgenev and England* (London: Macmillan, 1980)

Woodward, James, *Turgenev's Fathers and Sons* (London: Bristol Classical Press, 1996)

On the Web:
eis.bris.ac.uk/~rurap/novelsof.htm

EVERGREENS SERIES

Beautifully produced classics, affordably priced

Alma Classics is committed to making available a wide range of literature from around the globe. Most of the titles are enriched by an extensive critical apparatus, notes and extra reading material, as well as a selection of photographs. The texts are based on the most authoritative editions and edited using a fresh, accessible editorial approach. With an emphasis on production, editorial and typographical values, Alma Classics aspires to revitalize the whole experience of reading classics.

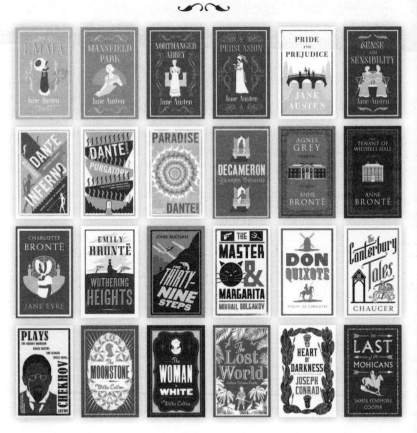

For our complete list and latest offers visit

almabooks.com/evergreens